Fallen Angel

Fallen Angel

The Unlikely Rise of Walter Stadnick in the Canadian Hells Angels

by Jerry Langton

John Wiley & Sons Canada, Ltd.

National Library of Canada Cataloguing in Publication Data

Langton, Jerry, 1965-
    Fallen angel : the unlikely rise of Walter Stadnick in the Canadian Hells Angels / Jerry Langton.

Includes index.
ISBN-13 978-0-470-83710-8
ISBN-10 0-470-83710-1

    1. Stadnick, Walter. 2. Hell's Angels. 3. Motorcycle gangs—Québec (Province)—History. 4. Motorcycle gangs—Ontario—History. 5. Gang members—Québec (Province)—Biography. I. Title.

HV6491.C3L35 2006   364.1'092   C2005-906436-6

Production Credits:
Cover design: Adrian So
Cover image: Used with permission from The Canadian Press

Printer: Printcrafters

John Wiley & Sons Canada, Ltd.
6045 Freemont Blvd.
Mississauga, Ontario
L5R 4J3

Printed in Canada

    2 3 4 5 PC 10 09 08 07 06

Structure of Hells Angels Outlaw Motorcyle Gang

President

↑

Vice President

↑

Secretary-Treasurer

↑

Full-patch Members

↑

Sergeant of Arms

↑

Honorary Members

↑

Prospective Members
and other associates
(can wear no colors and have no
official rights)

↑

Hang-arounds
(who are given three opportunities
to prospect and must get 100% approval)

Acknowledgements

Fallen Angel is a collaborative effort. It is the combined voices of dozens of police officers, bikers, lawyers, drug dealers, journalists, neighbors, politicians and all kinds of other people who had something to say. For reasons that are obvious, a significant proportion of them would rather I didn't use their names. They are the people—like Diane the nurse, Bob the cop and Vincent the, to use his own phrase, "wealth redistributor"—who are referred to by first name only and not always their real first name. Others are referred to by no name at all if their connection to the story requires no further context. Of course, some of my sources had agendas to push and some weren't always honest. There were times when two people would claim the exact opposite of each other with equal stridency. In those cases, I had to find the answer somewhere else or not at all.

Of the people who are named, there were some that I consider truly essential. Sergeant John Harris of the Hamilton Police Service rose above all others. His knowledge of crime in his city and the entire country is extraordinary and he delivers it all in such a wittily matter-of-fact way that I sometimes think he should be the one writing the books. Similarly, his fellow sergeant in Hamilton, Steve Pacey, added a remarkable amount of drama as the man who went face-to-face with the bikers so many times and was the one who exposed so much of the inner workings of the Hells Angels when he searched Stadnick's home. They may have been given the job of ridding the streets of outlaw bikers, but they both clearly understood that their adversaries—especially Stadnick—were people with rights and dignity and real, sometimes very deep, personalities. If there's a hero to this story from a law-enforcement perspective, it's Quebec prosecutor Randall Richmond. A man of courage, conviction and staggering intellect, he stood firm and repeatedly did his job brilliantly under bizarre conditions.

I could not have written much of anything without the people on the street who, through drug sales, drug use or simply hanging out in certain parts of certain cities and towns, gave me a perspective with more depth and color than I could have gotten from police and prosecutors. Thanks go to people like Brian and Mike and others who weren't entirely sure that being a Hells Angel was all that bad an occupation and kept reminding me that it's not us against them.

Many thanks also go to the great Leta Potter people and the folks at John Wiley & Sons Canada, especially to Don Loney for the pep talks at The Pour House pub. Thanks also to Eric in the Bronx for his research and perspective, to Mark for his constant guidance and mockery, and to Karen, who read the last few thousand words and shook me from my deeply held opinion that I am the worst writer in the world. And, of course, deepest thanks go to Tizz, Dida and the H-Dogg, the collective reason I do anything.

Introduction

Looking for help and maybe a little inspiration, I called Daniel Sanger. He'd just written *Hell's Witness*, an excellent book that follows the career of Dany Kane, the biker informant who played a significant role in the rise and fall of the Hells Angels in Canada, and it was clear he knew what he was talking about. When I told him that *Fallen Angel* would be in a large part about Walter Stadnick, he was mildly surprised. "Great subject matter," he said. "But you've got a lot of work in front of you."

Indeed I did. By all accounts, Stadnick is an extremely intelligent and capable man who excels at nothing better than keeping out of trouble. In the same period Maurice "Mom" Boucher was convicted 43 times, Stadnick received two traffic tickets. Of course he was arrested a couple of times, but could not be convicted until 2004, more than 20 years after he is said to have joined the Hells Angels. Every single one of the police officers, lawyers, politicians and journalists I spoke with were of the same opinion—that Stadnick was the man who built the Canadian Hells Angels from a bunch of cocaine-crazed louts on bikes in Montreal to the biggest, strongest and most efficient crime organization in the country. But none of them knew how or why. They all knew a part of the story and were eager to tell me their little bit. Putting it together, as Sanger told me, would be the hard part.

But *Fallen Angel* is not a biography of Walter Stadnick. If it was, it wouldn't do him justice. In *Fallen Angel*, the story of a remarkably complex and secretive man is just an allegory for the bigger picture. He was smart and charismatic, but he came of age in a time and place where his talents weren't worth much. When he started getting money and popularity through being a biker, he found his niche. He moved up through the minor leagues to the big time. Although he was tiny by biker standards and couldn't speak any French, he went to the Hells Angels' clubhouse in

Montreal, and before too long, he was their president. Stadnick traveled the country using charm and persuasion to sign up other men and other clubs, until his gang ruled the bikers from coast to coast. He then formed a new gang, the Nomads, who told the Hells Angels what to do. He did it all by staying a few steps ahead of the police and staying out of trouble. His story mirrors that of the Hells Angels, who started out small and without direction and quickly gained enough momentum to dominate organized crime in this country.

Chapter 1

Fresh from the gang wars in Kingston, Robeson David had seen his share of violence. Using public outrage over a massive tax increase as a ruse, armed gangs of men battled in the streets—raping, looting, burning and shooting with a callous casualness that caused ordinary citizens to create refugee camps in police stations. More than 500 people were murdered in less than two weeks. David, an officer in the Jamaican Defense Force's SWAT unit, led his men into the worst of the fighting. "It was more like war than police work," he said, his seriousness and Jamaican accent making him sound distinguished. "But desperate crimes call for desperate measures." He wasn't joking.

Despite his experiences on the front lines, even David had to admit his assignment for the morning of March 28, 2001, caused him some anxiety. He was told that he and his men would have to capture and arrest the kingpin of the Canadian Hells Angels. "This isn't about a bunch of boys with cricket bats anymore," he said. "This is the Hells Angels, professional killers—we didn't want to mess with them." Such was the reputation of the world's best-known motorcycle gang that an assault rifle-toting SWAT officer would rather face open gang warfare on the mean streets of Kingston than arrest one Angel at a luxury hotel.

The Ritz-Carlton Rose Hall, located just outside of Montego Bay, is a hell of a place. The 5,000-acre beachfront spa and golf club is easily the best hotel on the island. Nestled between verdant hillsides and the turquoise waters of the Caribbean, the beautifully appointed and tastefully decorated Ritz is the only Jamaican resort to earn AAA's coveted five-diamond rating.

Standing out amid all the luxury was a short man from Canada. Dressed garishly, even among the sea of tourists eager to party on the laid-back islands, he didn't present an impressive figure. At 5-feet 4-inches, his stout body and short limbs gave him an almost primitive appearance and his shoulder-length hair indicated that his profession probably didn't take him into an office every day. His face and hands, badly burned in a motorcycle accident 18 years earlier, did little to soften the edges of this hard-looking man. "Yeah, he was scarred up a bit, but that's not why he was funny-looking," said Shaun Plank, a hotel employee. "He had tiny, sunken-in eyes and a great big mouth. It made him look nasty—you don't play with a man who looks like that."

But Walter Stadnick was there to play. He had no business, official or otherwise, other than to celebrate his 22nd anniversary with his common-law wife, Kathi Anderson. Disappointed that the Ritz was booked, he spent the first part of his vacation at the Wyndham Rose Hall just down the beach.

The Wyndham is a nice place, too. It's not the Ritz, but at $395 a night for a decent room, it's out of reach for most hard-working Canadians. A former sugar plantation surrounded by 18 holes on an impeccable golf course, it mainly attracts well-heeled businessmen who like golf and women who'd like to meet them. Stadnick stood out there, too.

About 1,800 miles to the north, Steve Pacey wasn't sipping margaritas and checking out passing bikinis. If Stadnick looked out of place at a luxury hotel, Pacey stood out even more among the other cops in the Hamilton police force, even when he was with the men and women of the Ontario Provincial Police's Biker Enforcement Unit. At 6-feet 2-inches and 265 pounds, he was an imposing presence. With his shaved head, wild goatee, diamond stud earring and arms wrapped in tattoos, the man dressed in denim and black leather looked more like a prisoner than a colleague when he was with other cops. But he wasn't their enemy; he was their secret weapon. He went where the bikers went and, except for the drugs and violence, he did what the bikers did. To a newbie, he looked like another biker. To the bikers, he was close enough that they got sloppy around him after a few too many cold ones. Pacey knew more about Hamilton's bikers than anyone else. And he knew that, although most cops associate Hamilton with the traditional Italian Mafia, it was the bikers who called the Steel City home who really ran things in Canada, and it was Stadnick who called the shots for many of the bikers. "There are traditional organized crime members in this city who are very active," he said in 2001. "But in terms of sheer volume, Walter's influence spreads way beyond Hamilton."

At this point, it was pretty clear to everyone that Stadnick was not exactly Ned Flanders. Despite the fact that there exists no record of Stadnick ever holding a job, he lived pretty high on the hog. Unlike the more commonplace breed of *nouveaux riches* who expose themselves to scrutiny by buying an ostentatious mansion, Stadnick played it cool. He bought a small and comfortable house near the ridge of the 300-foot hill they call "the mountain" in Hamilton. Assessed for insurance purposes for an atrociously low $156,000, Stadnick's Cloverhill Road residence was an opulent, if not entirely tasteful, monument to the biker lifestyle.

From the street, the only indication that this wasn't an ordinary house was the oversized Canadian flag and the mailbox painted in the bright red and white of the Hells Angels. A few steps out back revealed that work had begun on an in-ground pool. Overlooking it was a recently finished second-floor balcony. A peek in the first floor windows would reveal a sumptuous glass, black marble and gold plate motif worth well more than the estimated value of the entire house. Climb up to the second floor and you'd see an office with a PC, scanner, fax and—what every legitimate businessman needs—a paper shredder. Next door was a bathroom featuring a new whirlpool with a wall-mounted TV. Beyond that was the red-and-white master bedroom with an expensive four-poster bed and a his-and-hers closet filled with custom-fitted Armani suits and enough women's shoes to make Imelda Marcos envious. Parked out front on most days were a late-model Chrysler luxury car, a Blazer SUV and, perhaps most revealing, a brand-new Jaguar with Quebec plates. The beloved Harleys lived in the garage. Stadnick's attempt to blend in didn't fool the cops. As one Hamilton officer mused aloud: "How can you have a guy like Stadnick—who's never had a job in his life—living in a gorgeous little house, with a place in Quebec, a place in Winnipeg—traveling all over the world wearing Armani suits?"

While the logical answer is crime, the legal answer is more complex. Or at least more elusive. When asked what his client did for a living, Stadnick's high-priced lawyer Stephan Frankel said: "I don't know, I really don't know." After a long, uncomfortable silence, he said: "It wasn't something that would generally come up; it wasn't really something that I needed to know . . . I don't know if it's strange necessarily—Walter is a really private person." Too private, apparently, to tell his lawyer what he does for a living.

Though his lawyer was oblivious, the police weren't. Although he was opaque in his business dealings, Stadnick wore his Hells Angels colours proudly, and always seemed to be at least on the periphery of trouble. A paid informant embedded close to the Hells Angels elite Nomads Chapter told his Royal Canadian Mounted Police (RCMP) handlers that Stadnick was not only deeply involved in the lucrative Southern Ontario drug trade, but that he was also making strategic alliances with biker gangs in Ontario and Western Canada in an effort to win them over from the Hells Angels' rivals, the Outlaws. Although cops in urban centers like Hamilton may view drug dealing as an unavoidable part of urban life—throw a Hells Angel in jail and someone else will take his place—the rumblings of a potential gang war were particularly worrisome. At least 157 people were murdered in the Hells Angels–Rock Machine conflict in Quebec and, when the Hells Angels rose from the battle victorious, they turned their homicidal attention to the government, killing two prison guards and threatening the lives of every guard, cop, prosecutor and judge in the province. Quebec was teetering on the edge of a Colombia-style government–gangster stalemate. "No, we don't need that here in Ontario," said another Hamilton cop.

* * *

Farther north in Montreal it was bitterly cold, one of those days that makes you wonder if winter will ever end. At 4:00 a.m., RCMP Sergeant Tom O'Neill arrived at the headquarters of the Sûreté du Québec (SQ) with armloads of coffee and doughnuts. He wasn't complaining about the cold or the early start or the long day he knew he had ahead of him—if anything, he was eager to get started. As NCO of Operation Printemps (Springtime) 2001, it was his job to coordinate a joint police task force consisting of 2,000 officers poised to pounce on 142 bikers.

Of them, two stood out in particular. Stadnick and Donald "Pup" Stockford were friends who grew up on the rough-and-tumble streets of Hamilton and, despite starting with no French skills and a pronounced size disadvantage, somehow managed to join the traditionally francophone Canadian arm of the Hells Angels; Stockford became president and Stadnick's right-hand man. At the top of the Canadian Hells Angels are the Nomads, an elite chapter of the Hells Angels founded, sources say, by Stadnick himself.

Stadnick and Stockford, along with such Montreal-based luminaries as Maurice "Mom" Boucher and David "Wolf" Carroll were among the Nomads management team who controlled not only the other Hells Angels, but associated gangs as well. A secret RCMP report read: "They'll have about a dozen members and will control all of Quebec as their territory. They'll put pressure on clubs that aren't doing a good job selling drugs." "Pressure" in Hells Angels' terms usually means violence. According to police, Stadnick's primary mandate was to recruit established biker gangs from Ontario and Western Canada into the Hells Angels family by any means necessary.

O'Neill knew that if the task force could put Stadnick and Stockford behind bars for a long time, they stood a very good chance of stopping or at least slowing down the gang's rapid and vicious western expansion.

In densely populated areas, and Ontario is no exception, the sex and drug trades are controlled by a number of organized crime groups. In approximate order of influence, they include the Italian and Irish mafias at the top, the biker gangs, Asian gangs, Jamaican gangs, and at the bottom the independent operators and other bottom-feeders. All of them live in a sort of uneasy tolerance of one another, with only the occasional head kicked in to maintain order. That hierarchy, as the authorities in Quebec found out, gets blown away when the Hells Angels arrive. Like a cunning retailer intent on eliminating the competition, the Hells Angels use their name and reputation, combined with smart marketing like cut-rate prices, free samples and other incentives to establish themselves as the dominant, if not only, dog in the yard. Unlike the Wal-Marts of the world, though, the Hells Angels reserve the right to kill whoever stands in their way. Competition becomes fierce; rival biker gangs often increase their activity in an attempt to show the Hells Angels they are worthy of membership or that they are powerful enough to remain independent. The Hells Angels can patch them in (give them membership), keep them as vassals or try to eliminate them. No matter which happens, the level of street crime and violence escalates.

Before the RCMP, the Sûreté du Québec (SQ) and individual police forces in Quebec started rounding up bikers in unprecedented numbers, O'Neill wanted to take down Stadnick and Stockford. On March 25, he set up a conference call with Pacey and a crew of eager young Hamilton police officers, telling them for the first time what the RCMP knew about the Hells Angels and particularly Stadnick and Stockford. The excitement was palpable. The Hamilton cops had been trying to bring down Stadnick for years, but the most they'd been able to nail him with were traffic tickets. "I could hear a lull," O'Neill said. "They'd obviously been trying to get him for years."

After O'Neill finished, one of the excited Hamilton cops asked: "You say there are murder charges—is that first degree or second?"

"First degree," O'Neill said with some satisfaction. Then he went on to read them the details of all 13 murder-one counts against Stadnick.

Another long silence. O'Neill wondered how his team in Hamilton was taking the news, until one of them couldn't help it any longer and shouted: "Oh man, we love you guys, you're the best!"

Stockford was easy. Ancaster is considered by many to be the nicest, certainly the most bucolic, of Hamilton's suburbs. Up on the mountain and far away from the smoke-belching factories of the city's North and East Ends, Ancaster is quiet, relaxed and safely removed from the squalor and poverty of inner-city Hamilton. When you see a police car up here you figure some kids got hold of some beer or something equally innocent. On the morning of March 26, however, a heavily armed SWAT team, complete with body armor and assault rifles, descended upon the Stockford residence. Taking no chances, the cops called to Stockford from a truck-mounted loudspeaker, informing him that they had a warrant for his arrest and a warrant to search his home. Almost immediately, Stockford came out of the house with his hands on the back of his head. Shivering in just jeans and a T-shirt, he was immediately whisked into a police car and taken to Hamilton for questioning. Inside, the cops found a treasure trove of evidence—everything from laminated index cards with the names, addresses and phone numbers of Nomads members, prospects and hangarounds to minutes of gang meetings to a tax return for Nomads Quebec Inc., and even a list of the bikers' favorite restaurants in Montreal. The police were surprised by how much incriminating material they carted away. For all his skill as an organizer, Stockford made a pretty lousy gangster.

Stadnick proved more difficult. Cloverhill Road is two blocks long and surrounded on two sides by a 90-degree turn in the forested cliff that separates Upper Hamilton from Lower Hamilton. It is about as isolated as you can get in a major city. That facade of calm was shattered on the morning of March 26 when eager police came racing down the street. Suddenly, they stopped in front of Stadnick's unassuming red brick house. There seemed to be some confusion. "Nothing happened for a few minutes," said one eyewitness. "Then a news van—with all the dishes on top—arrived and it all started going down." The police started blaring orders at Stadnick's house. Other than the light rustling of neighbors stirring and the white noise of police radios, there was silence. Again they pleaded for Stadnick to come out without violence. Nothing. Suddenly six large officers in full body armor came running out of a truck with what looked to one witness like "a log with handles." Two hits and the door was down. Two officers with their backs to the house each threw something into the opening where the door had been. Immediately there was a sound like twin thunderclaps and the inside of the house lit up "like it was daylight inside." Still nothing moved. One of the men who had thrown in a percussion grenade shouted "GO! GO! GO!" while windmilling his left arm. Armored men with assault rifles and shotguns stormed the house. Despite the fact that 24 hours of surveillance had shown no movement in or around the house, the police seemed surprised to find nobody at home.

Perhaps disappointed that their quarry had eluded them, they tore the place apart. After the raid, Stadnick's common-law wife, Kathi Anderson, complained that the house had suffered extensive damage from the grenades and that, even years later, the police were holding on to her computer and her "printer, monitor, keyboard, mouse, scanner and CDs and laptop." "They took my fax machine, my telephone, every VHS tape I owned, pictures right off the wall, dozens of photo albums . . . " and more. Complaining that the police had shown perhaps more zeal than efficiency, Anderson went on to say, "They also smashed the front and side doors in (although they are within 8 to 10 feet of each other) and left my home unwatched and open for five days." She also pointed out that in the Quebec arrests, police knocked on the front door.

Stadnick proved more discreet than his partner Stockford just up the road in Ancaster. The police found little in Stadnick's house that had any value in a courtroom aside from photos and a Valentine's card from a 10-year-old niece that asked "Uncle Wally" if he was "still in charge of the Hells Angels."

Pacey wasn't pleased. He called O'Neill in Montreal. "We haven't seen him around," he said. "Do you guys have any intelligence that he's away?"

O'Neill didn't know. He called RCMP intelligence and asked them to run a check on exit points. He was in luck. A few hours later, the phone rang. Stadnick and Anderson had flown from Toronto's Pearson Airport to Montego Bay in Jamaica. The cops even knew what hotel they were staying in.

It took the RCMP's Jamaica liaison officer, Richard Sauvé, six hours to drive from his office in Kingston to the Wyndham just outside Montego Bay. O'Neill's luck held. Sauvé spotted Stadnick in minutes. But then, there weren't too many longhaired, 5-foot 4-inch vacationers covered in tattoos and burn scars. "I saw him—he's sitting by the pool," Sauvé told O'Neill. "He's with his girlfriend."

O'Neill told Sauvé to sit tight and keep an eye on the suspect. With Stadnick in Jamaica, the arrest became an international operation. O'Neill was wise enough to make sure all his paperwork was in order before he made his move.

On the morning of March 28, the same day the Quebec arrests went down, Stadnick and Anderson moved from the Wyndham to the Ritz. The papers at the time, especially the vulgar Montreal tabloids, claimed that the couple had heard about the first few Quebec arrests by telephone or e-mail and were on the run, but Anderson says that they had dropped by the Ritz—the hotel they originally tried to book—the night before and asked if any rooms were available. When one was, they switched.

After settling in at the Ritz, the couple decided to relax by the pool. Stadnick knew instinctively from the sound of boots on pavement and the gasps of the vacationers that something was going down. When he looked up, he was staring at the hole in the end of an assault rifle. There were many of them, in fact, and they were all pointed at him and his wife. He said nothing. "Mr. Walter Stadnick?" asked a tall man with a prominently decorated uniform, even though it was clear he knew whom he was talking to. Walter nodded.

Sauvé stepped forward from behind the SWAT team and identified himself. "Mr. Stadnick, you are under arrest for 13 counts of murder, three counts of attempted murder, one count of conspiracy to commit murder, two counts of narcotics trafficking and two counts of attempting to smuggle narcotics." Stadnick went peacefully.

After a night in a tiny Montego Bay cell Anderson described as a "hell hole," Stadnick was transported to Jamaica's National Remand Centre in Kingston. Surrounded by razor wire and a 24-hour armed guard and obliged to use a communal toilet bucket, Stadnick waited patiently for his time in court. On April 2, he was led into Kingston's Half-Way-Tree Courthouse, where he confidently told resident magistrate Martin Gayle that he had no idea why the charges were being leveled against him and that he would readily waive his right to an extradition process so he could fight them. Granted.

The paperwork wouldn't be completed until April 10. When O'Neill and a partner from the Montreal Police arrived in Kingston, they were shocked at the atrocious conditions at the Remand Centre. Describing the scene as "a bit like [the 1978 prison movie] *Midnight Express*," O'Neill thought he'd find Stadnick desperate to get back to the relatively posh conditions of a Canadian jail. He was surprised by what he found. Sitting on the floor, chatting and laughing with some friends, Stadnick made O'Neill wait until he was finished his sentence before acknowledging him. Unruffled, O'Neill decided to play with Stadnick a bit. "So, Walter, how'd you like to stay here for a couple more weeks?" he asked. "It can be arranged."

Stadnick looked him straight in the eye and chuckled derisively. "Couple more weeks? I'd be running this place." Hoots of ominous laughter surrounded O'Neill and his partner.

Later, O'Neill admitted that he thought that the only white prisoner—and a short and funny-looking one at that—would have a tough time surviving in a Jamaican jail. He couldn't have been more wrong. "I thought they'd be frying him up," he said. "But he made some friends in there and left real cocky." As the two Canadian cops, aided by a phalanx of Jamaican guards with submachine guns, escorted the diminutive biker leader out of his cell, they were chilled by what they heard. Hoots, hollers, whistles and applause came from what seemed like every cell. "Yo, Walter!" they yelled. "We're with you, man!" Stadnick loved it.

Chapter 2

Joanne Carswell saw all her beliefs die in one day. At an event where she expected to celebrate the beauty of peace, togetherness, friendship and tolerance, she was instead a witness to a repulsive display of the strong preying on the weak. She saw a terrifying group of large armed men terrorizing young people, taking their money, assaulting them and generally destroying any idea she may have had about the fellowship of humanity. Before the day was over, Joanne would watch one of that group of men plunge a knife deep into the throat of a kid and see that kid crumple to the ground. She would witness a murder.

It was December 6, 1969. Three and a half months earlier, Woodstock, despite all its failings, had given young people all over the world hope that their ideals could work in real life. Originally intended to be held in Woodstock, a small town in upstate New York, the festival was actually realized 38 miles away on Max Yasgur's dairy farm in Bethel after officials in Woodstock and other towns turned it down. Hastily planned for up to 50,000 people, 400,000 arrived. The food, water, sanitary and security systems were immediately and absolutely overwhelmed. Almost nobody paid to get in—the promoters actually lost money until they started selling records a year later. Most people were forced to park at least 15 miles away, there were shortages of everything and people relieved themselves anywhere they felt like, leaving Yasgur's formerly idyllic farm a devastated, litter-clogged mud pit with all 450 of his cows "set free." Doctors, medicine, water and food had to be helicoptered in at taxpayers' expense. But, to the young people of the time, these were minor quibbles. They pulled it off. Woodstock worked. The hippies got together—almost a half million of them—and had a great time. Although at least three people died at Woodstock, none died as the result of violence. Let the establishment worry about such boring details as toilets, food and water. The people had put together the biggest party in history and proved that the ideals of peace, love and brotherhood had to be recognized.

One group of young men clearly recognized the importance of Woodstock. The Rolling Stones, the reigning kings of popular music since the decline of the Beatles, were conspicuous by their absence at the historic festival. According to rock mythology, author Ken Kesey came up with the idea of "Woodstock West" and presented it to a number of well-known bands. Eager to take advantage of the groundswell of enthusiasm for mega-parties, the Rolling Stones decided to end their 1969 tour with a bang.

Recruiting Woodstock alumni Santana, the Grateful Dead, Jefferson Airplane, the Flying Burrito Brothers and Crosby, Stills, Nash and Young, the Rolling Stones and the promoters managed to get everything together in just 110 days. As with their colleagues back East, the promoters were rebuffed by a number of potential venues. Frustrated, the band and their promoters turned to *Rolling Stone* magazine publisher Jann Wenner and he sent them to Melvin Belli, a lawyer famous for protecting the interests of California's conservative elite. A little more than 24 hours before the show, he hammered out a deal with Dick Carter of the Altamont Speedway. About as far away from San Francisco as Woodstock was from New York City, the sleepy, nearly bankrupt racetrack was just outside the dusty San Joaquin Valley town of Tracy.

Most of the same problems that plagued Woodstock—shortages of water, food and toilets—hit Altamont as well, and drug use was even more rampant. According to author Robert Sam Anson, the Hells Angels sold thousands of hits of LSD laced with methamphetamines.

That potentially deadly mix led to so many painful bad trips and psychotic episodes that the festival's first aid centers were swamped well before the first band went on. "There didn't seem to be any cops around, so people were doing all kinds of illegal drugs pretty openly," Joanne Carswell said. "It looked like the Hells Angels were in charge, and I don't think anybody thought they'd mind if we got high—hell, they all looked stoned."

Stoned or not, the Hells Angels were a formidable force. And as tensions mounted they reacted the only way they knew how. According to rock historian Philip Norman: "By halfway through Santana's set, swirls and flurries of violence, at first almost too quick for the eye to follow, were happening all along the stage—from there to its scaffolded corners where massed Hells Angels confronted the ordinary public." Although Altamont owner Dick Carter may have hired lots of cops and security guards, none could be seen anywhere near the stage once the concert had begun and the Hells Angels were holding sway.

The crescendo of violence at Altamont may have become a long-forgotten item of rock lore if not for the fact that a team of cameramen was shooting a documentary about the Rolling Stones tour. Called *Gimme Shelter*, the film shows a shocking amount of violence at Altamont, virtually all of it performed by the Hells Angels. Although the Hells Angels managed to intimidate most of the crew into not shooting, Stephen Lighthill came up with an ingenious and courageous way to record the event. Since his camera was mounted on a shoulder brace, he simply kept it running and pretended it was turned off. "Hells Angels were hassling me all day and telling me to stop shooting," he said. "All the stuff with people being beaten on with pool cues was shot by me, and as long as I wasn't looking at what the camera and the microphone were pointing at, nobody was the wiser."

The Angels, conspicuous by their leather jackets and the club's winged death's-head logo, were armed with sawed-off pool cues reinforced with lead. Although not quite a deadly weapon, a whack in the head with one would leave its victim a crumpled, helpless mess. In an attempt to calm the Hells Angels, promoters moved cases and cases of beer to their positions along the edge of the stage. The bikers began hurling full cans at fans they decided were out of line. Although it was later reported that the Angels were altruistically tossing beer into the crowd, they can be clearly seen in *Gimme Shelter* whipping full steel cans at kids in the crowd. One is said to have fractured a girl's skull.

Things got significantly worse during Jefferson Airplane's set and the fighting became the focus of more attention than the music. Frustrated, Jefferson Airplane singer Marty Balin told one of the Hells Angels, who was severely beating a young man, to stop. One of the Hells Angels on stage took offense at Balin's indiscretion and punched him in the face, knocking him out. The Grateful Dead and their entourage assessed the scene as too violent for them, packed up and left without playing.

The Rolling Stones, as headliners, didn't have the option of chickening out. They knew that 400,000 amped-up, pissed-off kids would riot. They went on and, to their credit, began a pretty good set. But a great many people in the crowd, especially those nearest the ridiculously accessible two-foot-high stage, had things on their mind other than music. Fights broke out all over. Fists, threats and even dirty looks were met with a smash in the face with a pool cue. Although Jagger pleaded with the crowd to "cool down," things seemed to ramp up as the Stones played their controversial hit "Sympathy for the Devil."

After that, things got weird. As the Stones finished their next song, "Under My Thumb," a young black man approached the stage. In *Gimme Shelter* it's clear he has something in his hand, but it's not clear what it is. Suddenly, he's confronted by a Hells Angel. A scuffle ensues and the two are almost instantly surrounded by a group of bikers. There's a flash of metal as a knife is plunged repeatedly into the throat of Meredith Hunter.

Carswell saw the whole thing. "They surrounded him and stabbed him over and over again," she said. "He wasn't dead when he was lying there, but he was clearly dying." According to Carswell, some of the kids in the crowd tried to help the poor young man convulsing in a pool of his own blood, but the bikers kept them away. "I heard one of them say, 'He's dying anyway' and another threatened some kids who were trying to help him," she said. "He told them, 'He deserves to die.'"

Altamont was a huge failure. When it was over, four people were dead. A couple in a sleeping bag fell victim to a hit and run, a teenager drowned in a drainage ditch and a young man was killed by the Hells Angels.

The police arrested 24-year-old ex-convict Alan Passaro, the biker who killed Hunter. Melvin Belli, recruited by the Hells Angels, got some of the film from the rough cuts of *Gimme Shelter* and showed it to the cops. He convinced them that the object in Hunter's hand was actually a gun. After a while, they agreed, but pointed out that the self-defense excuse would be no good unless the gun was found. Belli quickly made calls to "every lawyer in the area" to track down Ralph "Sonny" Barger, president of the Oakland chapter of the Hells Angels. The next day, Barger brought him a shoebox. Inside there was a gun that Barger claimed the Hells Angels had taken from Hunter at Altamont. The cops believed him and let Passaro walk. The Rolling Stones allegedly paid Hunter's mother $10,000 not to cause trouble.

By most accounts, the Hells Angels got away with murder at Altamont. Joanne Carswell certainly thinks so. "I saw it all. Hunter wasn't threatening Jagger; it's not like they were protecting him or anything," she said. "And even if he had a gun, and I still don't think he did, he didn't stand a chance against all those bikers."

It's unclear why the Hells Angels got off. Maybe it was racism, maybe it was Belli's charm or maybe it was the legendary reputation of the Hells Angels. Whatever it was, Altamont represented the end of the hippie era. The tragedy that sprang from the concert that was supposed to represent the anti-establishment ideals of the hippie generation instead showed the immense flaws in the peace and love philosophy. No matter how peaceful you want to be, there will always be bad men who want to take advantage of you. For every group of people who want to promote peace, equality and free love, there will be men with sawed-off pool cues and knives who will want to sell them drugs and bust their heads. Many saw Altamont as the death-knell of the hippie movement. Carswell, for one, took the flowers out of her hair and moved back home with her parents.

* * *

While the hippies lost their credibility, the Hells Angels increased theirs. The kind of young men who'd like to become Hells Angels were impressed and emboldened by what happened at Altamont. To them, the bikers at Altamont were doing their job, protecting Mick Jagger and each other from a black man with a gun. These were the kind of young men who saw all morality in absolutes, who saw violence as a natural retribution to those who break their rules and who saw a life outside the often incomprehensible laws of the state as logical, realistic and even romantic.

Such men have been flocking to the Hells Angels since they emerged in California after World War II. The organization was established as an entity in San Bernardino in 1947. Millions of men were coming back from the war and most of them wanted to return to their homes, wives, jobs and normalcy. But some didn't. "Like the drifters who rode west after Appomattox [during the American Civil War], there were thousands of veterans in 1945 who flatly rejected the idea of going back to their prewar pattern," said journalist Hunter S. Thompson, who wrote a book about the Hells Angels in 1965, *Hell's Angels*, after having lived with them for two years. "They didn't want order but privacy, and time to figure things out. It was a nervous, downhill feeling, a mean kind of angst that comes out of wars."

There were literally thousands of them—young men accustomed to the thrills and horrors of combat who could find nothing for themselves in normal civilian life. There was one thing, however, that came close. In the late '40s, motorcycles were very different than they are today. In that less sophisticated age, bikes were little more than engines, frames, chains and wheels. To make them even more dangerous and exciting, some riders would lengthen their bikes' forks and handlebars and remove their rear springs, giving birth to what we now know as "choppers." Many young men, fresh from the bloody fields of France or the vicious beaches of the South Pacific, needed something wild to satisfy their nihilistic urges—and tearing down the freeway on bikes was as close to fun as they could find.

These men didn't fit into the button-down conformity of the Truman/Eisenhower era and were well aware of it. They couldn't hang out with the squares any more than they could buy a tract house and drive a Ford Fairlane to the factory every day. Increasingly alienated from conventional culture, some combat-veteran bikers formed groups, at first loose and then later tight-knit, modeled after the units they served with in the military.

Many American units in World War II, particularly bomber squadrons, adopted the name Hells Angels. There was something about the concept of good men doing bad work (or bad men doing good work) that appealed to Americans in war. Perhaps the complex feelings aroused by dropping tons of high explosives and incendiaries on cities full of innocent civilians, all the while knowing it was the only way to combat fascism, created the quasi-religious paradox that brought about such an oxymoronic name.

Before America even entered the war, the Hells Angels existed. After Japan invaded China in 1937, what was left of Chiang Kai-shek's Nationalist government was desperate. With no real air force of their own, the Chinese bought 100 American P-40 fighters from the British and went looking for pilots. Chiang's wife hired Claire Chennault, a retired U.S. general, to recruit pilots under the guise of a civilian air transport company called the Central Aircraft Manufacturing Corporation. Chennault left the U.S. Army when he could not convince the brass that their bombers needed fighter protection and that using hit-and-run tactics would best suit the Americans' fast, rugged planes. A wise man who understood the complex emotions and motivations of young men, Chennault trolled the American military looking for pilots with drive, ambition and a deep dissatisfaction with the military hierarchy.

Going into action just after the attack on Pearl Harbor, Chennault's men, now known as the Flying Tigers, were a stunning success. Fighting over enemy territory, always outnumbered (sometimes by as much as 20 to 1), the Tigers used bravery, creativity and cutting-edge tactics to better the up-till-then invincible Japanese. While the regular American and British forces were being clobbered, the Flying Tigers were dominating. Despite ridiculous odds, the Tigers destroyed 286 Japanese planes for a loss of just six of their own.

The Tigers were individualists. At a time when most other planes were squeaky clean, theirs were emblazoned with lurid sharks' mouths, skulls, cartoon characters and funny or threatening slogans. And instead of numbers, the pilots named their three squadrons—the Pandas, the Adam & Eves and the Hell's Angels.

The name probably came from the controversial 1930 Howard Hughes film, *Hell's Angels*. At a cost of $3.8 million—inflated by

Hughes' pathological perfectionism which required 249 feet of film to be shot for every one that made it into the final cut—and three dead stunt pilots, the story of two charismatic American pilots who reluctantly fight for the British in World War I perfectly fit the image the Flying Tigers were trying to project.

After the Allies earned a toehold in Asia, the Flying Tigers were to be handed over from the Chinese to the U.S. Army Air Force. At first, it seemed like a good idea. The Flying Tigers had been operating in a devastated war zone with a minimum of food, ammunition and other supplies; getting a pipeline of goods from the States would help. But it didn't turn out that way. As volunteers under Chinese control, the pilots had no official tie to the American military and had to be enlisted. "The officious colonel who was recruiting started threatening the guys," said Dick Rossi, Pandas flight leader and six-kill ace. "He was one of those people with no combat experience who feels he knows it all." The tough-guy sales pitch failed. Only five of more than 100 pilots joined the China Air Task Force.

One who didn't join was Hell's Angels squadron leader Arvid "Oley" Olson. Noted among his peers for his fearlessness and ability to improvise, he once acquired some crated machine guns from an American boat that was thought to be totally destroyed by the Japanese in 1937. He and some of his squadron mates instead chose to join the Chindits, a British commando unit operating in Burma, who had the same self-determining freedom from a distant command structure that the Flying Tigers had.

When the war ended, Olson and his friends ended up in San Bernardino. They rode big, loud Harley-Davidsons. They rarely associated with anyone else. But they didn't become what we now know as the Hells Angels Motorcycle Club. Other units had used the name Hell's Angels—most notably the 11th airborne division and the famously hard-drinking 303rd bomber squadron in North Africa and Europe—so it could have emerged from another source. It's far more likely, however, the name's origin came from area bikers who came into contact with Olson and his friends and wanted to emulate them. There's no doubting they were cool.

All over America groups of young men were springing up who liked to ride bikes, party and live on the edge of the law or just outside it. Motorcycles were cheap; many were sold as army surplus after the war, and the men who rode them tended to cluster together because they didn't always fit into conventional society very well or at all. Of course, not all motorcycle riders in the late '40s, or even the majority of them, were outlaws. But the few that were tended to stand out and make things bad for the others.

The image of the antisocial trouble-making biker in a black leather jacket invaded widespread consciousness in the summer of 1947. Two motorcycle enthusiast groups—far from outlaws—organized a get-together for July 4th in the farming town of Hollister, California. Sanctioned by the American Motorcycle Association, the ride expanded to include races and hill-climbs. More than 4,000 bikers descended upon the town of 4,500.

Two groups in particular, the Pissed Off Bastards of Bloomington and the Booze Fighters, arrived with more on their minds than racing up hills. Drunk from the start, the Bastards and Fighters started racing and performing dangerous stunts in the streets, fighting, throwing beer bottles through windows and generally terrorizing the locals. Hollister's seven-man police force was helpless and called in 40 highway patrolmen who established a sort of informal martial law. Bars were closed, a threat of tear gas was made and the bikers skulked out of town. Those who remained were the 50 or so who were seriously injured—Frank McGovern of Chico had his foot nearly severed in a racing accident—and the more than 50 who wound up in jail.

Although the stories of a drunken orgy of violence that have circulated about Hollister are generally exaggerated and the famous photo that appeared in *Life* magazine of a shirtless biker passed out on a Harley was later admitted to be faked, the popular image of the rowdy biker was cast. Police chief Fred A. Earl called it "the worst 40 hours in Hollister's history." Joyce Lane, superintendent of nearby Hazel Hawkins Memorial Hospital, told the press that drunk and injured people were being admitted "too fast to keep accurate records." The AMA quickly distanced itself from the maelstrom by issuing a press release that labeled the troublemakers "outlaws" and referred to them contemptuously as "1 percent" of an otherwise law-abiding fraternity of riders. To this day, both "outlaw" and "1-percenter" are terms with great resonance among motorcycle gangs, and both are considered valuable titles to be earned.

After Hollister, a prominent Pissed Off Bastard named Otto Friedli split with the club and formed his own group on March 17, 1948 in Fontana, just west of San Bernardino. He called it the Hells Angels Motorcycle Club. They weren't much different from other clubs, except for the cool name. It got even cooler in 1954 when Otto's club merged with San Francisco troublemakers and Hollister veterans, the Market Street Commandos. The new members, now called the Hells Angels San Francisco Chapter, paid their mates back with what would later become a world-famous and fiercely protected trademark, the winged skull logo.

Later that year, Hollywood released a film that would do more for bikers than anything they could have done themselves. Inspired by the short story "The Cyclists' Raid," which was loosely based on the Hollister incident, *The Wild One* is about a biker gang that invades a motorcycle race and then clashes with a rival gang. Many consider Marlon Brando's portrayal of Johnny, the troubled, brooding biker, to be his best work. Johnny is seduced by the romantic, lawless life of the bikers, but is decidedly at odds with the pointlessness of their violent existence.

The film was a massive critical and financial success and it rocketed Brando to the apex of stardom. His rebellious look and style set the standard for alienated youth everywhere. Millions of wannabes popped up overnight and, even 50 years later, the leather jacket and jeans look still works on today's streets.

But the real bikers found Johnny to be a bit of a sissy. He didn't get it. All thoughtful and sensitive, he was a square pretending to be a rebel. Hell, he even rode a Triumph (Brando's bike in real life). No, the bikers preferred the film's villain. Based on notorious Booze Fighter Willie "Wino Willie" Forkner, Lee Marvin's Harley-riding Chino was derided by many as a sadistic brute. But to many bikers, he was the epitome of cool. So impressive was he that San Francisco Hells Angel (and later chapter president) Frank Sadilek rode to Los Angeles the day after he saw the movie to buy a replica of the blue-and-yellow striped shirt Marvin wore as Chino. Sadilek wore the shirt every day until it fell apart years later.

Armed with the new logo and the best bikes (Harleys only, no Indians or "foreign crap"), the Hells Angels were everything the legion of young men who saw *The Wild One* wanted to be. These weren't the pilots, paratroopers and bombardiers who took to motorcycles to relieve the tediousness of life after combat. These were more ordinary young men, rebelling against a post-war America that promised so much, but left many behind. Although it was a time of unprecedented wealth and freedom, not everybody got a piece and not everybody wanted to throw on a fedora, drive to the factory and come home to a wife, kids and a mundane house in the suburbs. Joining the growing trend towards franchising (McDonald's was emerging in the same area at the same time), Hells Angels chapters started sprouting up all over the west coast.

One of those disaffected young men was Ralph Hubert Barger Jr. Born on October 8, 1938 to a working-class family in a run-down stop on the highway appropriately called Modesto, Barger didn't have a great start in life. His dad was working down the road laying pavement on Highway 99 and his mother would take Sonny (as Ralph Jr. was called) and his big sister, Shirley Marie, on the bus to visit him every weekend. Whether it was the stress of handling two young children without a father or something she saw on her visits to Ralph Sr.'s motel, Kathryn Carmella Barger left the kids with a babysitter and ran off with a Trailways driver to Twentyninepalms, California.

There would be no picket-fence upbringing for Sonny. With mom out of the picture, he and his sister moved in with their grandmother in Oakland, one of the most violent and racially divided cities in America. Sonny was what they used to call a "problem child" and dropped out of 10th grade in 1955 to join the army. He finished 13 months of basic and then advanced infantry training before the army realized he was too young and gave him an honorable discharge. After that, he meandered pointlessly from one job to another— including a stint on a potato chip assembly line—before he bought a bike and started a club.

On April 1, 1957 (a date still tattooed on his arm), Barger's club became the Oakland Chapter of the Hells Angels. A year later Friedli went to prison and a new national president was needed. Through the force of sheer charisma, the wiry, fidgety little man from Oakland won the job. Barger immediately went to work. He moved the Hells Angels headquarters from Berdoo (as the Club rechristened San Bernardino because it was too long to fit on their jackets) to Oakland. Writing up a code of behavior that included things like a $5 fine for fighting between members and the ban on messing with another Angel's "old lady," he made a blueprint for a franchise that would eventually spread across the U.S. and a dozen other countries.

* * *

Despite their rebellious aspirations, Barger gave the Hells Angels a pseudo-military hierarchy and they have become one of the most stringently self-policed organizations in the world. Each chapter has a president, either elected or unchallenged, who has ultimate control of all club decisions. Despite his power, the president of one chapter has no jurisdiction over other chapters. Even the national president has no immediate power over other chapters, although he is always listened to and treated with respect and even reverence. The chapter president rides on the front left of the Angels' two-column formation. Beside him is his right-hand man, the road captain. His duties are to take care of all the unpleasant necessities like planning trips, carrying cash and dealing with police. Behind them ride the vice-president, the president's choice to stand in for him when needed but not necessarily the next in line for his job, and the secretary-treasurer, who controls meetings, fines and dues and keeps a list of all members' names and addresses. After these come the full-patch members of the club. The last of these is the sergeant-at-arms, who acts as the president's body-guard, club enforcer and general tough guy. Bigger clubs may have an assistant enforcer who rides alongside the sergeant-at-arms. Behind them ride the honorary members, who are retired members or close associates like lawyers, bail bondsmen or motorcycle parts suppliers who have helped the club in the past. At the very end are prospective members and other associates. As in a pack of wolves, everyone knows his place and any deviation from the established order is immediately and brutally put down.

Nobody is lower than friends—associates of club members who have no official rights and wear no colors but may be invited to parties or on rides. Friends who want to apply for membership must meet some qualifications. "Someone who comes around the club and wants to join must have a good motorcycle, a Harley-Davidson," said Clarence "Addie" Crouch, former vice-president of the Cleveland Chapter. "He must be white and 21 or older." A woman from Ventura, California, once attempted to sue the Hells Angels to gain membership, but failed because the club receives no government funding. "We don't get any money from the government; they can't make us do anything," said Barger years later. "Even if they could, we wouldn't do it." An applicant is expected to do everything he's told by anyone above him. He must also withstand a lot of "mud checking"—being beaten up by club members. Although he is expected to fight back, he will often be attacked by groups of two, three or more and usually knows better than to show a full member up by winning.

After a period that usually ranges from three months to two years in which the friend has proven himself trustworthy, the club members will vote on his status. Only if he receives 100 percent support from club members will he be promoted to a hangaround. Now he has more rights: he may be allowed in the clubhouse to work and he gets to hang around the clubhouse preventing the curious from getting close. A hangaround's primary duty is to keep a distance between club members and the public, but he may be asked to do anything by a member and he must do it. Chad Proctor, a former hangaround in Vancouver, described his life under the members as "intolerable" and called his bosses "tyrannical." But such is the allure of the Hells Angels that many young men fight for the opportunity to go through the procedure.

As his status rises, so does his risk. While a transgression by a friend may just result in his dismissal, it gets tougher for hangarounds. They are expected to be available to do any task a member dictates and they are on call 24/7. If a hangaround breaks a rule, he's exiled from the club forever. "If he does not go through a mud check, they run him off," said Crouch. "They beat him up, take his motorcycle, take his old lady, whatever; they run him off."

A hangaround is given three opportunities to become a prospect and must get 100 percent approval. If he fails, he'll be exiled. Unlike much of the operation of the Hells Angels, there's no set of rules surrounding the prospecting process. If a hangaround proves his worth and exhibits the right attitude, he'll be approved. The prospect's life is still tough, but in many ways is better than a hangaround's. He's allowed full access to the clubhouse and, far more important, he gets his colors. A leather jacket with the death's head logo and a top rocker (the text above the crest) that says "Hells Angels," the colors are said to be more important to a Hells Angel than any other possession or woman. The colors are precious and the rules around them are complex and absolute. They can't be touched by a non-member without punishment. A Hells Angel who forgets to wear his colors to a party or meeting will likely be beaten by other Angels. If he loses his colors, he will probably be exiled forever. To desecrate an Angel's colors is said to be an offense punishable by death, even when done by other Angels. The Angels are fiercely proud of their colors and will not tolerate imitators. Wannabes have had their unearned death's head tattoos removed by knife.

A prospect gets his full patch (the bottom rocker identifying which chapter he belongs to) when he becomes a member. Traditionally, the initiation ceremony for a member is as awful as everything he's had to endure thus far, and more disgusting. In a ritual that was as profane as the Cosa Nostra's is regarded as religious, the new member was forced to undergo a shower of vomit, urine, feces, blood and ejaculate and forbidden to wash his jacket ever again. What followed was a party where the initiate must prove his ability to withstand beatings, drink dangerous amounts of alcohol and perform sexual feats with women supplied by the club. The initiate was then given nine days to get a tattoo of the Hells Angels' logo (complete with rockers) and the date he joined. Most chose to tatoo an arm, but other body parts have been used, including the penis of some more dedicated members. If a member left the Angels honorably, he had to get the date of his departure added to his tattoo. If he was kicked out, he'd have his tattoo removed by other members. Although a few Hells Angels veterans have claimed that initiates must kill a person to gain full membership, that claim is almost universally regarded as a myth.

As horrible as it sounds, men lined up to join the Hells Angels. Existing motorcycle clubs either eagerly applied for acceptance or were forced to do so as the franchising operation sought dominance. For the next few years, the Hells Angels enjoyed riding, drinking and partying with celebrity status. They had so much notoriety and confidence that Barger found the chutzpah to express his hardcore patriotism by writing Lyndon Johnson in 1964 to offer help for the military in Southeast Asia.

Dear Mr. President,
On behalf of myself and my associates I volunteer a group of loyal americans in Viet Nam. We feel that a crack group of trained gorrillas would demoralize the Viet Cong and advance the cause of freedom. We are available for training and duty immediately.
Sincerely,
Ralph Barger Jr.
Oakland, California
President of Hells Angels

* * *

Things changed later that year. Two girls—one 14, the other 15—claimed to have been gang-raped by Hells Angels at a Labor Day run in Monterey. Although one of the girls later refused to testify and the other failed a lie-detector test, the damage was done. The Hells Angels emerged from the Monterey rape case an altogether different organization.

Members "Terry the Tramp," Marvin "Moldy" Gilbert, "Mother" Miles and Filmore "Crazy" Cross were indicted in the case and their defense was expensive. Despite their notoriety in the early '60s, the Angels were not rich. Still at that point a social club dedicated to bikes, booze and broads, many members committed some petty crimes to supplement paychecks, but were not riding to get rich. A few sold drugs, but nothing major. More often, the bikers would rent themselves and their vicious reputations out to the mafia as debt collectors and enforcers. The Hells Angels who were employed generally worked in low-paying menial jobs; Barger himself worked in a warehouse. By this time, Harley-Davidsons were becoming expensive and notoriously prone to costly breakdowns. Cops had it in for bikers and the constant barrage of tickets, bail and workdays lost for court appearances depleted the club's reserves. The club charged dues, regularly fined its members for minor infractions and needed a constant supply of beer, booze and food for its parties. Even the most decorated Hells Angels edged close to homelessness since keeping the club going and their bikes running was more important than things like rent.

Although a few younger Angels used and dealt things like marijuana on a small-time basis, the Hells Angels traditionally disdained illegal drugs. But it was a desperate time. With four brothers behind bars needing bail and lawyers, the club was on the brink of collapse. At a meeting, one member spoke about a friend who earned tons of money making a new kind of drug in his kitchen with ingredients bought at a pharmacy or grocery store. The other members listened and the Hells Angels, perhaps reluctantly, entered the crystal meth business.

Methamphetamines are stimulants that dilate the pupils and produce temporary hyperactivity, euphoria, a sense of increased energy and tremors. Crystal meth is the much more potent and smokable form of the drug. According to the U.S. Drug Enforcement Agency:

> Methamphetamine is neurotoxic, meaning that it causes damage to the brain. High doses or chronic use have been associated with increased nervousness, irritability and paranoia. Withdrawal from high doses produces severe depression. Chronic abuse produces a psychosis similar to schizophrenia and is characterized by paranoia, picking at the skin, self-absorption and auditory and visual hallucinations. Violent and erratic behavior is frequently seen among chronic, high-dose methamphetamine abusers.

It was the perfect drug for the Hells Angels. Made up of small white flakes or shards—earning it the nickname "ice"—crystal meth is easy to hide in a jacket or a motorcycle. In fact, many attribute the nickname "crank" to the fallacious idea that bikers hid the drug in the crankcases of their Harleys. Even better, since it was made locally in informal "labs," the notoriously xenophobic Hells Angels didn't have to rely on any "foreigners."

It was the '60s and the times were indeed a-changin'. The primary market for drugs was the burgeoning population of young people who were growing increasingly anti-establishment, but in an entirely different way than the Hells Angels were. Although they didn't care much for government and its rules, the bikers were fiercely patriotic and considered the legions of antiwar youths to be "commies." The animosity was not reciprocated. Hippies and their associates were as seduced by the biker mystique as anyone, maybe more so. When journalist Hunter S. Thompson was living and riding with the Hells Angels, he introduced them to pioneer hippie Ken Kesey. A strong advocate of drugs as a mind-expanding tool, Kesey traveled around the country in a multicolored school bus with a group he called the Merry Pranksters. He decided to put the two groups together and on August 7, 1965, the Hells Angels and the most prominent hippie group got together with assorted cultural and academic noteworthies for a summit and party.

About 40 Bay Area Hells Angels, led by Barger, showed up. At times disgusted with the hippies and the egghead intellectuals' left-wing pretensions, the bikers lightened up when they were introduced to all kinds of new drugs, primarily LSD and cocaine, and realized the implications. The hippies were delighted. The bikers seemed heroic. In the reactionary world of the '60s left, the Hells Angels filled the romantic niche of the rugged individualist soldier—much like the role of knights, cowboys and fighter pilots in other times and places.

After the party, the knights in leather armor went back to their regular way of doing things. On October 16, a throng of antiwar protestors (contemporary estimates were as high as 15,000) marched from the University of California campus at Berkeley toward the massive Oakland Army Terminal. The cops stopped them long before they reached the base and the demonstrators arranged an impromptu sit-in/silent protest as they had a couple of times already that year. Local bikers went to check on the situation. Angered by the brazen display of what they perceived as anti-Americanism, the Hells Angels went in and started busting heads. The cops stepped aside and let the bikers do what many of them probably wouldn't have minded doing themselves.

One cop did what he was paid for and tried to separate a Hells Angel from a hippie he was pummeling. Other bikers descended upon him and his leg was broken with a kick from a steel-tipped boot.

The top of the hippie hierarchy panicked. Kesey, Allen Ginsberg and others begged for an emergency meeting with Barger. He responded with a threat to derail a similar, larger march planned for November 20. But after much beseeching and offering of tribute from the hippies, he eventually relented and let the "commies" plead their case. What followed was a defining moment for the Hells Angels.

On November 19, Barger called a press conference and changed history. Although he pointed out his absolute disgust for what the protestors believed in, he ultimately chickened out. The Hells Angels put business before principle: "Because our patriotic concern for what these people are doing to our great nation may provoke us to violent acts," he said, "any physical encounter would only produce sympathy for this mob of traitors."

The demonstration went on as planned, uninterrupted by the Hells Angels. Some bikers showed up, but they didn't bust heads, they sold drugs. The bikers got a chance to sell drugs to the millions of anti-establishment youths who craved them. The people who told those youths what to think got lots of drugs, the glamor of the Hells Angels and a lot fewer trips to the hospital. The '60s "revolution" was able to happen in large part because the Hells Angels didn't interfere.

On that day, the Hells Angels transformed from a bunch of guys looking for thrills, women and good times into an organized crime syndicate.

* * *

Hells Angels chapters continued popping up all over California, especially in the Bay Area, and even beyond. Dozens of motorcycle clubs applied for membership and were refused. Donald "Skeets" Picard, the president of a club in Lowell, Massachusetts, had a novel and somewhat desperate plan. He offered to ride his whole club the 3,100 miles from suburban Boston to Oakland to prospect before the now

renowned Sonny Barger. Picard's offer was accepted and, by all accounts, the club was treated with extraordinary harshness. Picard's
gang was a whole country away and Barger and his men would have to
trust the Hells Angels before they could allow them to wear the colors.
After their brutal hazing and a six-month tour of California in which
every Hells Angel was visited, half of the 30 prospects became members and the rest were chased off. On April 17, 1967, Lowell became
the first chapter outside of the Golden State.

After that, applications came rolling in. Most were ignored, and
only one club was invited to join without applying. The Aliens, under
the iron-fisted rule of Sandy Alexander, were the scourge of a New
York City that was peppered with all kinds of gangs and a culture of
random violence. With chapters in the Bronx, Queens and Manhattan,
the Aliens committed crimes on their own and performed jobs the mafia found too difficult to carry out. These were badass bikers who didn't
need the Hells Angels, and that's probably why the Hells Angels wanted them. Unlike the dozens of wannabe clubs who begged for prospect
colors, the Aliens refused to wear them and told Barger that they'd only
accept Hells Angels colors after they were granted full membership. In
fact, the Aliens offended the Hells Angels by wearing red and white,
a color combination they violently reserved for themselves. When the
Aliens showed up at a rally in Laconia, New Hampshire, in red and
white, the Hells Angels threatened them with extinction. The Aliens
offered to fight for the right to wear whatever colors they wanted. They
clearly won Barger's respect and, after some tense negotiations, became
the Hells Angels Motorcycle Club New York City on December 5,
1969. At that moment, the Hells Angels became a nationwide organization with deep ties to the mafia.

* * *

Canada was not immune to post-war angst. If anything, it struck worse
there, particularly in Quebec. After more than 200 years of distant
rule from a sometimes callous federal government and the even more
intense and pervasive grip of the Roman Catholic Church, the youth

of Quebec were ready to rebel. Outside a narrow strip of Montreal, in the '50s and '60s, Quebec was practically medieval in its ossified judgmental conservatism, and it became a breeding ground for biker gangs. By the end of the '60s, police estimates put the number of biker gangs in the province at 350. With an eye on escaping the suffocating sameness of La Belle Province, the gangs came up with such names as the Black Spiders, Missiles, Atomes, Beatniks and the blatantly wannabe Pacific Rebels. It wasn't just the names. The Gallic gangs honored the Hells Angels by copying their clothes, their habits and their hierarchies. Only the Marxist Citoyens de la Terre stood out as any different—and not by much. All did some minor drug trafficking, mainly to high schoolers, and all were accused of rape and other forms of violence. So excessive in their behavior were the Black Spiders, that in 1978 they were actually set upon—like a scene from Frankenstein—by more than 100 townspeople armed with axes, farm implements and torches. But most violence was biker-on-biker, biker-on-debtor or biker-on-teenage girl.

But the Quebec gangs were small-timers lacking organization. One Canadian gang, however, had a level of sophistication rivaling the Hells Angels. At the time, the economy in Southern Ontario was booming, so much so that the people living on the half-circle around the western edge of Lake Ontario were proudly calling it the Golden Horseshoe. With prosperity came a taste for vice and rebellion. At a time when the Hells Angels had just 12 chapters, Satan's Choice had ten in Southern Ontario and another in the west end of Montreal, which was then a relatively affluent English-speaking enclave.

The club hit its peak in 1968 when the Hells Angels, always looking to expand, sent an emissary to Toronto to meet the Satan's Choice leaders in hopes of establishing a merger between the clubs. They greeted him at the airport, listened to his sales pitch, decided against it and sent him home before he even left the terminal.

After that, things began to unravel. Police and media hit the individual chapters of Satan's Choice hard and there were many arrests. When charismatic founder and leader Bernie "the Frog" Guindon was jailed, the organization fell apart. Chapters in Hamilton, St. Catharines, Windsor, Ottawa and Montreal defected one by one to the Outlaws, the Hells Angels' primary rival in the U.S.

The presence of the well-financed and well-equipped Outlaws in the West End did not go unnoticed on the other side of Montreal. After years of claiming it would never happen, the largest gang in Quebec applied to the Hells Angels for membership in 1977. The Popeyes had been the hardest gang in Montreal and were often employed by the mafia to take on their most unpleasant tasks. Although overwhelmingly French-speaking and prone to unnecessary and sadistic violence, the Popeyes were welcomed as the 31st chapter of the Hells Angels, the first in Canada.

Although the Satan's Choice-turned-Outlaws were hardly choirboys, the newest chapter of the Hells Angels had an unparalleled reputation for savagery. The Popeyes, now known as Hell Angels Montreal, followed an ethos established by their founder, Yves "Apache" Trudeau. Physically unimposing at just 5-feet 6-inches and 135 pounds, Trudeau compensated by striking out at those who crossed him. In September 1970, a loser named Jean-Marie Viel was unfortunate enough to steal a motorcycle that belonged to a Popeye. Trudeau tracked him down and shot him in front of the rest of the gang, setting a precedent he continued and expected the others to live up to. In July 1985, Trudeau admitted to 43 murders, making him one of the world's most prolific killers (though, notably, nowhere near the alleged Canadian record-holder Robert Pickton of Vancouver with 64). Many believe Trudeau was responsible for even more murders, but since he appeared psychopathically proud of his claims and wouldn't have suffered any more punishment for additional victims, it's unlikely.

After the Popeyes became Hells Angels, they attracted lots of new recruits. With their eye on dominating the Montreal drug market, the Hells Angels knew they needed soldiers, and young men volunteered in droves. But there was a definite rift between the original Popeyes, who were massively and unpredictably violent in their nihilistic efforts to find a good time, and the new Hells Angels, who were pragmatically concerned with making money by selling drugs and getting respect on the streets and in bars when they wore their colors. The new guys resorted to violence as a last resort; the original Popeyes considered it a reward, a perk of membership. But the Hells Angels would not tolerate infighting. Emissaries were sent from the Hells Angels East Coast headquarters in Manhattan to evaluate the situation. The solution was simple. On August 14, 1979, the Montreal chapter of the Hells Angels was split in two. One group, consisting mainly of former Popeyes and those who thought like them, established the Montreal North Chapter in the working-class suburb of Laval on an island just north of the city. The Montreal South Chapter, in Sorel on the south shore of the St. Lawrence, was made up mainly of newcomers and others who didn't adhere to the former Popeyes' code of brutality.

* * *

Tensions that had been simmering between the Satan's Choice and Popeyes boiled over after they became the Outlaws and the Hells Angels. The Laval chapter took a special interest in their oldest rivals. From 1977 until 1982, the Montreal Hells Angels, particularly the Laval chapter, waged a low-intensity war against the Outlaws. It wasn't just over bragging rights. The bikers in Montreal were the primary distribution source for drugs, especially cocaine, for both the Italian and Irish mafias. Unlike their militaristic and fiercely xenophobic neighbors south of the border, the Montreal Hells Angels had no problem with imported drugs. Besides, crystal meth wasn't really a Quebecker's drug. Most people in Quebec who did drugs smoked hashish—poor man's marijuana—while the hip Montrealers who considered themselves a cut above had a huge appetite for coke. But nobody in Montreal liked cocaine better than the Laval chapter of Hells Angels, especially Trudeau. The market was so competitive and the stakes so high that the streets of Montreal became a very dangerous place to be a biker. Trudeau himself claimed to have murdered at least 17 of the opposition as they faded out of the scene and eventually became extinct.

It was at this time that the boys from Laval experimented with explosives. The results were disappointing—two would-be bombers blew themselves up in an effort to explode a subway station in a protest over prison conditions and Robert "Ti-Maigre" Richard lost an arm when trying to assemble a similar device—but the concept remained a favorite with Quebec Hells Angels.

Though effective in dismantling the Outlaws, the Laval chapter was an embarrassment to the modern Hells Angels. Not only did they usually snort more cocaine than they sold, leading to all kinds of wild debts, they tended to assault people for no particular reason. If their violence could be tolerated, their stupidity couldn't. In 1982, Denis "Le Curé" Kennedy, who was almost as notorious a killer and cocaine user as Trudeau, fell into debt with the wrong person. Frank "Dunie" Ryan was the head of the notorious West End Gang, a remnant of the old Irish mafia, which still controlled much of the drug trade in Montreal.

In an effort to wipe out his debt and get back at his tormentor in one act, Kennedy planned to kidnap one of Ryan's children—either three-year-old Troy or seven-year-old Tricia—and use the ransom to settle his account. Proud of his supremely stupid plan, Kennedy bragged about it to his brothers in Laval. Before long, Ryan found out and decided to deal with the deadbeat. Rather than act on his own, Ryan went to Laval. His was a familiar and welcome face. As one of the richest gangsters in town, he'd often hired club members to act as muscle for debt collection. They respected him, feared him and didn't want to piss him off. He told them what happened. A vote was held and Kennedy, along with co-conspirators Charles Hachez and Robert "Steve" Grenier, a 23-year-old prospect, were given dishonorable discharges by a unanimous show of hands.

Within days, Kennedy, Hachez, Grenier and Hachez's girlfriend, the 25-year-old Marjolaine Poirer, were shot and sent to the bottom of the St. Lawrence in sleeping bags weighed down with concrete blocks.

Crisis hit Montreal's underworld again on November 13, 1984 when Ryan was assassinated by an ambitious member of the West End Gang. When the murderer, Robert Lelièvre, foolishly took pride in the hit, Ryan's No. 2 man, Allan "The Weasel" Ross, recruited Trudeau to take him out. Ross knew Trudeau could handle the job, having seen what he was capable of in the past, and offered him $500,000—$200,000 in cash and the rest in forgiven debts owed by various members of the Laval Chapter.

Since Lelièvre was holed up in an apartment with guards armed with submachine guns and a police station across the street, an assault was out of the question. Ross knew that Lelièvre and Paul April, one of the guards and an old friend and crime partner of Trudeau's, were both sports fans and Trudeau told him he noticed that the apartment did not have a TV. Ross then couriered a $25,000 advance, a TV, a VCR and 35 pounds of C4 plastic explosive smuggled out of a Canadian Armed Forces base by a Hells Angels–friendly soldier to Trudeau. Pretending to bring a gift to his old pal, Trudeau brought the TV and VCR (now jam-packed with explosives and a timer) to the apartment. For a little extra dose of realism, he included a copy of *Hells Angels Forever*, a documentary starring Sonny Barger and written by Sandy Alexander. "I told him I wanted him to have it to see how the Hells Angels operate," Trudeau said. "To see what they're all about."

Sunday, November 25, 1984 was a great day for a Montreal sports fan to stay inside. Not only was it unseasonably cold, but the new-look Canadiens were in Boston to take on the hated Bruins and the NFL season was heating up as teams jockeyed for playoff positions. It was a hard time for a betting man to be without a TV. At 3:30 p.m., Trudeau and veteran West End Gang hit man Michael Blass parked illegally in front of 1645 boulevard Maisonneuve Ouest, a 22-story luxury high-rise just a short walk from the southeast edge of Parc Mont-Royal. Trudeau didn't get out of the car. Instead, Blass carried the package up to number 917. He exchanged pleasantries with Lelièvre, April and two other thugs, Louis Charles and Gilles Paquette. They thanked him for the TV, but made it clear they had other things on their minds and weren't interested in socializing. April, in particular, seemed nervous and couldn't stop moving.

Blass said he understood and offered to set up the equipment. Desperate for a little normalcy, the gangsters thanked him and told him to go ahead. Blass unpacked it all and, with meticulous gentleness, assembled the equipment. His last task was to set the five-minute timer on the back of the VCR. He then feigned disappointment when the TV wouldn't turn on and mumbled something about getting a repairman. Lelièvre vetoed the idea. Charles half-jokingly suggested Blass take the TV back with him. Blass interrupted him and said he had a friendly repairman who knew how to keep his mouth shut. Lelièvre relented. Blass left. As soon as the door shut behind him, he ran for the stairs. Taking them two steps at a time, he tore through the lobby and into Trudeau's car. They laid rubber and were a block away before Blass's car door closed.

The blast could be heard throughout the city. At 4:10 p.m., Lelièvre's apartment (and everything in it) was obliterated. The walls of eight other units in the building crumpled. The elevators were destroyed. Windows all around the neighborhood shattered. "April found out exactly how the Hells Angels work," said Trudeau.

His job done, Trudeau went back to Ross and asked for his money. Ross said he couldn't pay him any more than the $25,000 he'd already advanced him and that Trudeau could get the rest by collecting debts owed to Ryan by members of the Sorel Chapter and the 13th Tribe, a gang slated to become the Hells Angels Halifax Chapter on December 5.

First he went to Sorel. They told him to fuck off. Why pay a fellow Hells Angel a debt they owed a dead man? Realizing there wasn't much he could do, he went to Halifax. Desperate to be Hells Angels, the members of the 13th Tribe struggled to comply. They gave him $46,000. A few weeks later, Grub MacDonald, by then president of Hells Angels Halifax Chapter, brought another $52,000 to Sorel. It was for Trudeau, but he didn't want to visit Laval. The boys at Sorel took the money—and it eventually made its way to Trudeau—but they mocked MacDonald for his fealty and he returned to Nova Scotia wildly embittered.

Réjean "Zig Zag" Lessard, president of the Sorel Chapter, called a meeting with Halifax and Sherbrooke, another chapter patched over on the same day as the 13th Tribe. It wasn't just the extortion. Trudeau and his gang of idiots were a black mark on the organization. Excessive cocaine use and drinking had led the Laval Chapter to bizarre behavior. Their wanton, random violence and their blatant, small-time crimes endangered them all. More important, their mounting cocaine debts were crippling the whole organization. After a vote, Lessard got what he wanted. Laval was to be eliminated. Two of the Laval bikers were to be offered membership in the Sorel Chapter, two others were to be forcibly retired and the rest were given a death sentence.

Naturally, Trudeau was the primary target, but he had the survival skills of a cockroach. Sensing that the hatred the other chapters had for Laval was on the verge of turning into retribution, Trudeau, who had snorted $60,000 worth of coke up his nose in the previous three weeks, checked himself into a posh Oka detox center on March 17, 1985. "I saw what was coming," he said. "I'd seen it myself in the past, what happened to members who drank or sniffed too much."

Sorel enforcer Robert "Ti-Maigre" Richard called the Laval, Sherbrooke and Halifax clubhouses to announce a party in Sherbrooke—about 100 miles southeast of Montreal—on Saturday, March 23. After the call, Georges "Bo-Boy" Beaulieu, president of the Sherbrooke Chapter, went to a local sporting goods shop and bought six sleeping bags. Store owner Daniel Raby later recalled that Beaulieu was in such a hurry, he forgot to take his receipt.

Less than half of the Laval chapter showed up. Incensed, Lessard and his men were forced to holster their guns and throw a party. He announced to the crowd that the meeting had been postponed a day so that the others could arrive, and that their attendance was absolutely mandatory. He booked every available room at the La Marquise motel down the street and put up the overflow at the Lennoxville a few miles away.

Most of the bikers woke around noon or soon thereafter. The remaining members of Laval, except Trudeau, of course, arrived in Sherbrooke that afternoon. Church, as Hells Angels worldwide refer to their meetings, was called for 2:30. Everyone showed and the slaughter began. Sorel prospects, forced to wait outside as usual, heard shouts. Someone mentioned the Outlaws. Another yelled something about guns. After that, it was just the booming of guns and the screams of the victims. Laurent "L'Anglais" Viau was shot in the head. Jean-Pièrre "Matt le Crosseur" Mathieu was similarly dispatched. Michel "Willie" Mayrand died struggling. Jean-Guy "Brutus" Geoffrion took a bullet in the head and another in the spine. Guy-Louis "Chop" Adam was shot seven times by three different guns. He died on the front lawn after fleeing through the front door.

The surviving members of the Laval chapter, Gilles "Le Nez" Lachance, Yvon "Le Père" Bilodeau and Richard "Bert" Mayrand (whose brother had just been murdered before his eyes) huddled in a blood-soaked corner. As the other Sorel members dragged the bodies into the garage and hosed the blood and guts off the floor, Lachance told Richard he had some blood on his boots. Richard took a moment to wipe it off.

Finished cleaning, the bikers gathered around Lessard. He told them that the men had died because they snorted too much coke and because Trudeau had leaned on his brothers because an outsider would not pay a debt. Bilodeau and the surviving Mayrand were told to leave. The others, some still spattered with the blood and tissues of their victims, surrounded Lachance. Lessard told him that they held no grudge against him and that he was free to walk away or join the Sorel chapter. Lachance eventually joined. One of the original Popeyes, he was still officially a Hells Angels prospect because he was in prison for manslaughter when the gang was patched over.

While a few prospects were forced to burn their dead brothers' possessions, Lachance and Sorel members Jacques "La Pelle" Pelletier and Robert "Snake" Tremblay drove back to Laval. When they get there, they found Michel "Jinx" Genest, the last surviving member other than Trudeau, all alone drinking beer. They told him what happened and that he was invited to join the Sorel chapter. He accepted and helped his new brothers pack some of his dead brothers' possessions into their trunk. Over the next few days the Laval clubhouse was looted and the apartments of the five dead bikers were emptied of anything of value, whether the murdered man lived alone or not. Lessard decreed the theft necessary to repay the Halifax Chapter and to provide a gift for Western Canada's sole chapter in Vancouver, a move he hoped would help soften the news of the slaughter. He sent a letter to the Hells Angels East Coast regional headquarters reporting that "the North Chapter has been closed down."

It had been closed, but not eliminated. Normand "Biff" Hamel, a former Laval prospect who joined Sorel, went to visit Trudeau in rehab. He told Trudeau what had happened and that he was dishonorably discharged and would have to get rid of his tattoo. Trudeau complied by blackening out the logo with an indelible marker. "I understood very quickly what it meant," he said.

Upon his release, Trudeau went to the ransacked Laval clubhouse. His bike and the $46,000 he had hidden in a wall safe were gone. He called Hamel who told him that he could forget about the money but could get his bike back if he murdered two people who might turn informant—including Mathieu's girlfriend Ginette "La Jument" Henri, who served as accountant for the Laval chapter.

Henri was also considered valuable to Sorel because she was one of the two living people who knew where Laval's drugs were stashed. Lessard knew she'd never turn them over to her boyfriend's killers, but he also didn't want them to end up as evidence. The only other person who could find them was Claude "Coco" Roy, a Laval prospect who was outside the Sherbrooke clubhouse when most of his chapter was exterminated. Genest was allowed to prove his worth to his new chapter by recovering the cocaine. He called Roy and told him to meet him with the drugs at the $20-a-night Ideal Motel in the boonies. As soon as Roy walked into the room, Genest smashed him in the side of the head with a gun, killing him. He then searched Troy's blood-spattered body and found five bags of coke in his underwear. Emboldened by a job well done and a sample of his booty, Genest called the dead man's stripper girlfriend and asked her for a date. She turned him down.

* * *

A police wiretap that had been in place at the Sherbrooke clubhouse since October 1983 finally paid a dividend. Officers from the Sûreté du Québec determined that five Hells Angels were missing and that something big had happened at the clubhouse. Armed with this meager evidence, the cops descended on the building. The front door was torn down with a backhoe and cops with metal detectors swarmed the grounds. Helicopters equipped with heat sensors powerful enough to discover fresh graves were brought in. They found nothing but a shirt with what they claimed was a bullet hole, some legal weapons and an amount of drugs too small to get anyone in real trouble.

Trudeau earned his bike back by murdering former Popeye Jean-Marc "Le Grande Guele" Deniger. It took a while, though. The Hells Angels will only accept media coverage as confirmation of a hit and nobody found Deniger's body. Frustrated, Trudeau finally called *Le Journal de Montréal* five days later and gave them an anonymous tip that they would find something of great interest in the back seat of Deniger's car.

The police kept hammering away at the Hells Angels, but found very little. They happened upon a treasure, though, when they arrested Trudeau on a weapons charge.

As the St. Lawrence got warmer, decomposition did what the police couldn't and the bodies started floating. First came the fattest, Geoffrion, on June 1st. Sûreté du Quebec (SQ) divers were sent down. Although the water was nearly opaque, with visibility no more than a foot, they felt around and found the remains of Viau, Adam, Mayrand and Roy. So crowded was the Hells Angels graveyard that one diver also discovered the skeleton of Berthe Desjardins, who was murdered by Trudeau—along with her husband and mother-in-law—on February 11, 1980.

The Quebec media went crazy. *Allô Police*, a lurid Montreal tabloid that often knew more about the underworld than the police did, ran an article claiming the Hells Angels had $50,000 contracts on the lives of Trudeau and Regis "Lucky" Asselin, a former Laval prospect who narrowly escaped two attempts on his life, once by driving a bullet-riddled van through the front door of a hospital. Sergeant Marcel Lacoste, the commander of the SQ's investigation into the murders, took a copy of the story to Trudeau, who was in Montreal's Bordeaux jail on an unrelated weapons charge. Trudeau, who was scheduled to be back on the streets in August, sighed, shook his head and said: "I killed for them and now they want to kill me—that's gratitude, eh?"

By October 2, 1985, 17 Hells Angels were charged with first-degree murder and warrants were issued for 10 more, all on the basis of tips and testimony from Trudeau and Gerry "Le Chat" Coulombe, a Sorel prospect who was horrified by the slaughter and wanted out. But the police knew their case was weak unless they could get an eyewitness to talk (Coulombe was at the scene, but was outside the building for most of the shooting and was hiding when Robert "Snake" Tremblay shot a fleeing Adam on the front lawn).

It didn't take long. Gilles "Le Nez" Lachance, now a Sorel member, had seen everything. The SQ arrested him on a minor charge, but they knew exactly how valuable he was. They offered him immunity for a laundry list of crimes if he would tell them everything that had happened in the Sherbrooke clubhouse in March. Terrified that he might be next on the hit list and more than happy to avoid prison, he cooperated readily.

Superior Court Judge Jean-Guy Boilard brought down his gavel on the case on December 19, 1986. After two trials—a main one and a separate one for Genest—complete with a media circus, countless calls for mistrial, 12 people cited for contempt of court, a judge scolding the SQ for "incompetence" and one juror admitting he was bought by the Hells Angels for $25,000—Lessard, Pelletier, Michaud and Genest were found guilty of murder. Richard was acquitted. The rest plea bargained their way to lesser sentences.

With six bikers dead, Lessard, Pelletier, Michaud and Genest in prison and Trudeau, Coulombe and Lachance in protective custody, the people of Quebec thought the Hells Angels were a spent force. They were dead wrong. After an aggressive recruiting drive and the patching over of a number of small, rural clubs, the Hells Angels were replenished with eager young men ready to make money from drugs and show off their death's heads. In fact, one Hells Angels veteran told a Montreal paper that he was grateful to the cops for cleaning out the club's deadwood.

Sonny Barger and his Bay Area buddies defined the Hells Angels through rules, rites and uniformity. They put together a self-sustaining entity that attracted new members who were willing to die for their brothers simply because of what they believed in. Years later, men like Lessard, Trudeau and Lachance set a precedent for Canadian Hells Angels that would be repeated again and again. Brotherhood has its place, but not if it gets in the way of money or the drug trade. The penalty for going against the club is a bullet in the head and a trip to the bottom of the St. Lawrence. The life of a Canadian Hells Angel isn't about the thrill of the open road or the company of a club of freedom-loving brothers. Instead, it's a sleazy, low-rent existence in which members must sell drugs, plant bombs, hire themselves out as muscle and commit other crimes without knowing if, when or why they could end up facing the small end of a shotgun.

Chapter 3

Kelly has driven over the Skyway Bridge twice a day for 12 years but she still looks every time. And she always looks on the same side. Lake Ontario is just another big lake, but Hamilton Harbour has some real character. Even from a quarter mile away, the water looks greasy. On the south side of the harbour, the Hamilton side, there are sinister-looking steel factories from one end to the other. On most days, it's hard to see much of them through the smoke and fog. But the fires are always visible. Sometimes red, purple or even bright blue, the tongues of flame reach three or four storeys into the air. They are there to burn off poisonous gases, but their smell remains. Almost as tall and just as imposing stands another by-product of steelmaking, slag, which shows up as hundred-foot high piles of gray stones. Much of what you see of Hamilton from the Skyway is actually built on slag dumped into the harbour to make more room for even more factories. If you look closely enough, Kelly pointed out, you can see a junkyard with a fence made of old buses turned on their sides, their windows now shattered and their tops and sides covered with threatening graffiti. It's not a pretty sight.

"It's like a bad car wreck, isn't it?" she said as her silver Toyota Echo swayed in the high winds over the bridge. "Just can't take your eyes off it, eh?" Like most people from Hamilton with any ambition, she got out of town as soon as she could. "To tell you the truth, I don't even know many people back there any more," she said. "I was one of the last of my friends to move out." She now lives in Oakville and commutes to her job with an insurance company in the city. Even though she's abandoned her home town and freely speaks derisively of it, Kelly still considers herself a Hamiltonian at heart. After all, there is no Oakville in Oakville. As she says: "It's really just a few thousand nearly identical houses, a gas station and a 7-Eleven." Hamilton may be smelly and ugly, but at least it's a city with a culture and an identity. She's proud to be from Hamilton and finds herself defending it at dinner parties. "Besides, it's way better than it used to be," she said. "Back when I was in high school, Hamilton was a very different place—dirtier, smellier, nastier and more violent."

Kelly grew up in Birdland. Tucked away on the mountain in the southwest corner of Hamilton, as far away from the factories of the northeast as possible, Birdland is more like the suburbs than part of a major city. Originally called Cardinal Heights, the planned community of look-alike houses and identical cul-de-sacs got its more popular name from the fact that all the streets are named after species of birds. The neighborhood joke is that the residents of Titmouse Court wanted to change their street's name because property values might be affected by the mention of mice. Away from busy streets, Birdland was a quiet, well-treed neighborhood where most people knew each other and generally got along. Barbecues and pool parties were commonplace and there were always kids playing some sort of sport in the round part of the cul-de-sacs, while watchful parents worked, relaxed or socialized. Growing up on Bobolink Road, Kelly went to Hill Park High School.

She was even prettier then. It was 1970 and she was a long-legged blonde who got good marks and kept mainly to herself and a few good friends. Since she spent a lot of time with Rodney, her boyfriend, who was already in college at Mohawk, she didn't socialize much with other students after class. But after three years at Hill Park, she basically knew who everybody was.

Even if she had been more outgoing, she probably wouldn't have spent much time with Walter Stadnik. He wasn't really her kind of guy.

Born 18 years earlier, on August 3, 1952, at St. Joseph's Hospital at the base of the mountain, Wolodumyr Stadnik was the third son of Andrew and Valentina Stadnik. Living at 98 East 16th Street, a few blocks north of Birdland, he grew up around a different set of kids. Consisting of smaller, less attractive houses filled with scores of immigrant and transplanted farmer families—most of whom had found work in the city's factories, although Andrew Stadnik was a tree surgeon employed by the city—Stadnik's neighborhood was entirely less friendly than Kelly's. It was a place where people generally kept to themselves, preferring to socialize with extended families instead of neighbors. It was nothing like inner-city Hamilton for violence and squalor, but it bred a more rough and tumble kind of kid than Birdland.

But Stadnik—soon called Walter or Wally by everyone but his parents and beginning to spell his last name "Stadnick"—hardly fit the mold of a juvenile delinquent. People who remember him as a child uniformly report that he was intelligent, quiet, polite and generally well behaved. He went to church every Sunday with his parents and seemed to be a pretty good kid. As happens with so many other boys, though, Stadnick changed when he hit puberty. Although he was one of the first kids in his class to clear 5 feet, he soon grew to 5-feet 4-inches and never got much taller. As the shortest boy in class by grade 11, he had to try harder and would often act out in school—and not in ways that educators would approve of in the late 1960s. "He clearly had a great deal of natural intelligence, but he was impossible to motivate," said a former teacher who didn't want to be named but couldn't hide his frustration. "It was almost like he didn't want to succeed." Stadnick's marks were good enough to get by, but no better. His best marks came from auto shop, where he showed a great deal of mechanical inclination and an organized mind well-suited to solving complex problems.

While no academic, Stadnick did find some success in the school's social circles. He had an undeniable charm and was very popular with a small segment of the school population and was well known by the rest of it. "Of course I knew Wally, everyone did," Kelly recalled. "It's not like we were best friends or anything like that; but I knew him well enough to say 'hi'—although I don't think I would have unless he did first." But they traveled in different circles. Kelly, quiet, studious and ambitious, spent all her time in class or the library. Walter, on the other hand, could almost always be found in the smoking area if he wasn't in class and often when he was supposed to be. "He was what we used to call an 'occie'—someone who only took courses that prepare you for a specific occupation, like auto mechanics, electrical or metal shop," she said. "But he was better than the rest of them; he never called me names or tried to grab my rear end or anything; he seemed nice enough."

And there was more; Stadnick had even more reason to be popular. According to most people who knew him in high school, he made friends by selling drugs. It was the '70s and drugs were everywhere. High school kids had grown up with almost heroic stories of drug use in the '60s and were anxious to try them out. "I never took drugs myself, so I can't really say," said Kelly. "But I had lots of friends who did, and they told me they always got them from Wally."

It wasn't just fellow students who knew about Stadnick. The police were aware of him, but not because they ever caught him doing much. "It was hard in the '70s," said a Hamilton police officer who was very familiar with the Hill Park students of the era and wanted to be identified simply as "Bob the cop." "Before that, and again afterwards, it was easy to tell the bad boys from the good boys, but in the '70s, they all looked alike—skinny kids with long hair and denim jackets." But a dedicated officer could tell the difference by driving the streets, seeing who had an improbably affordable new bike or car, by looking into the faces to see who was putting on a tough-guy attitude or by talking to principals and vice-principals. "Of course we knew who Stadnick was," he said. "We were sure he was distributing hash, but unless you see him doing it or someone tells on him, there's nothing you can do about it." Stadnick was arrested once in 1971 for possession of a small amount of hashish. He spent four months in the old Hamilton jail and was put on two years' probation.

Hashish is a dark, putty-like substance made from resin collected from the cannabis plant. It contains the same active ingredient (tetrahydrocannabinol, or THC) as marijuana, but in far lower quantities. It is often smoked in pipes, but younger and/or poorer users tend to inhale the smoke of hash burned on the end of a needle or on the blade of a heated knife. While marijuana is stronger, easier to smoke and less likely to be contaminated with impurities, hash is popular in places where cannabis is hard to grow because it can be molded into almost any shape and is very easy to smuggle over borders. Back in 1970, before the days of hydroponics and grow-lights, growing cannabis in Eastern Canada was virtually impossible and hash was king. Cheaper and easier to conceal than weed, it was the perfect drug for high-schoolers. In the 1970s, big pieces of hash were called cakes and smaller ones were called nuggets.

By 1970, people who knew Stadnick well were calling him "Nurget." Although this nickname has mystified police and journalists for years, its origin is pretty clear to some. "People in Hamilton have a funny way of talking; they like to play with words," said Bob the cop. "They'll call Tim Horton's 'Horny Tim's' or they'll call a bargain a 'bargoon'—they're not trying to be funny or anything, it's just the way they speak." After Stadnick was arrested in Jamaica a quarter century later, confused Royal Canadian Mounted Police (RCMP) officers and lawyers asked him why the other Hells Angels called him "Nurget." He simply smiled and kept quiet, helping further a reputation he had for being secretive and mysterious. They should have asked Bob the cop. "That's an easy one," he said. "He was called 'Nurget' because he always had a nugget—or, as the kids in Hamilton would say, a 'nurget'—of hash on him." Others say his name had nothing to do with hash but that it actually stemmed from his small size.

Whether he was dealing hash or just carrying it for a friend, as he maintained in his 1971 trial, he certainly appeared to have lots more spending cash than the other kids in the neighborhood. Looking for something more thrilling than a ten-speed or the old man's Delta 88, Stadnick bought a motorcycle. It was old and needed work—that was no problem for a mind like his—but it was really something. A few of the kids at Hill Park had cars, mostly junkers, but nobody else had a motorcycle. Even though the Canadian climate makes motorcycles useless for about six months a year and the summer vacation means that you can only ride to school for a few weeks, a motorcycle can turn an otherwise forgettable guy into a big man on campus. Stadnick's star was clearly rising.

The start of the '70s was a hard time to be coming of age. After Altamont, the hippies, with their peace and love, were beginning to be seen as ridiculous. It was a cynical and pessimistic time. More important for teenagers in Hamilton, the Canadian economy was suffering through the beginning of its worst period since the Depression. For the first time since then—and in defiance of basic economic law—it was undergoing a combination of stagnant growth combined with runaway inflation. While retail prices were getting higher, wages were not keeping up and the level of unemployment was staggering. Hamilton was hit particularly hard. After years of feasting on the success of the auto, aerospace and military goods industries as a primary supplier of steel, Hamilton's economy took a nosedive as those businesses slowed down considerably. With fewer users and plunging prices, the market was flooded with cheaper steel from places like Japan, Iran and Taiwan. Layoffs were the only way to keep the factories alive, but it put hundreds of men out of work and effectively closed off the only natural employment opportunity for many young people.

"The days when they opened their doors to anyone who showed up were long gone," said Justin Pietzcerak, whose dad had worked at Stelco and brought his sons up to believe they would too. "Even when they weren't laying people off, you had to have an 'in'—someone like a father or uncle who already worked there—just to push a broom." Frustrated by the lack of factory work, young people in Hamilton looked to other industries and other places where the recession hadn't hit as hard. Thousands sought work in Toronto or the United States and even more, like Pietzcerak, went to Alberta. "At the time, it seemed like the thing to do," he said. "While the steel and car factories back East were getting rid of people, the oil and gas drillers in Alberta were hiring all the time."

For those who stayed behind, real opportunities were scarce. College and university graduates were having trouble finding work and those who had banked on a guaranteed factory job or just hadn't planned ahead were in a far worse state. A city that was built around and dependent on a single industry, Hamilton suffered a domino effect when the steel factories were idled. Stores, restaurants and other services that were accustomed to a steady stream of customers now had to make do with long stretches of inactivity and minor spikes in business twice a month when government assistance checks arrived. "It was a joke at the time that the biggest employer in Hamilton wasn't Stelco or Dofasco, but the Unemployment Insurance Commission," said Bob the cop. "It wasn't far from true."

For young people, the effect was devastating. With no jobs or opportunity, with boarded-up stores and houses and massive government cutbacks, many of the most law-abiding young people were beginning to believe that the system had failed them and their faith in it foundered. A large number of them turned to things like welfare fraud, cigarette smuggling and under-the-table labor to supplement their incomes. Some went a bit farther. The market of stolen items, especially car stereos, became a big business. Flea markets, where nobody asked where the merchandise came from and all transactions were cash-only, flourished. But there was an even easier way to make money for those with guts. "Of course it's wrong, but you can understand why they'd sell drugs," said Bob the cop. "It seemed like no matter how little money was around, people could always scratch up enough for a little hash or weed—the opportunity to make a quick buck was definitely there."

Although nobody will go on record to admit ever having bought hash from Stadnick, he was widely reputed—by both his peers and police—to have been a major seller. By the end of high school, he had two motorcycles and an impressive wardrobe of clothes and jewelry despite there not being a scrap of evidence of him ever having held a job. He looked like he was doing better than his peers who had paper routes or put in a few shifts at McDonald's. Wherever it came from, Stadnick had a flamboyant way of showing off his new wealth. The hippies themselves may have been dying out, but their wild styles, often with black, Latin or far Eastern roots, began to filter down to Sears and Kresge's.

At the same time, Alice Cooper and other hard-rock musicians were experimenting with their own shocking looks and, as they always had and still do, teenage boys began to imitate their heroes. The result, in Stadnick's case, was an eye-catching mismatch of colors, styles and messages. "Walter wore some pretty strange clothes; you could tell they were expensive, but they looked bizarre with his regular outfits," Kelly recalled with a chuckle. "He'd wear tight, tight jeans and have like this really expensive purple and black patterned silk shirt underneath an old denim jacket with patches all over it." And he began a lifelong love affair with ostentatious jewelry. "Oh, he loved jewelry; very few of the other guys would ever wear more than a simple chain," she said, "but Wally always had rings and chains."

Silk shirts and jewelry notwithstanding, it's unlikely the other boys would question Stadnick's masculinity. "He wasn't much to look at, but he was a tough little guy," Kelly said. "He had a fight with this one really big guy—Stewart, I think his name was—and totally destroyed him; after that nobody ever thought of challenging him." Besides, it wasn't always easy to get to him. By 12th grade, Stadnick was usually surrounded by a group of friends, associates and other hangers-on. In the smoking area, at the mall or anywhere else, Stadnick could be seen with a group of guys clad in cheap versions of the same denim-and-leather uniform young toughs have been wearing since *The Wild One*.

After school ended, when the other graduates were headed for college, looking for jobs or moving to more prosperous cities, Stadnick and his pals were hanging out and enjoying life. One by one, they got motorcycles. They didn't have Harleys, mostly old British bikes actually, but they were all on two wheels. The bikes were financed at least in part, Bob the cop suggests, by Stadnick. "He was a biker; they were his friends," Bob said. "If they wanted to keep up and he wanted to keep them, they had to get bikes." Before long, they were riding together, dressing alike and holding regular meetings. But they weren't a gang until they had a name. They found their identity through Stadnick's other interests. It was an iconoclastic time, and heroes were out. Young men no longer idolized fighter pilots or cowboys or anyone who could be judged in historical context. Instead, Stadnick and his followers went further back in history.

"Like the kids who are into *Dungeons & Dragons* or *Lord of the Rings* today, they loved the medieval stuff," said Bob the cop. Proud of his Ukrainian roots, Stadnick called his group the Cossacks. Derived from the Turkish word "kazak," meaning "free man," the Cossacks are historically considered to be a group of men from Southeastern Europe who banded together after denying the authority of their local leaders. Famed for their independence and fighting abilities, the Cossacks, particularly their cavalry, were frequently used as mercenaries. They developed a reputation as vicious, bloodthirsty fighters who answered to no ruler. Perfect heroes for a teenage motorcycle gang.

So great was Stadnick's influence that he actually convinced his followers to wear a sort of ponytail on the tops of their heads in the mistaken belief that this was how Cossacks looked. He even figured out a way to put holes in the tops of their helmets to pull their hair through. "Yeah, we knew about the Cossacks, we didn't think much of them," said Bob the cop. "They were pretty small-time, a little bit of trafficking, a little fencing, but we never really caught them doing anything important—it really seemed like all they wanted to do was make noise and look tough."

Normally a group of criminally intent teenagers on motorcycles with their hair pulled through helmets would garner a bit of attention, if not fear, on the streets of any city. But this was Hamilton in the 1970s. The Mafia under the control of Johnny "Pops" Papalia still held sway and what was left of the organized crime spoils was divided up by the Satan's Choice and Red Devils motorcycle gangs. Although the Cossacks were easy to identify by their hair, the rest of the look was pure biker with the leather, denim and patches that had been made the industry standard by the Hells Angels. But it's unlikely they were intentionally copying them. Without any Canadian chapters, the Hells Angels seemed distant, foreign and even mythical when the Cossacks were formed. They were more likely emulating the local gangs, who in turn were imitating the Hells Angels. Unlike the odd, almost comical Cossacks on their low-horsepower British bikes, the members of the senior gangs were the real thing. Satan's Choice had a membership and reach approaching that of the Hells Angels and the Red Devils were the oldest motorcycle gang in Canada. Both were headquartered on the Beach Strip, a narrow isthmus of land that connects Hamilton with Burlington and is dominated by the Queen Elizabeth Way superhighway that brings traffic from Toronto and the Niagara region. With their focus on the north and east sections of the city, the members of the Satan's Choice and Red Devils tolerated the existence of the Cossacks. "The big guys weren't bothered by them," said Bob the cop.

Although Stadnick was clearly pleased to be in charge of his own creation in the Cossacks, most police officers who knew him at the time agree that he'd much rather move up to the major leagues. As tough and charismatic as he was, neither the Satan's Choice nor Red Devils ever called, so he jumped at the chance to join the Wild Ones. Named, probably unwittingly, after the movie that helped spawn the entire outlaw biker phenomenon, the Hamilton mountain–based Wild Ones were a much more serious and sophisticated gang than the Cossacks, but still a step below the big boys. Closely associated with Satan's Choice, the Wild Ones acted as a sort of minor-league farm club, sending prospects up to the parent club once they had proved themselves at a lower level. According to Hamilton cops, members of the Wild Ones could make names for themselves by performing tasks for members of Satan's Choice or the mafia. Members would often act as hired muscle, either protecting debt collectors or serving as a warning to those who didn't want to pay protection money. The most effective way a member of the Wild Ones could earn his stripes, cops have said, was to punish a recalcitrant debtor. One of their favorite methods was to plant bombs in small businesses. Not only was this said to be an excellent scare tactic, but it also allowed the bikers a chance to make another visit after the insurance settlement. The system worked exceedingly well. The mafia hired the bikers who intimidated the businessmen who paid the mafia or suffered from the bikers. "It was quite a sophisticated operation," admitted Ken Robertson, a Hamilton–Wentworth police sergeant who investigated some of the bombings and later became the force's chief. And they were never short of business.

But in the fall of 1978, the ever-ambitious Stadnick began to realize that he and his gang were on a treadmill. He and his fellow Wild Ones did all the hard work, took all the risks and got only a tiny portion of the proceeds. Satan's Choice got their share simply by hiring their underlings out and also got the glory of being the top of the local biker heap. Tired of doing all the hard and dangerous work so someone else could get rich, Stadnick decided to take matters into his own hands. He took aside a few of his best friends from the Wild Ones and told them what he thought. Using his abundant charm, Stadnick did his best to convince them that they were being used and that if anyone should benefit from their muscle and courage it should be them. He told them about another gang, a much bigger gang, called the Hells Angels. They were cool; they wouldn't exploit them like the Satan's Choice did. He said he'd talked to some Hells Angels and that they had it easy—they rode, they partied, they made money and had a good time. He told them that he'd set up a meeting with them in Montreal.

Two of the Wild Ones were sold on the idea; the rest told Stadnick it was too dangerous. So on October 12, 1978, the three of them took off up the QEW to the 401 and on to Montreal.

* * *

Le Tourbillon is as seedy as most bars in the east end of Montreal. Other than a few old rummies and the dancing girls who work there, the Hells Angels usually have the place to themselves. With a low-intensity war against the west end–based Outlaws heating up, the nondescript little bar near Jarry Park in the heart of Hells Angels territory seemed the most safe and appropriate place to hold a meeting. Stadnick and his fellow Wild Ones—Gary "Gator" Davies and George "Chico" Mousseau—took a table in the back and pretended to watch the girls on stage. A round of beers didn't take the edge off them. This was the biggest night of their lives. Yesterday they were just a bunch of Hamilton mountain street toughs who were busting their asses to be noticed by the Satan's Choice, and today they were being courted by the mighty Hells Angels.

At exactly the time agreed upon, the delegation from the Hells Angels appeared. Despite the war, the Hells Angels conspicuously wore their full colors. The men they sent were big, hairy and well decorated—they were trying to make an impression on their potential recruits from Hamilton. Louis "Ti-Oui" Lapierre, Bruno Coulombe and Jean Brochu squeezed into the booth with the Wild Ones and had beers placed in front of them before anyone said anything. Neither Stadnick nor Davies spoke any French and the Hells Angels at the table had only rudimentary English skills, so Mousseau did the translation. A few jokes were told, partially with facial expressions and hand signals, and the ice was broken.

They were just about to get down to business when they were temporarily blinded by a shaft of sunlight as the door opened. In the glare they could make out the silhouettes of two men.

As the door closed and their eyes adjusted, they saw two young, muscular men they didn't recognize. With short hair, nylon wind-breakers over golf shirts and no visible tattoos, they obviously weren't Outlaws. Lapierre almost certainly would have recognized their faces if they had been. Instead, he identified them as undercover cops and, transcending the language barrier, put his index finger on his lips to indicate to everyone at the table not to say anything incriminating.

Everyone understood and the conversation switched over to the weather and the differences between women in Ontario and Quebec. The jovial group fell silent as the short-haired men stood up and turned towards the booth.

Lapierre, who was in no mood to be harassed by cops when he was trying to make an impression of strength and security to the Wild Ones, turned to them and began to tell them off. He didn't get many words out before one of the men drew a large pistol and shot him in the shoulder. The other assassin pulled out a sawed-off shotgun and start-ed pumping shells into the booth. Instinctively, Stadnick slid under the table. His friends weren't as smart or as lucky. The assassins sprayed bullets and shells into the wooden booth until they were sure all the men were dead, then fled. Under the splinters, shards of upholstery, broken glass and the shredded corpse of Mousseau, who had been sit-ting beside him, Stadnick moved. He was surprised that he was still alive. When the smoke cleared, Mousseau and Brochu were dead on the scene. Davies was lying on the floor in a pool of his own blood and died in an area hospital a few days later. Lapierre and Coulombe suf-fered life-threatening injuries, but eventually recovered most of their abilities. Stadnick suffered minor injuries, when what may have been wood splinters or bone chips grazed his face. Rather than wait around for the cops, he jumped on his bike and rode home.

On the way back to Hamilton, the astute Stadnick put together an accurate re-creation of what had happened at the bar. One of the Wild Ones who knew about his plan but didn't join him, had gone to the Satan's Choice and told them what was happening. Informing on your peers is usually frowned upon in the criminal world, but with bikers, it can get you a promotion. The top guys in Satan's Choice then told their higher-ups in the U.S.-based Outlaws. Not wanting to allow their bitter rivals in the Hells Angels a toehold in the lucrative Ontario market, the Outlaws decided to put a stop to Stadnick's plan. They hired two non-biker hitmen (one from Detroit, the other from Miami) because they thought their clean-cut appearance would make them less conspicuous and harder to track. They were right on both counts; the killers were never found.

When he returned, Stadnick met with the Wild Ones he thought he could trust and told them to stay cool. They didn't have the man-power to take on the Satan's Choice in an outright war, so the best they could do was lie low, and hope that the whole mess would blow over or another gang—maybe the Red Devils or even the Hells Angels— would be open to a strategic alliance. But the problem didn't go away and nobody came to the Wild Ones' rescue. The slaughter continued a week later. One of the remaining Wild Ones woke up and couldn't find any coffee in his Hamilton mountain townhouse. He and his stripper girlfriend had been drinking pretty heavily and his hangover gave him a crying need for a good old greasy breakfast. Too sick to walk the three blocks, he left his sleeping girlfriend behind and grabbed the car keys. The old Firebird didn't always start right away and he was low on gas, but his head was pounding and his joints ached something awful. He got in, pulled on his seatbelt, turned the key and was blown to bits. The explosion and fire were so intense that when his girlfriend called the fire department she told them that her boyfriend had been murdered. Less than a week later, another car bomb tore off a Wild One's right leg, ending his career as a biker. In a friend's garage, two surviving Wild Ones, Derek Thistlewaite and Peter Michael Urech, built a bomb they were intending to use to intimidate a rape victim into not testifying at a fellow biker's trial. A combination of limited intellect, inexperience, volatile chemicals and a few beers resulted in the garage being blown to bits and the would-be bombers obliterated.

With that last pathetic blunder, the Wild Ones ceased to exist. Those who weren't dead were permanently disabled, scared off or absorbed by other gangs. Except for one. Stadnick, who somehow managed to escape the slaughter that he instigated unscathed, kept riding around Hamilton. He had no gang, few friends and little to do but wait. He knew he would either die or succeed, but he would do it as a biker. Ever since his trip to Montreal, he was focused on joining the Hells Angels, an organization he knew was far more powerful than the Satan's Choice, or even their American masters the Outlaws, could ever hope to be. While the surviving Wild Ones had given up and gone straight, Stadnick held out. According to Hamilton biker cop Sergeant John Harris, who followed Stadnick's career very closely, "I think Stadnick thought 'this will never happen to me, I'm too smart for this—the ones we're losing now are the careless ones.'"

Chapter 4

There are lots of guys like Vincent in Montreal. He's about 6 feet tall, but looks as if he weighs no more than 100 pounds. You can get a good idea of how old he is by the deep lines on his face around his goatee. And although his hair goes down to his shoulder blades, it's receding in the front, especially at the temples. His entire wardrobe consists of T-shirts, denim and leather, perfect apparel for his part-time job at an area scrapyard and his less official and more lucrative duties.

He's not just willing to talk about his illegal activities, he's proud of them. He says he made a lot of money smuggling cigarettes into Quebec from the United States. "That business has dried up a little now, though," he said. "But I have other things on my plate." The other things, he says, include marketing stolen electronics and car parts and occasionally selling some hash. He also receives a small check from the government, but won't say why. "I make lots of money," he said.

One of the other scrapyard workers said something quickly in French and he and two other guys laughed. Vincent translated. Although he has a French last name and has lived in or around Montreal since the mid-'70s, he was born and raised in Ontario and English is his mother tongue. "I'm rich but I look like a bum because I spend all my money on strippers and hookers," he said, smiling widely to reveal a missing incisor. "What can I say? I have an addiction to the ladies." Then he explained how using prostitutes made much more sense than conventional dating because they didn't discriminate based on looks or income and they don't waste your time with anything other than sex. "The best part is that you can tell them to leave when you're done with them," he said proudly. "Try doing that with your girlfriend or your wife." Encouraged by his own logic, he then explained how cigarette smuggling and the sale of someone else's electronics and car parts were, to him, victimless crimes. "The only people who lose out are the tax collector, rich people who can afford it and insurance companies," he said. "I just provide normal people with things they couldn't afford by taking them away from the people who make them so expensive in the first place."

His delusions of being a modern-day Robin Hood aside, Vincent is a pretty popular and important person in his community, where many people share his philosophy. He operates in a world in which the government is a distant and foreign entity that exists simply to be bilked. Laws are arcane rules of a game he'd rather not play. "Rich people just make laws to keep normal people from getting ahead," he said. Instead, the normal people in his world make money by breaking the law so that they can pursue items and activities that are also illegal. It's a life that frequently takes him into the bars and clubs of Montreal and into contact with the Hells Angels. It's how he got to know Walter Stadnick.

"He's a hell of a guy—people don't usually just show up and join the Hells Angels," said Vincent. "But he did, and he didn't even speak a word of French." Although it's often repeated in Montreal that Stadnick just appeared one day at the club's Sorel headquarters, knocked on the door and talked his way into membership, it's not exactly true. In fact, he had been in irregular contact with the Sorel chapter since his ill-fated attempt to make a pact between them and the Wild Ones in the fall of 1978. By the time the Wild Ones had become extinct, his was a fairly familiar face at parties and other Hells Angels events.

And the Hells Angels gained even more of his trust by not forgetting what happened at Le Tourbillon in October. Telling him

that revenge would be sweet, the Montreal Hells Angels intensified their war against the Outlaws, mainly by taking the muzzle off
Apache Trudeau. Less than a month after the hitmen destroyed the
Wild Ones–Hells Angels summit, Trudeau went to the west end
and knocked on the door of former Outlaws president Brian Powers.
Suspecting nothing, Powers opened the door and took nine bullets in
the head before he hit the ground.

Every Quebec and many Ontario Outlaws turned out at Powers's
funeral. Their numbers were swollen as two Toronto-based gangs—the
Vagabonds and the Para-Dice Riders—appeared to show their respects
and impress upon the Hells Angels that Ontario was still the exclusive
territory of the Outlaws and their friends.

It didn't impress Trudeau. A few weeks later, on December 8,
Trudeau went back to the west end and saw someone he thought he
recognized as an Outlaw. Casually, he asked the stranger—a non-biker
named William Weichold—if his name was "Roxy." Before Weichold
could answer, Trudeau shot him in the head. He later told police that he
couldn't stop laughing when he read about his mistake in *Le Devoir*.

He laughed again on March 29, 1979. When Roland "Roxy"
Dutemple turned the key in his Camaro that morning, it exploded
and he was incinerated. According to informants, it was Dutemple
who told the Outlaws' assassins where Stadnick's meeting was taking
place. Trudeau had finally gotten the right guy.

The man was on a roll. After a rumor surfaced that the Huns, a
non-affiliated suburban Montreal gang, were interested in patching
over to (merging with) the Outlaws, Trudeau took action. Five days
after he killed Dutemple, Trudeau found prey closer to home. In the
Laval neighborhood of Faberville, he walked up to the home of Robert
Labelle. Through the front window, he saw the 25-year-old former
president of the Huns. Labelle had quit the post to devote more time
to his import-export business, which acted as a cover for a large-scale
drug trafficking operation. Trudeau rang the bell, Labelle answered
and Trudeau shot him in the head. Whether the rumor was real or not,
the merger never happened.

Although Trudeau was leaving a trail of Outlaw and Outlaw-
sympathizer bodies, he had yet to murder an underworld heavyweight.

That changed on Tuesday, May 9. Donald McLean was, physically and intellectually, a big man among the Outlaws. Although he held no official rank, he was considered a rising star and a future president by many. And he didn't exactly hide his status. One of the most highly decorated Outlaws, he wore his colors when others considered it unsafe and he rode a motorcycle that drew attention from blocks away. His customized 1963 Flathead was louder than thunder and was flashily customized with tons of chrome and airbrush art. With his 22-year-old girlfriend Carmen Piché on the back, McLean kicked the starter and the couple were blown to bits. The ignition was hooked up to a bomb made and planted by Trudeau and fellow Hells Angels Yves "Le Boss" Buteau and Jean-Pierre "Matt le Crosseur" Mathieu.

* * *

Although he was almost completely lacking in French language skills and none of the Canadian Hells Angels could boast better than rudimentary English, Walter Stadnick proved popular and was made a prospect without having to go through the hangaround process. His time as a prospect was also made much easier than most as he was allowed to continue living in Hamilton and he only had to attend club meetings and functions when he could. "The guys from Sorel really liked Wally right away," said Vincent. "He was small but very tough and he had lots of ideas; he seemed a lot smarter than most of the guys they had hanging around."

He was even allowed to bring along a friend from Hamilton, another former Wild One. Noel "Frenchy" Mailloux earned his nickname in his overwhelmingly English-speaking home town with his ability to speak French. When he and Stadnick went to Montreal, he acted as an interpreter when necessary. "Noel was always around and Wally was able to speak through him," Vincent said.

Although his personal charm and bravado shouldn't be underestimated, Stadnick had the good luck to show up exactly when the Hells Angels needed more members, especially smart and ambitious ones.

The late '70s saw the Hells Angels in the United States again experience a significant change. In 1973, Sonny Barger went to prison for possession of heroin and marijuana. When he was released on parole in February 1977, he found a very different world and a larger, more aggressively businesslike Hells Angels. Although use of marijuana and injected drugs like heroin actually declined while Barger was in Folsom, the popularity of ego-enhancing stimulants—particularly cocaine and its country cousin crystal meth—was skyrocketing. As the brotherhood and free-love ideals of the Age of Aquarius were giving way to the narcissism of the Disco Era, the Hells Angels were making huge profits.

As would happen with any big corporation, an increase in business created a need for more manpower. Luckily for the Hells Angels, there was a new talent pool emerging, many of whom had excellent skills and were highly motivated. Combat veterans from Vietnam were an even better fit for the Hells Angels than previous generations who had seen action in World War II or Korea. Not only were Vietnam Vets more likely to be well-versed in covert and guerilla operations, but they had a deep contempt for a government they felt had betrayed them, as well as no love for a public that had ignored, mocked or reviled their best efforts in Southeast Asia. Bored, disillusioned, misunderstood and unable to readjust to conventional American life, many Vietnam combat vets turned to the Hells Angels and other biker gangs for the brotherhood, excitement and patriotism they felt was missing outside.

Of course, the explosive expansion of business and membership did not escape the notice of Uncle Sam. In June 1979, the federal government arrested Barger, his wife and most of the Oakland Chapter and charged them with offenses under the Racketeer-Influenced and Corrupt Organizations (RICO) law. Federal prosecutor G. William Hunter told the media: "the cornerstone of this illegal drug enterprise was the manufacture and sale of methamphetamine."

It looked like the feds had stacked the deck. RICO had been used against the mafia, Weather Underground, Black Panthers and other groups with the desired effect. Bail for Barger was set at $1 million and the judge appointed was Samuel Conti, who had earned the nickname "Hanging Sam" after doling out some pretty harsh punishments in very high-profile cases. The San Francisco courtroom looked like an armed camp. The proceedings were protected by bulletproof glass and guards with shotguns and submachine guns. Anyone entering the room was checked twice for weapons, and belt buckles larger than two inches wide were confiscated.

But the case didn't work out as planned. After eight months and a parade of more than 100 prosecution witnesses, the sides were stalemated. It was clearly established that the members of the Oakland Chapter used and sold all kinds of drugs—Barger himself admitted to selling heroin—and used intimidation and even murder to protect their businesses, but it was not proven that they did so as a group. Since it was the organization that was on trial, not the individuals, Conti, who actually fainted twice from exhaustion during the proceedings, declared a mistrial. Barger's bail was reassessed at $100,000 and he was freed. Charges against him, his wife and 19 other Hells Angels were dropped less than a week later. A few months later, the 11 remaining members were put on trial again and the jury couldn't reach a verdict. In February 1981, the government dropped all charges, in effect declaring that the Hells Angels were not a criminal organization, although it clearly does have criminals among its membership.

RICO, the law that crippled the mafia in the U.S., proved impotent against the Hells Angels. Instead, the feds were punished for their hubris as the bikers emerged as grassroots heroes. "Free Sonny Barger" T-shirts sold well nationwide and Hells Angels membership ballooned.

As always, things were slightly different in Canada. Although the cocaine market had taken off, the reach and membership of the Hells Angels hadn't. Canada was not involved in the Vietnam War and the draft dodgers that came north to avoid it weren't the sort to join or be accepted by the Hells Angels. There were drug-dealing biker gangs all over the country in the early '80s, but the Hells Angels were limited to Montreal. And, although police estimated that Montreal had a bigger cocaine market than any city in North America other than New York and Los Angeles, the Hells Angels weren't cashing in. The members of the Laval chapter had no business sense and preferred to snort cocaine and run up immense debts rather than sell it. The Sorel chapter tried its best, but with its membership full of unpolished, inexperienced and often less-than-bright young men, it hardly made a dent in the huge Montreal drug scene.

It was a perfect time for Stadnick to show up. Smart, likeable, ambitious and tough, he was exactly what the Montreal Hells Angels needed. Even better, as an English speaker from Ontario with, as almost everyone who knows him alleges, wide and successful experience in selling drugs, he had the potential to help the Hells Angels expand into other, more lucrative Canadian markets. On May 26, 1982, not long after he showed up on their doorstep, Stadnick was initiated as a member of the Hells Angels Motorcycle Club Montreal South Chapter.

From a social standpoint, he didn't disappoint. "I remember him from those days. He was wild," said Vincent. "At Sorel's fifth anniversary party [in December 1982], he out-drank, out-fought and out-partied everyone—Wally was the last man standing."

He may have had an immense capacity for alcohol, but unlike many other Montreal Hells Angels, Stadnick didn't suck the club's profits up his nose. If Stadnick had felt any temptation to acquire a heavy cocaine habit, he could see examples of why he shouldn't all around him. Although the Sorel members didn't have anywhere near the blow problem that their brothers over in Laval had, many members showed signs of overuse—psychosis, random violence and, most prominently, paranoia.

Stadnick saw it first-hand when he and Mailloux went back home for Christmas in 1982. Because Hamilton's drug trade was still largely run by Satan's Choice at the time, it was an Outlaw town and Hells Angels were not welcome. Stadnick was cool. He lay low and kicked back with a few cold ones with friends and family. Mailloux, a heavy coke user, found it harder to settle down. Always known to be a bit suspicious, Mailloux let his paranoia take over his personality. In Hamilton, he was twitchy, nervous and irritable. He carried a .357 Magnum with him wherever he went and he checked every car—even taxis—for explosives before he would enter.

His girlfriend noticed, but she didn't complain. Connie Augustin was also a cocaine user whose hobby had gotten a bit out of control. Thin but shapely, the 24-year-old Augustin was a successful stripper who took her act to different clubs around the area and billed herself as a former "Miss Nude Ontario," although she never specified when she won the title or who gave it to her. She lived in a nice but modest rented townhouse on Garth Road on the west side of Hamilton Mountain, not far from where Mailloux and Stadnick grew up. She shared it with her four-year-old son, Stewart Hawley, and Mailloux when he was in town. Hawley's father lived in Kitchener and rarely visited.

The rest of the story came out later in court. From Christmas until Valentine's Day, Augustin estimated that she and Mailloux went through about $21,000 worth of cocaine. When the stash he had brought from Montreal ran out, Mailloux went to an old friend for more. Mario D'Alimonte worked as a bouncer for a disco at the Royal Connaught Hotel downtown and had access to all kinds of drugs. When Mailloux and Augustin first showed up on February 17, D'Alimonte joked about how frazzled they looked and suggested they needed a good night's sleep more than another binge. He noticed that Mailloux seemed to tense up after that, so he cut the small talk and gave them what they had come for. The couple then raced back up the mountain to use the coke. After about two hours, Mailloux got up to use the phone. He was screaming obscenities at someone—but Augustin was used to that—and when he hung up, he seemed extremely agitated. He was shaking and freaking out. He had a hard time looking her in the eye for more than an instant. Getting caught up in the coke and the paranoia, she began to get nervous. He told her that D'Alimonte's coke was no good, maybe even dangerous. She started to worry. Then he convinced her that D'Alimonte was hired by the Outlaws to kill him. He tried to flush the rest of the coke down the toilet (Augustin stopped him) and pulled out his gun.

Back downtown, the phone conversation unnerved D'Alimonte so much that he loaded two shotguns and kept them with him wherever he went, even taking them to bed with him.

Mailloux ordered Augustin to turn all the lights out, lock all the doors and pull all the shades. He sat on one of Stewart's tiny stools at the front window, aiming his gun at everyone who walked by. He cocked and almost fired on the one person who walked up the steps to the porch until he recognized her. He screamed for Augustin and she ran to the door, grabbed her friend before she could press the doorbell and pulled her into the house.

Cindy Lee Thompson was a friend of Augustin's from work. Younger, prettier and less angry than Augustin, she made a lot more money. Although the 18-year-old had only been dancing for about six months, she had done well enough to be driving a brand-new Lincoln Continental and living in a bigger house and a better neighborhood than Augustin. Because of her age, she had to get special permission from the Liquor Licensing Board of Ontario for the right to work in an establishment that served alcohol; she even needed a letter of permission from her legal guardian. Although it got her a stripping license, the note's signer has never been identified and his address (56 Sherman Avenue North) was fictitious. Because she wasn't shy about showing off her near-instant wealth, Thompson made few friends among her peers, but she found one in Augustin. They shared clothes, went out drinking and snorted cocaine together.

Without explaining what was going on, Augustin hurried Thompson into the kitchen, where they finished the last of the coke. When they finally started whispering about the situation, Thompson convinced her friend that in the state he was in, Mailloux was a lot more dangerous than any Outlaws could be. She also pointed out that if any other bikers were out there, they were out to get him, not her. Augustin thought about it for a second and made a plan. She tiptoed up the carpeted steps to Stewart's room and carried him down to the kitchen. With the small boy clutched in her arms, she and Thompson ran out the side door and into the front bench seat of her 1975 Buick. But Mailloux heard them and pursued. Just as the ignition fired, he and his gun vaulted into the back seat. Before she could say anything, he pushed the cold, thick barrel of the gun into the back of Augustin's neck and ordered her to drive.

Without asking where, she drove. She stopped at the first red light, Stone Church and Upper James, and made her decision. At that point, Upper James is six lanes wide and at 3:40 a.m., there is virtually no traffic. Augustin figured the best way to save her son's life would be to run. After all, Mailloux didn't have anything against Stewart or Thompson, it was her, his girlfriend, who would have betrayed him by trying to run. It was her he would be after. In a desperate bid to save her son's life, she opened the driver's side door and ran as fast as she could.

She was dead wrong. Mailloux's immediate reaction was to fire. He shot her in the back and the bullet emerged through her right breast. Then he shot both Stewart and Thompson in the backs of their heads.

They both died instantly.

When he looked out the blood-spattered windows, he saw something he didn't expect. Augustin—still alive—was running toward a car stopped on the other side of Upper James. He opened his door and started chasing her, shooting wildly. She had managed to get to John Perrins's car and was desperately pulling on the door handle screaming "he's going to kill me!" Perrins looked over and saw Mailloux storming at his car and reloading his gun. He fired again and Perrins stomped on the accelerator.

Augustin stumbled, got up and ran over to the next car. Kevin Pomeroy worked with Perrins at Dofasco and had been at the same party that night. He was heading home to Mount Hope when he noticed that he'd lost a hubcap. He stopped and looked for it, and when he gave up, got back into the cab of his pickup. Less than a second later, Augustin got in beside him and was screaming. She was trying to tell him what was going on, but he couldn't understand her. At the height of the confusion, he saw Mailloux through the passenger window. He was pulling on the door handle, but Augustin had wisely locked it. She was screaming at Pomeroy to drive, but he was frozen with fear and confusion. He heard a crash and a burning sensation in his chin; then he floored it and his truck fired across the intersection. A block later, he realized he'd been shot in the chin. But he didn't panic. He drove two long blocks south to Rymal Road—the junction locals called Ryckman's Corners—and stopped the truck in the parking lot of Target Variety.

Bill Verrall was behind the counter and he recognized Pomeroy right away. The Target, open 24 hours, was the only late-night stop on the way from Hamilton to Pomeroy's home in Mount Hope and he'd stopped in there many times for cigarettes or Cokes. When Pomeroy came in screaming something about being shot, Verrall thought he was joking. He changed his mind when he saw the blood. He called an ambulance. As he watched Pomeroy bleed, he decided it was smarter not to wait any longer and told his brother Paul, who had been stacking cases of soda, to drive him to the hospital. Pomeroy told them about Augustin, and the three men ran to the truck. They pulled on the doors, but she wouldn't let them in. Pomeroy put his key in the door, but she kept pushing the locks down. After a few frantic minutes of trying, Paul drove Pomeroy to the emergency room at Chedoke–McMaster Hospital. Despite Bill's entreaties, Augustin wouldn't leave the truck until an ambulance arrived. With two bullet holes in her, she collapsed on the way to ICU at Henderson Hospital.

When he saw Pomeroy's pickup drive Augustin away, Mailloux knew he wasn't going to be able to kill her that night and he fled. Without many options, he ran into Dr. William Cornell Park and hid in the bushes. Alerted by Bill Verrall, the Hamilton–Wentworth police sent four officers after him. Following the tips of eyewitnesses, they ran with their guns drawn and searched the park. One took a thorn to the eye and had to turn back, but the others combed through the trees and bushes in near-total darkness. The best of them, Sergeant Charles Bramlett, a former army NCO, spied a movement in a growth of cedars and approached it with his weapon drawn. Less than 100 feet away from each other, Bramlett and Mailloux both had their guns aimed at the other man's head. Without blinking, Bramlett walked toward Mailloux. He didn't take his aim off Mailloux's face, but he didn't fire either. When the two men were less than 20 feet way, Bramlett heard it. "Bang!" Mailloux, out of bullets after having shot at least 30 times that night, kept squeezing the trigger, hoping that somehow the gun would fire. Every time he pulled, he yelled "bang!' as loud as he could. Bramlett called the other officers over and they took Mailloux, shivering and babbling incoherently, back to the station.

The next day, Augustin's house was a very busy place. Neighbors, all of whom have asked to remain anonymous, reported that the place was visited at least three times. But it wasn't the police who were collecting evidence. The first visit was early Friday afternoon. An older woman who lived on the other side of Garth Street said that "two guys in leather jackets drove their motorcycles right onto her front lawn." The "tough-looking" pair "knocked on the door, looked in the windows, looked all around the house and then took off." About an hour later, a different neighbor, a man two doors down from the first, saw a long-haired man in a black leather jacket ride up to the house. He parked on the street. He and a blonde woman who was also on the Harley walked up to the door and let themselves in. The witness did not notice if they used keys or not, but he was sure that they didn't knock or use the doorbell. They spent a few minutes inside the house and left.

About 90 minutes later, more bikers showed up. This time they brought a small pickup truck along with the bikes. They backed it up over the curb and onto Augustin's lawn and dropped the tailgate. "They all looked the same with their black leather jackets and their beards and their long hair," said a witness. "They were all scruffy-looking guys and they kept going in and out of the house; they were taking things out and throwing them into the truck." After they were satisfied that there was no important evidence left in the house, they left.

When the police searched the house, they found a lot to link Mailloux to the Hells Angels, including his colors, which they reluctantly returned when a judge declared them inadmissible as evidence, but no drugs.

*   *   *

Stadnick returned to Montreal and was welcomed with open arms. Although Mailloux had totally fucked up, the Hells Angels didn't hold it against Nurget. The boys from Sorel were used to watching guys taking too much cocaine and going nuts. What impressed them was that Stadnick had shown the courage, intelligence and resourcefulness to make sure that Mailloux would go down alone and that the cops would never find any connection that would jeopardize the club. They had wanted Stadnick to succeed, and when a crisis arose, he handled it with aplomb and efficiency.

His stock rose even further when the Hells Angels learned that his presence in Ontario had thrown some fear into the local Outlaws. While former Hamilton Outlaws president Richard Williams was being tried for alleged possession of eight handguns and four sticks of dynamite, his lawyers convinced Crown Attorney Laverne Urban and Judge Walter Stayshyn that he should be allowed to carry a gun after his release from prison because of the danger posed to his life by the "Hells Angels presence" in town. Smart, good in a crisis and certified by the courts as a major threat to the Outlaws, Stadnick was clearly the man the Sorel chapter wanted to lead the club's charge into the rest of Canada.

Although his translator was gone, Stadnick got by. His French never evolved beyond a pidgin level, but many of the other members of the chapter had improved their English for the express purpose of communicating better with him and with the East regional office in Manhattan. Before long, Stadnick found himself riding farther and farther forward in the lineup of bikes.

From the way he handled himself—his confidence, charm, bonhomie and ability to resolve disputes—many of the guys at Sorel began talking about how much Stadnick reminded them of Yves Buteau, who had since become the chapter's president. It was strong praise. A close friend of Sonny Barger's, the big, blonde Buteau was the only Canadian with his permission to wear the "Hells Angels International" patch. A former Popeye, Buteau is generally considered responsible for bringing them into the Hells Angels family by making them the dominant gang in Montreal. Brutal when he needed to be, as when he fueled the murderous war between the rival Atomes and Gitans to ensure the Popeyes' success or when he, Mathieu and Trudeau put the bomb on McLean's bike, Buteau's real talent was tact. When he heard that ten Popeyes had walked out on a lavish bill at a biker-friendly restaurant, he leapt onto his bike, rode to the bistro and paid their tab in full. Unlike many bikers, particularly among the free-spirited Popeyes, Buteau showed a restraint and a knack for public relations that earned him the chapter's presidency and the nickname "Le Boss."

Like Barger before him, Buteau knew that if the Hells Angels were to succeed as a business they would have to clean up their act. He encouraged members to shave and wash their clothes every once in a while and consider cutting their hair. He wanted to present a less relaxed look to clients and suppliers and discourage police harassment. Under Buteau, Hells Angels were instructed to keep a low profile, avoid petty crimes when possible and avoid confrontations with police, even backing down when necessary. All of Buteau's rules were breakable except for one. Any Montreal Hells Angel caught using cocaine would receive an instant death penalty with no excuses and no appeals. Buteau had seen what excessive and even recreational use of the drug could do as many of his friends in the Popeyes went crazy or were crushed under mounting debts. With his wild past behind him and the ambitious dream of a coast-to-coast Canadian Hells Angels, Buteau knew that cocaine use was bad for business. "It's like he [Buteau] always used to say: 'Letting an addict sell drugs is like having a dog run a butcher shop,'" said Vincent, who knew Buteau when he was a Popeye and a Hells Angel.

As good a manager as Buteau was, he was an even better diplomat. He'd gone to British Columbia to scout a gang called the Satan's Angels. With three chapters, the Satan's Angels had done a very good job dominating the drug trade in the Vancouver area. Modeling themselves after the American Hells Angels, the Satan's Angels formed alliances with and supplied drugs to lesser B.C. gangs like the Coffin Cheaters of suburban Vancouver and the Devil's Escorts of Kamloops. After a hugely successful police crackdown on heroin in 1981 crippled the industry, the Satan's Angels successfully shifted their business interests to cocaine and prostitution. Impressed with their efficiency, reach and willingness to use violence, Buteau offered them membership in the Hells Angels. Thrilled that their heroes would accept them, the Satan's Angels jumped at the chance to became the third, fourth and fifth chapters of the Canadian Hells Angels.

Many of the top Canadian Hells Angels flew to British Columbia for the patching-over ceremony; some rode cross-country, but Laval's Michel "Jinx" Genest and Jean-Marc Nadeau decided to take the bus. Eight hours into their trip, Genest fell asleep with his back to the window. Four Outlaws, including vicious Hamilton boy Mario "the Wop" Parente, who happened to pass the bus on Highway 17 just outside North Bay, Ontario, were shocked by what they saw. Although Genest's face couldn't be seen, his winged-skull Hells Angels logo was clearly pressed up against the window. Knowing how harshly the Hells Angels dealt with non-members who wear their logo, the Outlaws realized that one of the enemy had blundered into their midst. While one biker was left to tail the bus, Parente and the others sped to Sault Ste. Marie to pick up some weapons and an inconspicuous car. When they finally caught up with the bus again, it was heading north along the eastern edge of Lake Superior. They followed it at a discreet distance until it turned off on Highway 101 to Wawa.

An old mining town of about 3,500, Wawa didn't have an actual bus terminal. Instead, the bus stopped in front of Mr. Muggs, a 24-hour coffee shop that specializes in chocolate fudge doughnuts. Genest, Nadeau and a 17-year-old girl who was traveling with them got off the bus to eat.

Fifteen minutes later, as the passengers were getting back on the bus in the dark, a car drove by with the windows open. With no target more specific than the bus itself, the men in the car, later described as having long hair, beards and leather jackets, opened fire. In the ten seconds or so of shooting, screaming and glass shattering, startled bus riders dove to the ground and instinctively covered their heads. Nobody was seriously injured, but the bus was a mess. All the passengers could do was sit in Mr. Muggs and wait for the police to come. In their investigation, the Ontario Provincial Police (OPP) found 56 hits of PCP hidden in a cigarette box in a trash can. Genest, Nadeau and the girl were interviewed separately and exhaustively about the shooting and the drugs. Unable to get them to crack, the police released them. Genest and Nadeau waited in Mr. Muggs for the next bus back to Montreal and the girl accepted a ride with police back to Sault Ste. Marie. No fewer than 20 witnesses noticed the "Support Your Local Outlaws" bumper sticker on the back of Parente's car.

The party went on without Genest and Nadeau, and on July 23, 1983, the Hells Angels had expanded to the Pacific Coast as chapters from Vancouver, Nanaimo and White Rock received their patches. With the westward expansion Buteau, always a respected biker and leader, established himself as something of a statesman.

* * *

At the opposite end of the underworld spectrum lurked Gino Goudreau. Nervous and small, the 22-year-old Goudreau was a minor league criminal who sold stolen goods and drugs, including cocaine when he could get his hands on it. He worked very hard to fly under the Hells Angels' radar. On the few occasions he encountered them, he slunk away, chastened, claiming that he was just hanging out. They thought he was comical and never took him seriously.

Perhaps they should have. Ever ambitious, Buteau was always meeting with representatives from other clubs, hoping to forge alliances. On the night of September 8, he and René Lamoureaux, a Montreal Hells Angel with strong ties to the Eastern headquarters in Manhattan and the best English-language skills in the chapter, were entertaining an important visitor in a Sorel strip bar called Le Petit Bourg. Guy "Frenchy" Gilbert was in town representing the Kitchener chapter of the Satan's Choice, one of three chapters that hadn't patched over to the Outlaws, and they were discussing setting up the first Hells Angels outpost in Ontario.

Goudreau and his girlfriend rode up on his motorcycle and parked out front. His older brother was an Outlaw and he'd always wanted to be one, too. He waited until a few minutes after 1:00 a.m. when Buteau, Lamoureaux and Gilbert emerged. The three friends were laughing and sipping their rum-and-Cokes on the sidewalk. They were clearly enjoying each other's company and the warm late summer weather. Gilbert lit up a joint and the others started laughing. They scanned the street and didn't see anything important. "Watch this!" Goudreau told his girlfriend as he leapt off the bike and pulled a .38 from under his jacket. He put two bullets into Buteau's chest, another in Gilbert's stomach, one in Lamoureaux's stomach and another through his scalp. The patrons inside Le Petit Bourg hid under their tables and the girl on stage crawled nude into the men's washroom. Buteau fell face forward and was dead before he hit the pavement. Gilbert managed to stumble into the bar, leaving a trail of blood before he died clutching a stool. Lamoureaux collapsed on the sidewalk and waited, holding his stomach and rocking, until an ambulance came. He survived. Goudreau hopped on his bike and fled. He got his Outlaws membership the next day.

With Buteau out of the picture, Sorel had to be rescued from disarray. Réjean "Zig-Zag" Lessard was elected chapter president and Michel "Sky" Langlois took over as national president, overseeing Sorel, Laval and the three isolated and independent Pacific Coast chapters that Buteau had patched over in July.

Although Langlois had a more impressive title, Lessard had the real power. He got his start with the Marauders, a particularly violent gang from the dying mining town of Asbestos who were notorious for dealing drugs to children, raping girls and selling cars they didn't own. Because the Marauders often partied with the Popeyes, Lessard had known and trusted Buteau for many years and when the Popeyes became the Hells Angels, Lessard joined.

A consummate Eastern Townships tough guy, the tattoo-covered Lessard fit right in with the rowdy members of the Laval chapter. Before long he became known as a vicious fighter and a big-time seller and user of huge amounts of cocaine. His excessive drug use caught up to him in the spring of 1983 when he suffered a series of psychotic episodes that culminated in epileptic seizures. He immediately swore off cocaine and found himself rapidly returning to health. As he recovered, he saw how stupid, reckless and violent his friends in Laval could be. They were wasting money and wasting their lives on the white powder when they could be selling it and getting rich. Disgusted with the chapter, he and his friends Luc "Sam" Michaud and Robert "Ti-Maigre" Richard defected to the more businesslike Sorel chapter that summer. A close association with Buteau guaranteed immediate credibility for Lessard and before long he was acting as his Number 2. So when Buteau was assassinated in September, it was hardly surprising that Lessard was chosen to fill his spot.

His first act as president was stunningly successful. He managed to orchestrate a lavish funeral for Buteau on September 12. So great was Buteau's reputation that more than 2,000 mourners filed through a small church in Sorel. Some mourners who were wanted by police—most notably West End Gang hitman and enforcer John "Jake the Snake" McLaughlin—paid their respects from a number of rented windowless vans parked outside. After the service, a fleet of almost 200 bikers made the slow 45-mile drive to escort the casket to a Drummondville cemetery. Although many of the bikers came from the U.S. and even the U.K., it was an impressive show of strength that gave the Lessard regime instant credibility.

Lessard admired Stadnick and the change in leadership did nothing to dull his star. The police who were watching the Sorel chapter noticed that Stadnick would occasionally wear a "Filthy Few" patch on his jacket. The patch means different things to different people. In the '70s, the Oakland cops noticed that all of the Hells Angels they arrested for murder or suspected of being murderers wore the Filthy Few patch. They made the natural, if presumptuous, assumption that committing a murder was the entry fee into the Filthy Few fraternity. But in his autobiography, Sonny Barger gave a different account. He wrote: "The Filthy Few patch signifies 'The first to the party and the last to leave' after someone once said, 'Man, by the time the last of you leave, you're fucking filthy,' so we came up with the name the Filthy Few." Of course, it would be in Barger's best interest to deny that the Hells Angels committed and rewarded murder as an organization. And it would have also helped the police to disagree. No matter which account you believe, Stadnick wore the patch.

A year after Buteau's death, Lessard was less worried about the Outlaws than he was about his former chapter in Laval. Their random and excessive violence was leading to unnecessary arrests, any of which could lead to dangerous secrets being spilled, and their voracious cocaine use was leading to crippling debts. His plan was to gather both chapters together for an event, so that the guys from Sorel could talk or beat some sense into those from Laval. A memorial service and party commemorating Buteau's death seemed like the perfect occasion.

It could have been, but the timing was bad. On September 8, 1984, Pope John Paul II landed at St. John's, Newfoundland, to be greeted by throngs of faithful and curious Canadians. Easily the most popular pope of the modern era and a genuine worldwide superstar, John Paul II was the first pope ever to visit Canada. He was mobbed everywhere he went. In heavily Catholic places like Newfoundland and Quebec, the local population considered it an event of unparalleled magnitude. Pope John Paul, a man of considerable charm, endeared himself to Canadians by praising them, telling them they had won his heart and referring to Canadian beer as "good, honorable and tasty."

Montreal, despite its reputation for cynicism about religious matters, was no different. At 10:26 p.m. on the evening of September 10, the Pope's train pulled into Montreal's Windsor Station almost 90 minutes late. The train had been slowed to 35 km/h (22mph) because of the more than 35,000 people who had lined the tracks from Quebec City to Montreal in an effort to get just a glimpse of the man. His plan for the following day was a quiet morning visiting two shrines—the tombs of Brother André and St. Marguerite Bourgeoys—to be followed by an open-air mass at Jarry Park in the afternoon and a massive youth rally at Olympic Stadium. The excitement was palpable; the city was abuzz. Mayor Jean Drapeau, the man who brought the Olympics to the city, called the Pope's visit "the biggest event in Montreal's history." Throughout the city, thousands of people were chanting "JP!" and "Vive il Papa!" At least 350,000 faithful braved the constant rain to see him at Jarry Park and many more got stuck on the way. That day, Montreal traffic, already notorious, became by turns stuck and violently fast.

It was a bad day to hold the Buteau memorial, but Lessard was adamant. Although other drivers had a habit of getting out of the way when the Hells Angels showed up, the sheer amount of traffic made it nearly impossible for any group to get past Montreal without getting caught in the quagmire. Lessard thought that the Hells Angels could avoid the worst of the traffic by taking rural roads. It worked at first. The motorcade crossed the St. Lawrence and headed to Drummondville on a series of ancient two-lane highways that cut through the red and gold woods, cornfields and cow pastures. Traffic was light, but the poorly paved roads were slippery, as it had been raining lightly but almost constantly since about 10 o'clock the night before. Heading south on Route de Monsignor Parenteau through the tiny farming village of Saint-Pie-de-Guire, some of the riders slowed to take the sharp downhill turn east. Lessard and most of the top members sped right through. About a quarter-mile behind, baby-faced prospect Daniel Matthieu was at the front of a big group of bikers when he saw a battered old Mercury going down Rue St-Michel at a pretty good clip. But he also saw that it was headed for a stop sign, so he twisted his right wrist and accelerated through the intersection.

Inside the car was an elderly small-parish priest who was desperate to get to Montreal in time for the Jarry Park mass. It promised to be the biggest event of his life and he didn't want to miss it. Not only had he overslept that morning, but he'd been delayed by parishioners who couldn't make it to the big city and wanted to give him items to be blessed or tell him their sad stories so he could ask the Pope to pray for them. Their delays and outlandish, unrealistic requests had made his already stressful morning almost unbearable. It had been almost 20 years since he had driven to Montreal and he wasn't sure of the way. So, with a road map on his passenger seat and a prayer, he set off for the city. When he was driving down Rue St-Michel, he was thoroughly lost. Saint-Pie-de-Guire looked like hundreds of other little villages on the South Shore, with nothing to distinguish it other than a name. Whether it was the map, the rain or the stress, he didn't see the stop sign and he didn't see the bikers.

The old Mercury slammed into Matthieu and his bike with such force that Matthieu's legless body was found almost 100 feet away from the twisted wreckage of the Harley. Stadnick, who was just behind Matthieu, couldn't stop in time and his bike crumpled as it plowed into the passenger door of the old car. His elongated forks became dislodged and were rammed into the bike's custom gas tank. The car, the bike and Stadnick were consumed in a massive fireball.

The rest of the bikers leapt off their bikes in a desperate attempt to help. With the fire enveloping Stadnick still too large to brave, two prospects opened the door of the car and dragged the driver out. About to deal a deadly blow, the biker's hand was stopped when he saw the priest's collar. He escaped the accident and the aftermath totally unharmed.

There was no helping Matthieu, who was lying in pieces. But when they finally managed to pull Stadnick from the flames, they were shocked to see that he was somehow still breathing.

Chapter 5

John Harris is so big he's scary. The 6-foot 6-inch former defensive end for the University of Minnesota and the Hamilton Tiger-Cats is the kind of big and strong you can't get from steroids. It's so natural that it seems like he was born that way. Worse yet, he has a look on his face that says he's not just aware that he can kick your ass, but he'd be more than delighted to do it. Give him a big gun, a big stick, a bulletproof vest and a uniform and he's a bad guy's worst nightmare. That's probably why the Hamilton–Wentworth police made him their biker cop in 1980. "It helps when you're the biggest guy in the room," he said. "When you can intimidate them, your job becomes a lot easier." And he did his job so well, the force was reluctant to remove him. "They told me that nobody should do this job for more than two years—the danger, the stress were too much," he said, laughing. "That's why I did it for ten."

Harris knew Walter Stadnick from his days as a uniformed officer in the '70s and didn't have a very high opinion of him. "He was the kind of guy you'd never notice no matter how hard he tried," said Harris. "You wouldn't see him in a crowd if he was naked." Harris followed Stadnick's movements and his rise through the Montreal Hells Angels and did his best to remind him of his presence every time the biker was in town. "I'd stop him from time to time, just to let him know I was out there and I was watching him," said Harris. "He was always co-operative, but never said a word more than he had to—I thought the whole thing was pretty funny, but he never seemed to get it." Their paths crossed frequently as Harris stopped in the bars, strip joints and other haunts of Stadnick's. "He was civil enough, but he never had a sense of humor," said Harris. "One time I said to him: The last time I saw cowboy boots that small, they were on a keychain—and he didn't react at all; that was Walter."

In 1984, Hamilton was still very much an Outlaws city and, after Mailloux imploded and left Stadnick as the only Hells Angel in town, Harris was much more concerned with keeping tabs on Mario "The Wop" Parente and his gang. But in September, he received a call from Kathi Anderson, Stadnick's common-law wife. Harris had known her for a while and thought she was pretty okay considering who she lived with. She held a day job at a Canada Trust branch downtown, was smart, well-spoken and almost refreshing compared with all the coked-up, air-headed strippers most of the bikers spent their time with. Without a hello, she said, "John, Walter needs your help."

The accident that killed Daniel Matthieu had a catastrophic effect on Stadnick. When his gas tank exploded in his face, the heat was so intense that it melted most of his helmet and fused his hands to the grips on his handlebars. When the other bikers tried to pry his blackened, smoldering body from the still-flaming wreckage, they were pretty sure they were carrying a dead man. But when the medevac helicopter arrived, they began to get optimistic.

Three days later, Stadnick woke from a medically induced coma screaming in pain. He may not have been entirely sure of where he was or why he was there, but the seriousness and gravity of the situation quickly became apparent. His screaming and thrashing soon drew a nurse into his room and she started trying to calm him. Her soothing tones did little to calm him down because he couldn't understand a word she said. While she was speaking to him in French, he was screaming at her in English and neither had any idea what the other was trying to communicate. She sedated him.

When visiting hours began the following day, Anderson was there, as she had been since arriving in Montreal after the accident. She knew it was him under the bandages, but had no idea what he would look like when they came off. The doctor, who spoke English, told her that Walter had received third-degree burns over much of his body and that he was lucky to be alive. He'd lost two-and-a-half fingers and the tip of his nose to the flames and was scarred all over his upper body, especially his hands, arms and face. He woke screaming again. Even the most comprehensive pain-management program can do little in the face of third-degree burns; some of Walter's went all the way to the bone. After Kathi was able to calm him down enough to talk to him, she realized that he couldn't stay in a hospital where none of the nurses could speak English. No matter what he needed, they just pumped him full of drugs. It was not the place he needed to be.

Anderson called Réjean "Zig Zag" Lessard, the president of Stadnick's chapter in Sorel, and told him what was happening. He was eager to help; he told her that the club would pay to move him to Hamilton and even provide some protection. The 13th Tribe, a Halifax-based club prospecting for the Hells Angels, would be given a chance to prove themselves by standing guard outside Stadnick's room.

Bikers and cops alike suspected it was Parente who had shot up the bus in Wawa because he saw some Hells Angels on it, and there was little chance he'd let Stadnick recuperate in Hamilton, their shared hometown. "Mario wasn't the smartest guy in the business, but he had all the nerve," said Harris. "A lot of guys acted tough, but he was the one who would do everything he promised he'd do."

Parente earned his reputation honestly, with incidents like the time he and local tough guy Jimmy Lewis got into a fistfight at Bannister's, a biker-dominated strip joint in downtown Hamilton. The fight eventually spilled outside, where it was broken up by bouncers and club patrons. Without a word, Parente got on his bike and sped off as Lewis returned to the club. Parente rode to the Outlaws' Birch Street headquarters, grabbed a shotgun police had just returned to him after it was declared inadmissible as evidence in another case, rode back downtown and shot Lewis dead. He was convicted and served three years.

The 13th Tribe were a pretty tough bunch of guys who could probably hold off the Outlaws if it came to that, but they could only stand guard during visiting hours. Otherwise, security was lax. Parente or one of his men could easily sneak in and kill Walter, and it wasn't as if he could defend himself. Desperate, Anderson turned to the only person she thought could protect her husband. She called Harris.

Hamilton cops regularly earn extra money working as security for concerts and other events. In fact, just a month earlier some officers had come under investigation for improper conduct while working at Flamboro Speedway, a racetrack just outside the city. But this was different; Anderson was talking about hiring police to protect a Hells Angel (in Harris's eyes, a criminal). "I told her I couldn't authorize something like that, and that my first instinct was to say no," said Harris. "But he is a human being with rights, so I told her I'd ask the chief."

Much to Harris's surprise, Hamilton–Wentworth Police chief Ken Robertson agreed to allow officers guard Stadnick while he was in hospital. His reasoning was that while protecting a Hells Angel would certainly lead to bad press, bringing a full-scale biker war to the city would be far worse. The day before the burned biker was to be moved to the city, Harris met with Anderson and Stadnick's lawyer, Stephan Frankel, to establish terms.

* * *

Built in 1848, Hamilton General Hospital looks even older. It has since undergone an extensive facelift, but at the time Stadnick was there it had a sinister, industrial revolution–era atmosphere inside and out. Situated on one of the worst sections of Barton Street—just two blocks from the jail—everything about the General belies its reputation as one of the best hospitals in Canada. Its burn unit was and still is particularly well respected.

Diane was a nurse at the General at the time Stadnick was there and remembers his stay well. "It was crazy; most of the day there were these big, burly bikers outside his room," she said. "And the rest of the time, it was these big, burly cops—it's like he was a rock star or something." There was not much affection between the 13th Tribe and the Hamilton–Wentworth Regional Police. "You could tell the bikers were small-town boys; they weren't used to cops like we had here in Hamilton," she said. "They used to taunt and tease the bikers all the time—trying to start a fight, eh?" Despite the best efforts of the police, the bikers couldn't be persuaded into anything illegal. "After a while, things seemed to calm down and the two sets of guys seemed to at least tolerate each other," said Diane. "But the cops always referred to Mr. Stadnick as 'French Fry' and the bikers always called the cops 'the Doughnut Gang.'"

Visiting hours were busy. Anderson was there as much as her job would allow, and Stadnick had frequent meetings with his lawyer and many local friends. Stephan Frankel was shocked at how badly his client had been burned. "He was beyond recognition. The only way I knew it was him was when I saw Kathi sitting beside his bed," said Frankel. Don Stockford, a friend of Stadnick's family who'd always wanted to be a biker, dropped by regularly and earned Hells Angels prospect status with his kindness and loyalty. And, of course, Harris visited every once in a while. "I just wanted to remind him I was around," he said. "And annoy him a bit." The Outlaws never showed up and the 13th Tribe earned their colors, becoming the Hells Angels Halifax Chapter on December 5, 1984.

When he was released from the General, Stadnick was a very different person. The crash and burn had cost him two and a half fingers, the tip of his nose and much of his skin. He was scarred over much of his upper body, especially his arms and face, but the incident also affected his personality. "It's not like he was an attractive guy before the accident, but he was real hard to look at afterwards," said Harris. "And it seemed to change him even more mentally than physically; he seemed isolated and depressed afterwards." Those changes didn't affect Anderson and Stockford, both of whom stayed loyal to Stadnick. "You have to hand it to Kathi," said Harris. "She stuck by him after the accident; not many people would have."

* * *

While Stadnick was recovering at home in Hamilton, Réjean Lessard was declaring war in Montreal. Upset by the fact that the members of Laval were snorting more cocaine than they were selling and were accumulating horrendous debts, Lessard decided to "close" the chapter.

He decreed death sentences for the primary offenders and invited the entire chapter to a party at the headquarters of the Gitans (formerly the Dirty Reich), a Sherbrooke, Quebec, club prospecting for the Hells Angels. The slaughter, later known as the Lennoxville Massacre after a nearby suburb, was a qualified success. Lessard and his men shot and killed five members of the Laval chapter, but missed Yves "Apache" Trudeau, their primary target, who had checked into rehab a week earlier. For their participation, the Gitans were awarded the honor of becoming the Hells Angels Sherbrooke Chapter.

Before the bodies started floating up to the surface of the St. Lawrence River, word of the Lennoxville Massacre had spread through the Quebec underworld and divided it sharply. Some were impressed by Lessard's decisiveness and ability to impose his will, while others were appalled by the Hells Angels' ability to turn on their own kind. No organization was split more deeply than the SS, a loose-knit gang of East End lowlifes with a racist bent. The division was so profound that it actually broke the SS up. One member, Salvatore Cazzetta, was so appalled that he and his brother Giovanni formed their own gang in opposition to the Hells Angels. Realizing how dangerous it would be to flaunt their existence in front of Lessard's men, the new gang—the Rock Machine—identified its members not by colorful jackets, but with rings emblazoned with a stylized eagle's head.

Cazzetta made it clear when he formed the new gang that it was because he did not want to be part of the Hells Angels. "Sal once told me: 'Those guys, they operate their club in such a way that I didn't want to join them,'" said Fred Faucher, a veteran of the SS and one of the Rock Machine's original members. With the charismatic Salvatore Cazzetta's close ties with the Montreal mafia, his new gang had no lack of business and soon grew strong and large. They gained even more strength and credibility when two notable SS veterans—the immense Paul "Sasquatch" Porter and the cold-blooded André "Curly" Sauvageau—joined the new club.

One of Cazzetta's closest friends and a founding member of the SS, Maurice "Mom" Boucher, disagreed. A hardcore tough from the nastiest streets of Montreal who dropped out of high school to become a full-time drug dealer and enforcer, Boucher was in prison when the SS broke up. He'd been found guilty of sexually assaulting a woman while holding a knife to her throat and had served 23 months of a 40-month sentence when he was released to a new Montreal. While he was inside, one Hells Angels chapter had butchered another, the SS had disbanded and a major new gang had emerged. Naturally, the Cazzettas tried to recruit him for the Rock Machine, but Boucher wasn't interested. He didn't want to be part of the third-best biker gang in Montreal. In fact, Boucher actually admired what Lessard had done—he'd seen a problem and taken care of it. Boucher had always wanted to be part of the best gang and the way Sorel had handled Laval showed him that the Hells Angels were indeed the top of the heap. Rather than take a primary position with the Rock Machine, Boucher rode his bike to Sorel and asked to join the Hells Angels. They were more than happy to accept him as a prospect as long as he promised never to use cocaine again. That was okay with him; he'd switch to alcohol.

When the bodies of the Laval members started to appear, the police knew who had murdered them. But it wasn't until a chance arrest of Trudeau coincided with a tabloid article that claimed he was being targeted as Sorel's next victim that the case broke. His testimony against the Sorel chapter was exactly what the police needed to cripple the Hells Angels in Quebec. After a long and exhaustive inquest, prolonged by numerous challenges by Hells Angels lawyer Léo-René Maranda, Crown attorney René Domingue charged 17 Sorel members with murder and issued warrants for ten more on October 2, 1985. Fear caused two more Hells Angels, Gerry "Le Chat" Coulombe and Gilles "Le Nez" Lachance, to agree to turn informant. Lachance's testimony was especially damning, as he was an eyewitness to the Lennoxville Massacre and was desperate to escape what he thought was a death sentence from Sorel.

Things were little better for the Hells Angels on the East Coast. A Halifax prostitute who was enraged when the bikers started demanding 40 percent of her gross earnings in exchange for advertising and protection, went to the cops and told them everything. On May 30, 1986, all eight full-patch members of Hells Angels Halifax Chapter were arrested and charged with conspiracy to live on the avails of prostitution; they were eventually sentenced to one-year terms. The clubhouse and what remained of their business was operated by prospects and hangarounds until Michel "Sky" Langlois, who became president after Lessard was arrested, was informed by Eastern headquarters in Manhattan that a chapter must have a minimum of six full members or face potentially permanent suspension, as had happened in Buffalo, New York, a few years earlier. Desperate, Langlois dipped into the Sorel and Halifax coffers to pay to fly full-patch B.C. members to operate the chapter in two-week shifts.

The national network of Hells Angels chapters that Yves "Le Boss" Buteau had envisioned and begun in earnest was in shambles. Laval was extinct, all the important members of Sorel and Halifax were behind bars, ratting on their brothers or hiding from police, while the B.C. chapters were busy on a cross-country commute trying to keep the entire club from falling apart. And, despite repeated forays, the club had no footing in Ontario, Canada's richest market for drugs and prostitution.

The Hells Angels' misfortunes didn't escape the Outlaws' notice. Traditionally less aggressive than their rivals, the Outlaws began to exert themselves in Quebec. They began by posting leaflets all over the Montreal area which illustrated "Hells Angels Brotherhood" with crudely drawn pictures of dead bikers at the bottom of the St. Lawrence. At an April 10, 1986, open-air rock concert in the tiny village of Verchères on the South Shore just down river from Montreal, the normally discreet Outlaws arrived in full colors. According to eyewitnesses and tabloids like *Allô Police*, they also conducted drug sales without fear of interruption by police or rivals. In hopes of hosting an international Outlaws party, the Montreal Chapter bought a farm in Dundee, Quebec, just walking distance from the U.S. border. Before any events could take place, the tipped-off Sûreté du Quebec (SQ) raided the farm and found 200 handguns, 30 hand grenades and a box of dynamite, but made no significant arrests. The Outlaws' new assertiveness was complemented by the Evil Ones, a prominent Hells Angels puppet gang, who stopped wearing their colors in public. When Langlois found out, he was enraged. He sped to the Evil Ones' clubhouse and threatened their president, Marc Bourassa. Unless the Evil Ones showed more backbone, and their colors, he told them, they would be stripped of them and, he hinted, they could find themselves at the bottom of the river. Bourassa and his men complied and sweetened the deal by donating the proceeds of local stickups to the Hells Angels' defense fund.

* * *

Stadnick, out of the hospital, was recuperating at his trailer in Courtcliffe Park in Carlisle, Ontario, just outside Hamilton. Courtcliffe is a friendly place where people kick back, relax and get to know each other generation after generation. As in Hamilton, Stadnick's country neighbors found him quiet, unassuming and eminently likeable. "He never caused any problems; he was always friendly," said a man who had a trailer near his. "I didn't even know he was a biker—he always drove a car up here." While Stadnick never rode his Harley or wore his colors up to Carlisle, he did bring at least one piece of the underworld with him.

In the summer of 1986, a neighbor was mowing the area around his trailer when he came across a large white Tupperware container in the underbrush. When he opened it, it was full of pills. Sensing something was wrong, he called the police. Since most of the Hamilton–Wentworth force knew Stadnick was up there, the case was forwarded to Harris. "It was full of amphetamines, and we knew it was his," said Harris. "So we put the container back where it was found and kept an eye on it." But Stadnick must have realized what had happened, because he never went back to retrieve the pills. "He was pretty smart," said Harris. "If nothing else, he had an ability to keep himself out of trouble."

Harris wasn't the only one Stadnick had to worry about back then. Although the Hells Angels had no official presence in Ontario at the time, Stadnick had business to conduct and kept his local associates close. Rather than meet at his house, Stadnick held meetings on the other side of town. "Someone else's name was on the papers, but we knew it was really Walter who owned Rebel's Roadhouse," said Harris. "It was a great set-up, he had a bar in the front and an office in the back." With its biker/Western/Confederate decor, Rebel's was a popular meeting and drinking spot, despite being owned by a Hells Angel in an Outlaws town, and it made plenty of money legally. But in the back, out of earshot, was where the real action was. Stadnick, with his now-omnipresent right-hand man Stockford, met with many regional heavyweights and old friends. "Walter was extremely careful in Hamilton," said Harris. "He surrounded himself with friends who had legitimate and useful businesses."

Kathi Anderson helped to handle Stadnick's investments and taxes. She also held a job with Canada Trust. Stockford ran West End Talent, an agency that supplied strippers to area bars.

Some of Standick's other old friends who had cut their ties with biker organizations included former Wild One John "Cataract Jack" Pluim became a prominent real estate agent, while another good friend, Alvin Patterson, still owns and operates AL Choppers, a shop that specializes in Harley-Davidson repair and customization. Another, George Freeborn, owned a successful paving company that eventually won the contract to pave the new Hamilton Mountain police station. "Those guys stayed clean and helped Walter in legal ways," said Harris.

Aside from Stockford, none of Stadnick's Hamilton friends ever got in serious trouble with the law, although Patterson was the sole Canadian importer of *Easy Riders*, a magazine for bikers published by a Hells Angels puppet company, which was illegal in this country until 1984. The police never really bothered him about it.

The Outlaws couldn't ignore Stadnick's growing influence in the area. If they couldn't keep a single full-patch member from succeeding in their city, how could they prevent the Hells Angels from taking over the province? Stadnick had to be removed, but it wouldn't be easy. He was as careful with the Outlaws as he was with cops. Bombing his car wouldn't work; he was just too smart for that, so they decided to hit him at Rebel's. Through Outlaws in New York State, the Hamilton Chapter managed to get their hands on the perfect weapon. The M-72 Light Antitank Weapon (better known as the LAW) is a single-shot rocket launcher similar to the bazooka from World War II. Collapsing down to a two-foot tube weighing just five pounds, the LAW is easy to conceal, but it packs an incredible punch. From 200 yards, an armor-piercing LAW shell can penetrate a foot of solid metal and create havoc on the other side. The plan was to put one shell through the front door of Rebel's while Stadnick was inside and have another one ready in case the first one missed.

They never pulled it off. A nervous informant within the Outlaws called Harris and told him everything, including the location within a nearby provincial park where the weapons were buried. There was no way Harris would leave the LAWs there to see who'd dig them up; it was way too dangerous. "I think they were relieved when I found them; they didn't have the heart to pull off something that dramatic," Harris said. "When Parente was running the show they would have done it; but after he went to prison, they didn't have the guts."

* * *

When Stadnick returned to Sorel, it was a very different place. Most of his friends were in prison or living in fear they soon would be. With their numbers reduced, the Hells Angels were rapidly losing ground to the formerly second-fiddle Outlaws. Always on the look-out for rising talent, Stadnick noticed a fearless and decisive young prospect in Maurice Boucher and quickly befriended him. It was an odd pairing. Strapping, handsome Boucher couldn't speak much English and tiny, disfigured Stadnick was even less comfortable in French. But the two recognized that they needed each other. Boucher was ruthless, but not reckless the way Trudeau had been. He had the muscle and courage to impose the Hells Angels' will. And Stadnick was smart, meticulous and forward-thinking. He had the ability to charm, recruit and formulate a strategy for a Hells Angels comeback. Together they would form the future of the club in Canada, and they knew it.

But it wasn't them, or any other Montreal Hells Angel that would make the first successful and lasting inroads with an Ontario club. In the huge expanse of Canada between Quebec and British Columbia, there were dozens of clubs that tried their best to remain neutral in the Hells Angels–Outlaws rivalry. In fact, the three biggest non-aligned clubs of the time—the remaining Satan's Choice in Ontario, the Grim Reapers in Alberta and Los Brovos in Winnipeg—created an informal alliance specifically aimed at frustrating the advance of the Outlaws and Hells Angels into their territory. Toronto was no different. Home to drug and prostitution markets at least double the size of Montreal's,

Toronto had long been home to a number of clubs that lived in an uneasy tolerance of one another. There was a tacit, but strictly followed, agreement that no Toronto club would associate with either of the superpowers. That changed in August 1986, when the Para-Dice Riders, Toronto's biggest club, partied with the Hells Angels in British Columbia.

Rick Ciarniello was a member of the Vancouver Chapter and, if you believe the police, the de facto leader of the B.C. Hells Angels. He frequently denied that the Hells Angels were a criminal enterprise—claiming they were "just a bunch of nice guys who rode motorcycles"—but he lived in a massive house in a great neighborhood and drove a brand-new Lincoln with vanity plates that read "ANGELS." It wasn't just individual members who were getting wealthy in British Columbia; the local chapters put their savings together and bought a beautiful wooded piece of land just outside Nanaimo on Vancouver Island. Angel Acres, as they called it, featured a dirt track, a large in-ground pool, a bandshell and a set of trailers for overnight stays. It was a perfect place for bikers to drink, party and blow off steam without worrying about neighbors or police. On the first weekend of August 1986, the B.C. Hells Angels threw a birthday bash to celebrate their third anniversary. More than 3,000 bikers showed up from all over North America, including all 39 members of the Para-Dice Riders, who had driven all the way from Toronto. They drank, they partied and they met with the Hells Angels brass, including Stadnick, but made no deals other than to promise to return for the party next year.

* * *

Back in Montreal, both Stadnick and Boucher (who became a full-patch member on May 1, 1987) were gaining in influence. Their complementary skills made them a powerful team, and they were soon calling the shots for Sorel. They were ready when their chance came.

Despite an official salary of $400 a week, Langlois had a house in the mountains that put Ciarniello's to shame. He also had a luxury car, an award-winning custom Harley and a private airplane. After the top of the chapter went to prison, he was the natural choice to take over as president. Not only did he have seniority, but he'd proven his ability to make money and escape prosecution. But his reign came to an abrupt end in the spring of 1988. When word spread that a Hells Angels associate in Montreal's Bordeaux prison was willing to betray Langlois for his part in the Lennoxville Massacre in exchange for a reduced sentence, the president panicked. Rather than face his chances with police and courts, he fled. Packing as much as they could, Langlois and his wife flew to Morocco. For two years, they disappeared in the North African country where French is widely spoken and European tourists are common.

Stadnick took the initiative and called an emergency meeting. Every member showed. After a long and sober night of discussion and argument, he called a vote. It was close, but a clear winner emerged. Walter Stadnick, the tiny tough guy from Hamilton, the guy who used to pull his hair through a hole in the top of his helmet, the guy who was scarred almost beyond recognition and still barely spoke a word of French, got what he always wanted: he was president of the Canadian Hells Angels.

Stadnick's first act as president was an astute one. He took Boucher aside and let him know that he would be the top Hells Angel in Quebec and that Stadnick would concentrate primarily on recruiting clubs in English-speaking Canada and other strategic goals. It made perfect sense: besides the obvious language problem, Stadnick realized he didn't have a very firm grip on the cultural differences between Quebec and the rest of Canada. And he liked what he saw in Boucher, who could be charming and likeable when he wanted to be and had kept his promise to stay off drugs. He was a natural leader, and he also appeared to be a loyal friend who understood that Stadnick possessed organizational skills and a strategic intellect he would never have.

Reinforced with a strong new leadership team, the Hells Angels again went on the offensive. A Quebec City club, the Vikings, had been prospecting for the Hells Angels and many members had become skeptical about the organization after Langlois fled. They didn't know Stadnick well and were dismayed that a runty Anglophone was now in charge of the mighty Hells Angels. On May 28, 1988, the Sorel chapter rode down the river and partied with the Vikings. Stadnick negotiated the deal, while Boucher translated and made friends. It was so successful, they patched over the Vikings—who became the Hells Angels' Quebec City Chapter—that night. Little more than a year later, October 17, 1989, the SQ executed a search warrant on their clubhouse with a backhoe. After knocking down two outside walls and a ceiling but finding nothing incriminating, the police shrugged their shoulders and left. The Quebec City chapter called Sorel for help. Stadnick told them to sue the police and gave them the names of some lawyers. They won their case and the SQ was forced to pay for the clubhouse repairs.

* * *

When Stadnick returned to Hamilton, he was a different man. Or at least, he looked like one. "I first realized he'd been elected president when he showed up with the company car," said Harris. Instead of his familiar Pontiac Bonneville, Stadnick was driving a brand-new black Jaguar with Quebec plates. And his wardrobe changed too. Always a flamboyant dresser, Stadnick pushed the limits after he became president. "He wore his colors more and more and decorated them with patches and red leather fringes," said Steve Pacey, a Hamilton cop who took over the biker beat in 1999 and had known Stadnick since high school. "He was very ceremonial, like a king; but sometimes he reminded me of Michael Jackson."

He may not have impressed the cops, but Stadnick was beginning to increase his influence in his hometown. On August 23, 1988, he was arrested at the home of Douglas Freeborn, a former president of the Hamilton Satan's Choice chapter who had decided to quit when the Outlaws took over. Just over 11 ounces of hash was found in the couch they were sitting on, and both men were charged with possession with intent to distribute. What happened next surprised everyone, particularly Harris. For reasons that have never been made entirely clear, Freeborn claimed that all the hash was his; Stadnick was free to walk.

The case made Stadnick famous in his hometown. *The Hamilton Spectator*, a daily newspaper as old as the city itself, acted as though it was the first time they had heard his name. On September 15, 1989, it ran an article claiming that Stadnick was in Hamilton recruiting potential members in an effort to establish a chapter there. "He is a bona fide Hells Angels member, and he does have permission from the national president to start a chapter here," the article quoted Bob Slack, head of the Hamilton–Wentworth Regional Police vice and drug departments, as saying. Obviously, he didn't know that Stadnick was national president at the time.

Other police disagreed. "Clearly he wanted to move the Hells Angels into Ontario, but he wouldn't establish a chapter in Hamilton," said Harris. "He didn't want that kind of attention in his backyard." Although Harris was right, it didn't matter. The idea had been planted, and Stadnick was better known and more feared than any other biker in Hamilton.

* * *

Emboldened, Stadnick and the Montreal Hells Angels began to exert themselves again. Days after setting fire to the old Laval clubhouse, the Sorel chapter showed up at a party held by the Vagabonds, a non-aligned club in Toronto. "When the Hells Angels show up in Toronto, they are always welcome now," said a Sorel prospect who attended the Vagabonds party. They were greeted with hospitality, but when discussions turned to patching over, the Vagabonds were noncommittal. Stadnick did manage to hammer out a working relationship with Vagabonds president Donald "Snorkel" Melanson, in which members of the Toronto gang could buy drugs from the Hells Angels individually and sell them locally, but there would be no official contact between the two clubs.

While Stadnick was preaching the Hells Angels gospel across the country, Boucher was consolidating the club's power at home in Quebec. He fired his first salvo on September 15, 1989, when the Hells Angels rode into Danville, located in the Eastern Townships between Sherbrooke and Asbestos, and fire-bombed the Outlaws' heavily fortified clubhouse. The next day, Darquis Leblanc, president of the Outlaws' Danville chapter, showed up on the steps of the Sorel clubhouse and asked to defect. Boucher accepted his offer, but told him that he could never be a Hells Angel, a prospect or even a hangaround. Instead, he would serve the club as an associate, doing the dirty work Hells Angels found beneath them. Leblanc quickly agreed.

To press the point that Quebec was their turf, large groups of Hells Angels and their puppet clubs started showing up in Outlaw towns and in Outlaws bars in full colors. Now it was the Outlaws who were beginning to worry about wearing their colors in public.

The Hells Angels punctuated their statements on September 15, 1990. Montreal Outlaws president Claude Meunier took his Harley to a repair shop in the Côte-Saint-Paul section of the city. As he was parking his bike out front, he looked over his left shoulder to see a car creeping slowly along the curb. When he turned back around, a man in the back seat of the car opened fire. Meunier died slumped over his handlebars, with four bullets in his chest and another in his neck.

Meunier's funeral drew hundreds of Outlaws from Canada and the United States, and one surprise guest. Leblanc, who had befriended Meunier before they were Outlaws, appeared to show his respect. Despite the presence of dozens of uniformed and plain-clothes cops, the enraged Outlaws who recognized him started insulting him, spitting on him and pushing him around. Leblanc fled and a number of Outlaws took off after him. Once they were satisfied he was gone, they gave up the chase. But a group of police kept following him and saw him desperately pull on the door of a parked white van, only to be refused entry and start running again. When the police searched the van, they found two Evil Ones and a Hells Angels associate inside with a .30-caliber machine gun and two .44 Magnum handguns.

Three weeks later, Tony Mentore, Meunier's old friend, was waiting for his brother outside their dad's store in Joliette. A young man with a map approached him, apparently looking for directions. Mentore rolled down his window; the stranger pulled a handgun from under his map and shot him three times in the head.

The murders and the increased presence of the Hells Angels and Evil Ones on their turf had a devastating effect on the Montreal Outlaws. By December 1989, deaths, defections and hasty retirements had rendered the once-powerful gang impotent. They had been had reduced to just ten members who rarely wore their colors. Their new president, Johnny "Sonny" Lacombe became a virtual recluse, leaving his Chateauguay home only when necessary and always with at least two armed bodyguards.

With the Outlaws eliminated as a viable threat in Montreal, Leblanc had outlived his usefulness. On the snowy night of February 21, 1991, he and his brother-in-law, Yvan Martel, were found shot dead less than 100 feet from the Sorel headquarters. Their cars were parked in the clubhouse parking lot. When the police questioned the Hells Angels, they all denied they had ever met Leblanc or Martel.

One immediate reward of the war with the Outlaws was the addition of another Quebec chapter. One of the oldest clubs in the province, the Missiles, had a checkered history but were well-known as expert drug traffickers. First based in Jonquière, they moved to Chicoutimi and later Trois-Rivières after repeated arrests made their members well known to local police forces. Finally, settled in a fairly large city where they could blend into the crowd, the Missiles were so successful that they were courted by both the Hells Angels and Outlaws for years. After the Stadnick-led Hells Angels forced the Outlaws underground, it was no contest. On June 14, 1991, the Missiles patched over and became the Hells Angels Trois-Rivières Chapter.

* * *

After a string of small successes, Stadnick's Hells Angels endured their first crisis on May 16, 1992. A random search of a prisoner's cell in Archambault Prison in Sainte-Anne-des-Plaines just north of Montreal revealed a sobering surprise. Inside his refrigerator was a list of the names, home addresses and Social Insurance Numbers of more than 260 prison guards from across Quebec. Chillingly, more than 60 of the names were underlined or marked with asterisks. Although the inmate had proven ties to the Sorel chapter, he refused to talk and nothing stuck to the Hells Angels.

Since no Hells Angels of any significance were hurt or arrested during the war with the Outlaws, Stadnick was well insulated from police. They often saw him back in Hamilton, escorting his now elderly parents to church, but he was also spotted in Winnipeg with increasing frequency.

By 1990, cops and informants were constantly exchanging information on the movements and activities of bikers like Stadnick. "As soon as a biker crossed into Ontario from Quebec, the Ontario Provincial Police (OPP) would tail them, often in unmarked cars," said Frankel. "And the police from the individual forces would watch them whenever they were in a city." Although that kind of cooperation proved vital in countless investigations, it also compromised sensitive information on at least one occasion. Kevin Roy Hawkins was a respected cop who took over the Kitchener–Waterloo biker beat in 1987. Things started going downhill when he met Cherie Graham, a stripper who worked at the Breslau Hotel just east of downtown Kitchener, and fell in love. Within weeks, he left his wife and moved in with Graham. Their relationship wasn't always loving; Graham complained to other police officers that Hawkins could get physically abusive when he drank too much. More important, however, was his relationship with her talent agent. Claude Morin was not just in the business of handling strippers: he was also president of the Kitchener Satan's Choice chapter. Between alimony and his new girlfriend, Hawkins ran into severe financial trouble. Graham told him that Morin could help him out. The men met and Morin paid him $5,000 for some information. If it proved accurate and useful, Morin promised to pay him $10,000 more. The next time they met, Hawkins told Morin about a drug bust that was going to go down in Hamilton that week. From the information supplied, Morin deduced who Hawkins' informant was and had him killed. "At first we thought it was a drug deal gone bad," said Harris. "But when Hawkins went down and we found out what happened, we were all more careful about what we said."

Chapter 6

While Quebec, Ontario, British Columbia and the East Coast of Canada were either under control or being fought over by the Hells Angels, the parts in between were largely no-man's-land. Right in the middle of the country was Winnipeg, an urban area at least as big as Quebec City or Hamilton, where all the highways, railroads and airlines stopped to serve the prairies. Naturally, it was a huge market for drugs, strippers and prostitutes and even boasted, according to the Royal Canadian Mounted Police (RCMP), the biggest gang population in all of Canada. But there was one big difference: in Winnipeg the overwhelming majority of those "gangsters" were teenagers—many still in high school—not the hardened criminals who made up organizations like Satan's Choice and the West End Gang.

The city did boast two large biker gangs with roots going back to the 1960s—Los Brovos and the Spartans—but they had always been more interested in riding and drinking than getting involved in organized crime. The two gangs united under the name Los Brovos in the early 1980s, but a number of disgruntled bikers left to form a new gang, the Silent Riders. Under the leadership of hardcore tough guy Darwin Sylvester, the Silent Riders were more ambitious than Los Brovos. They had made repeated advances to the Hells Angels, including riding out to

British Columbia to meet with the chapters there, but when Sylvester went to prison on drugs and weapons charges in 1984, their ambition ended. Unhappy with the upstart gang and sensing its weakness, Los Brovos decided it was time to retire the leaderless Silent Riders. The resulting war was distinctly one-sided. Without Sylvester, the Silent Riders were quickly routed and forced to burn their colors.

When he was released from prison in 1990, Sylvester was too late to save the Silent Riders, but he did recruit some of the survivors and enough disgruntled Los Brovos to form a new club, big and tough enough to resist a forceable takeover. He called his new gang the Spartans, returning Winnipeg to the status quo—two biker gangs who lived in basic tolerance of each other because a full-scale war would be too costly. That situation could hardly be more perfect for the Hells Angels. Winnipeg had a large, decentralized drug trade and enough biker manpower and competent leadership to dominate it. "Winnipeg is the chokepoint for the drug trade in Canada," said Rick Lobban, the city's biker cop in the early 1990s. "We knew the Hells Angels were going to come; it was just a matter of time."

It didn't take long for Stadnick to become a regular visitor to Winnipeg. He started spending a great deal of time in the city, generally with members of Los Brovos. Police said Stadnick found them more efficiently run than Sylvester's thuggish Spartans. As he had in Toronto, Stadnick liked to wear either his colors or audaciously expensive outfits and was always surrounded by a phalanx of bodyguards. One of them, a drug dealer originally from Thunder Bay, Ontario, named Donald "Bam Bam" Magnussen, almost never left his side. They made an odd pair and drew many stares. Stadnick, a neatly attired man of limited stature, looked even shorter and more garish next to Magnussen, a huge man who preferred to wear old T-shirts and battered jeans, no matter what the weather.

Although the members of Los Brovos and the Spartans were proud of their independence, they were impressed by Stadnick's ability to buy booze, drugs and other entertainments. And the power and fame of the Hells Angels preceded him. "This was *the* club," Ernie Dew, president of Los Brovos, said of the Hells Angels. "You've gone from the farm team to the major leagues."

Despite his power in the underworld, things weren't always easy for Stadnick. Lobban had followed him to the airport on the morning of June 16, 1992, and tipped off the security officers. As Stadnick traveled through the metal detectors, one of the officers asked him to step aside and gave him a little extra frisk. Inside his belt, the authorities found just over $81,000 in cash, and Stadnick was arrested on the spot for possession of the proceeds of crime. Within hours he was out on bail and on the next plane back to Toronto, since the next flight to Hamilton was almost a week away. Stadnick preferred to use Hamilton's John C. Munro Airport, because, Harris asserted, it had no on-site police detachment.

In August, the next time Stadnick was back in Winnipeg, he was entertaining a few Los Brovos, Spartans and local call girls in a downtown rock 'n' roll bar called the Rolling Stone Cabaret. The drinks and conversation were flowing and everyone was having a good time, when a pair of unwelcome guests dropped in. Two off-duty Winnipeg cops, already drunk, sauntered into the bar and took a table near Stadnick's. As soon as they sat down, they started in on the assault. Making fun of Stadnick's height, clothes and scars and questioning his relationship with the ever-present Magnussen, the cops probably intended to raise doubt about the Hells Angels, but only managed to make themselves and their employers look bad. When they finally became frustrated at the lack of reaction they were getting, the two cops stumbled out of the bar, still flinging insults and accusations. Outside the bar, the cops got a bit bolder. No longer content with calling the bikers names, they started pushing them around and slapping them. There was no reaction until one of the cops mounted a Los Brovos' Harley. In an instant he and the other officer were leapt upon by the bikers and beaten badly. Both officers wound up in local emergency rooms, treated for a variety of injuries. Stadnick, Magnussen and another biker were arrested.

Police nationwide rejoiced as they finally had the elusive Walter Stadnick. Not only had he been arrested for assault—and on a police officer yet—but it had happened when he was out on bail. "I couldn't believe it," said Harris. "It was like Walter, who was so careful here at home and in Montreal, went crazy out west."

But their celebration was short-lived. On October 4, 1993, Stadnick came to trial for the airport arrest. His lawyer argued for a stay on the grounds that the *Winnipeg Sun* had run an article about Stadnick's career with the Hells Angels, which he maintained would jeopardize his client's chances of getting a fair trial. He also questioned the accuracy of the article, and he argued to get the reporter to reveal her sources. Before the trial, the woman who wrote the story, Melanie Verhaeghe, noticed she was being followed by a large man with long blond hair in a Jeep (he was later identified as Magnussen), and she told Stadnick's lawyer, Sheldon Pinx. She expected him to be surprised and helpful, but actually found him quite threatening. He pointed out that he had a thick file on her and had had her followed by a private investigator who had shot some pretty interesting videotape of her daily life. The judge didn't agree that the article would make a difference and the trial went on as planned. Despite hours of testimony, the prosecution could prove nothing. Although there are laws against earning money selling drugs, there is no law against having $81,000 in cash, and, since it could not be linked to any criminal act, Stadnick was free to go.

A few weeks later, Stadnick was back in Winnipeg for the inquest for the assault trial. No sooner had the judge read the charges than he, chuckling, dismissed the case. Clearly, he pointed out, the drunken off-duty police officers had provoked the bikers. Again, Stadnick was free.

While the Hells Angels still had no official presence in Manitoba, Stadnick considered his work there successful, despite his run-ins with the police and the press. He had Los Brovos and the Spartans not only talking, but partying together. He had, according to police, good business relationships with both gangs, with the Hells Angels supplying drugs, prostitutes and strippers, which the local clubs marketed to hungry Winnipeggers.

* * *

The situation in Ontario was far less welcoming. The Outlaws were the dominant gang, so Stadnick courted the next biggest, Satan's Choice. He could often be seen escorting Bernie "the Frog"

Guindon, national president of Satan's Choice, to Oshawa strip joints and even fine Toronto restaurants. "He'd make a round trip of it," said one OPP officer. He'd see Guindon in Oshawa, take him out for the night, drive over to Hamilton to take his folks to church and then fly off to Winnipeg." Satan's Choice was one of many different biker gangs to emerge from Southern Ontario in the middle 1960s. The key difference was the leadership of Guindon, who assumed club presidency in 1965. While not major players in organized crime, the gang made a name for itself by fighting, and sometimes destroying, neighboring gangs. Rumbling with clubs like the Golden Hawks, the Fourth Reich, the Chain Men and others, Satan's Choice became the most feared and respected bikers in the province.

And, as the gang grew, it added chapters. Every summer, Guindon hosted an all-members meeting and party in the resort town of Wasaga Beach, about 75 miles northwest of Toronto. It was a habit that didn't always go down well with other vacationers, but rarely led to any legal trouble. "Oh yeah, it was awful when they came," said Ian, who had a cottage in Wasaga Beach in the '60s and '70s. "They'd camp out right in your front yard without asking and throw garbage and bottles around—and some of them just smelled awful." Intrusive and obnoxious as they may have been, the bikers had little to fear from the cottagers. "There's no way we would have called the cops; there were just too many of them and they were mean-looking—real thugs," said Ian. "We just stepped around them and went about our business as best we could."

That tolerance was tested in August 1968 when a *Globe and Mail* photographer infiltrated the party and took pictures of one of their games, in which a live chicken was placed in a ring with about two dozen bikers, who quickly tore it to pieces. The winner of the competition was the biker with the biggest chunk of flesh. When the photos ran, the public was outraged. The Ontario Humane Society even offered a substantial reward for information leading to the arrest of anyone involved in the game. Nobody came forward.

A few arrests for animal cruelty wouldn't have made a difference anyway. Satan's Choice was big and rapidly getting bigger. At its peak in the early 1970s, Satan's Choice was the second-biggest biker gang in the world—far bigger than the Outlaws and second only to the Hells Angels—with chapters in Hamilton, Oshawa, Guelph, St. Catharines, Preston (now part of Cambridge), Peterborough, Ottawa, Kingston, Windsor, Montreal and Vancouver. The primary reason for the club's success was the leadership of its national president, or "supreme commander," as he preferred to be called.

A former Canadian amateur light-middleweight boxing champion, Bernie Guindon was a smart man and a natural leader. He became Satan's Choice president at the age of 22 and recruited area clubs in much the same way Stadnick would decades later—wining, dining and using force when necessary. Satan's Choice became so impressive that emissaries from the Outlaws and Hells Angels came to Canada and attempted to recruit them, only to be turned down without specific reasons. Guindon was also known for quelling dissension within the club. In 1973, a fight at a strip joint caused the Toronto Satan's Choice chapter to become enraged and declare war on two major independents, the Vagabonds and the Black Diamond Riders. When Guindon heard, he called a summit meeting with the presidents of both clubs and negotiated a peace treaty without informing the Toronto chapter until afterward. They accepted their commander's decision without question.

The success of his mutual tolerance pact gave Guindon an idea. Aware that the Hells Angels were hungry for a foothold in Ontario, he played one superpower against the other. He called his contacts in the Outlaws and they jumped at the chance to form an alliance that eventually also included the Vagabonds and Toronto's biggest independent club, the Para-Dice Riders.

Arrested in 1973 for aggravated sexual assault, Guindon went to prison and worked on his boxing. Although he was a model prisoner, claiming that he wanted to represent Canada in the 1976 Olympics or teach kids how to box and avoid the mistakes he'd made, he had a hard time with the parole board. The sticking point was always the same: they wouldn't release him unless he stayed away from unsavory characters, and the other members of Satan's Choice fell under that definition. "They're the only friends I have," he told a *Toronto Star* reporter. "I'm not going to give them up." He served his full sentence.

The Chicago-based Outlaws saw their opening. Almost as soon as Guindon was behind bars, they sent a group of emissaries with a tempting offer. In exchange for marketing their drugs in Ontario—an attractive proposition in and of itself—the Outlaws offered to treat Satan's Choice members as equals, and Outlaws chapters in border states even promised to alter their patch to include a maple leaf and a tongue of flame in honor of the Canadian club. Within two months of the alliance being formed, two U.S.-based Outlaws were arrested attempting to re-start their lives under different names in a different country. James "Blue" Starrett, who was running a successful business called Charlie Brown Painting Contractors in St. Catharines, was arrested and deported for escaping a Florida prison, where he was serving time for the shotgun murder of a woman at an Outlaws party. Five weeks later, William "Gatemouth" Edson was caught leaving a Kitchener Liquor Control Board of Ontario (LCBO) store. As an Outlaw in Fort Lauderdale, Florida, he'd murdered three Hells Angels, beaten the girlfriend of a Bandidos member and tortured a woman with heated spoons and lit cigarettes because he saw her wearing an Outlaws T-shirt. His fake Ontario driver's license identified him as Dennis Lupo. Similarly, the most wanted member of Satan's Choice, a murderer named Howard "Pigpen" Barry was arrested in North Carolina with a Florida driver's license claiming his name was Tim Jones. He was wearing Outlaws colors at the time.

Despite the increased trouble with the law, Guindon honored the alliance when he came out of prison, reasoning that it was better to work with the Outlaws than to be at war with them. He was also impressed by the efficient, almost corporate, way they ran their drug business and he certainly didn't mind the sudden wealth it brought. But it was that industrial style of drug manufacturing that eventually brought down Guindon and his independent biker gang. It happened where the bikers considered themselves most safe. Oba Lake is a remote fishing and hunting spot about 150 miles northeast of Sault Ste. Marie, accessible only by train or floatplane. There were only two buildings on the lake. Next to the train tracks was a lodge where wealthy, mostly American, sportsmen stayed when they were after walleye or moose. The lodge was owned by Alain Templain, an important member of the Oshawa chapter of Satan's Choice, who flew his own floatplane up north every summer. The other building was much smaller and newer. On an island in the middle of the lake, the Outlaws built a sophisticated drug lab and staffed it with members of Satan's Choice. Guindon and Templain were there on August 6, 1975, when the island was raided by OPP officers who were posing as fishermen and staying at Templain's lodge. Caught with nine pounds of PCP and 236 pounds of unfinished PCP with a total value of $6 million, Guindon and Templain went away for 17 years.

Almost as soon as the commander was in prison, his hand-picked successor, Garnet "Mother" McEwen from the St. Catharines chapter, called a summit meeting. That night he convinced the presidents of the Montreal, Windsor and Ottawa chapters to burn their colors and join the Outlaws. Dissenting members were to be forcibly retired. For the summer of 1977, the party moved from Wasaga Beach to Crystal Beach, just ten miles from the U.S. border, where it became a massive patching-over ceremony.

When Guindon found out, he offered $10,000 of his own cash for McEwen's head. But it was too late; the onslaught of giant American super-gangs had begun. The Outlaws had established a massive presence in Ontario and a beachhead in Quebec. The remaining chapters of Satan's Choice eventually either joined the Outlaws or, without Guindon's guidance, faded into relative obscurity while he was behind bars. Nobody ever collected on Guindon's reward. McEwen was eventually exiled by the Outlaws for embezzling $30,000 and fled to Alberta, where he tried to go straight with a job at a hotel. He last showed up in the public eye in 1990 when a biker—unaware of his identity—beat him severely with his own artificial leg.

An alliance of major independents kept the Outlaws out of Toronto until the summer of 1984, when the local drug supply dried up. Outlaws leaned heavily on local dealers and suppliers to keep any drugs from getting into the hands of area bikers. The siege broke in September when Robert "Pumpkin" Marsh convinced his fellow Iron Hogs to patch over and become the Outlaws Toronto chapter. "They were a bunch of idiots," said Harris. "But it got the Outlaws into

Toronto." And it also helped form a new anti–Hells Angels alliance, including the Outlaws, the Para-Dice Riders, the Vagabonds and even the Satan's Choice, minus Guindon.

By 1986, when they patched over the Holocaust motocycle gang based in London (formerly the Queensmen), the Outlaws had become the dominant biker gang in Ontario, with other chapters in Toronto, Hamilton, Windsor, St. Catharines, Ottawa, Sault Ste. Marie and Kingston. The Kingston chapter was especially successful, as it was very close to the U.S. border and even closer to Canada's largest prison population, an excellent market for drugs. Their success frustrated the Hells Angels, who were established in Quebec, Nova Scotia and British Columbia, but were hungry for a chance at richer markets. They were forced to audition clubs that the Outlaws had passed over, like Sudbury's Coffin Wheelers, Kitchener's Henchmen and until they fell apart, Stadnick's own old gang, the Wild Ones of Hamilton.

When Guindon was finally released from prison in 1991, he returned to Oshawa and resumed command of what remained of Satan's Choice. Stadnick, now president of the Hells Angels, showed up almost immediately. He met with Guindon repeatedly, taking him to Toronto's most expensive restaurants and the area's most prominent strip bars. They were always joined by a squad of burly bodyguards, as much to show the power of the Hells Angels as for protection. Guindon loved the free food, booze and entertainment, and he never turned down a meeting with Stadnick. But he always deferred giving him a firm answer on whether the Satan's Choice would ever patch over to the Hells Angels. What Stadnick didn't know was that Guindon had no intention of ever patching over. As fiercely xenophobic as the original Hells Angels, he didn't want his club, which he considered a Canadian institution, to become a franchise of an American supergang. He played Stadnick, not just for the free nights out, but because friendly relations and the potential to patch over made sure the Hells Angels wouldn't enforce a hostile takeover.

When Stadnick's patience finally wore thin, he decided to show Guindon who was boss. With 150 Hells Angels and associates behind him, Stadnick rode from Montreal to the Satan's Choice's old haunts in Wasaga Beach on June 18, 1993. Many independent clubs were invited to the party, but Satan's Choice was not. The OPP stopped the procession twice, but found no reason to detain any of them. One officer paid the Hells Angels a huge compliment by telling *The Toronto Star*: " . . . you can expect a pretty violent summer this year." At the party, Stadnick met with lots of bikers but spent most of his time in the Alliston Hotel (he rented every room) with the Loners.

The man he met with was Frank Lenti, the Loners' president. Even by Canadian biker standards, Lenti was a strange guy. Vain, constantly preening and prone to violent temper tantrums, he had a habit of giving up on projects when things didn't go exactly the way he wanted. Originally a member of the Rebels, a decidedly racist North Toronto gang with a Confederate flag emblem, he got bored with their hierarchy, took some friends and formed his own gang. The original Loners carved out a small niche for themselves in Woodbridge, Lenti's hometown just north of Toronto. Since the Rebels had incorporated the Confederate flag into their logo, the Loners steered well clear of the Rebels.

Things were working out well until the other Loners caught their president stealing from club funds. Rather than face his accusers, Lenti flew to Italy until tempers cooled. While he was gone, the rudderless Loners fell apart. When he returned in 1981, Lenti joined the Toronto chapter of Satan's Choice. He had a rough time there, too. His me-first attitude and penchant for whining didn't endear him to the guys at the top, and Lenti grew more and more alienated from the rest of the club. In 1984, he collected some other malcontents and formed a new gang, again called the Loners. Although they managed to terrorize a few blocks of Woodbridge, they made little impact and most other bikers called them "the Losers." From all reports, Lenti's meeting with Stadnick did not go well. Lenti, an Italian, tried to impress the Hells Angels president with his connections to the mafia. Stadnick, who had actual ties to the mafia from the days when the Wild Ones were blowing up bakeries in Hamilton, and more recently from Montreal, wasn't impressed.

But expansion into Ontario would have to wait. The biggest drug bust in Winnipeg history went down on September 16, 1993, and it caused a crisis on the streets. The cops confiscated $18 million worth of heroin and cocaine after raiding 70 houses, including the Los Brovos clubhouse. Sixteen people were arrested on drug and money laundering charges, but none were bikers. The busts created a very enviable situation for the Hells Angels. The police took a huge amount of drugs and a number of drug dealers off the streets, while leaving the desperate drug users and eager bikers behind. Days later, police spotted Stadnick in Thunder Bay, a city not far from the Manitoba border, where he met with members of Satan's Choice, spending at least 90 minutes alone with Kitchener president Andre Wateel, before flying to Winnipeg the next day. The drug shortage in Winnipeg seemed to disappear overnight. As always, Stadnick frustrated police, who believed he was involved in illegal drug operations, but couldn't find a scrap of evidence to prove it. "He was extremely careful," said Harris. "He always insulated himself."

Although Stadnick was a highly visible character in his outlandish outfits and with his troop of giant bodyguards, he conducted business in stealth mode. Police recorded many hours of Stadnick engaging in personal conversations with other bikers and underworld personalities, but nothing close to incriminating (even in code) ever emerged. Instead, Stadnick and whoever he was doing business with would leave the bugged area and talk in places like busy street corners, abandoned alleys, front lawns and even parks, where he was confident the police couldn't eavesdrop.

* * *

Despite his success in Winnipeg, Stadnick was frustrated by his inability to move the Hells Angels into Ontario. It had become Outlaws territory under the forceful leadership of Parente, who shot at Hells Angels on sight. Satan's Choice, which still had a solid network and quality leaders like Wateel, represented a perfect opportunity to create a serious rivalry, but Stadnick eventually realized that they would never become Hells Angels as long as Guindon was in charge. And, after meeting with Lenti, he assessed the remaining nonaligned clubs as unworthy of the colors. Unable or unwilling to recruit Ontario bikers, Stadnick decided to import his own.

His plan was to send Quebec bikers loyal to the Hells Angels into Ontario to set up puppet gangs and drug operations there. He agonized over who he would appoint as their leader, but finally decided on Dany "Danny Boy" Kane. Unlike so many of the other bikers, who seemed slow-witted if not entirely stupid, Kane impressed Stadnick with his intelligence, ambition and gregarious personality. The president also noticed that, despite a lack of effective English-language skills, Kane had quickly and smoothly aligned himself with Stadnick and his East Coast lieutenant, David "Wolf" Carroll, president of the Halifax Chapter, formerly the 13th Tribe. Kane had a lot going for him, including a history of courage, resourcefulness and loyalty.

An unplanned pregnancy in 1988 had led to Kane getting a job alongside his girlfriend's father at the Tissues et Fibres d'Amoco plant in industrial St. Jean on the South Shore. But the mind-numbing tedium of operating a thread-making machine all day, every day of his life depressed him. In an effort to alleviate his frustration, he bought a Harley. It was a 1946 Knucklehead model, 23 years older than he was, and he lovingly parked it in what he planned would become the baby's room. His girlfriend, Josée, liked the bike, but wasn't sure they could afford it. But the rumbling bike and the leather jacket emboldened Kane to the point where he told his boss he just couldn't take the thread machine any longer and quit. With a girlfriend and newborn son at home, Kane needed money. His own family was in no position to help him and asking Josée's parents, who had two other grandchildren from their two other unmarried teenage daughters, was out of the question. So when Josée's old friend Pat Lambert offered Kane a job, he jumped at the chance.

Lambert was a member of a notable Hells Angels puppet club called the Condors. Little known outside the South Shore, the Condors were well respected by the Hells Angels and other gangs. Unlike the Evil Ones, who operated in the area just to the west of them and always seemed to be in trouble with the police, the Outlaws or the Hells Angels, the Condors were quiet and efficient. Although police in the area called them small-timers who were nothing to worry about, the Condors actually dominated the regional drug trade right under their noses. Lambert was one of their best dealers and a rising star. He offered to pay Kane $700 a week to deliver drugs to area bars and pick up the cash they owed Lambert. The pay was more than three times what Kane made at the thread factory, and he could set his own hours.

That winter, Josée drove Kane, who only had a motorcycle license, from bar to bar on the South Shore in her ancient Hyundai Pony. She and their son Benjamin waited outside shivering because the Pony's heater didn't work very well—while Kane did his business inside. Then he would guide them to the next small-town bar. Ever gregarious, Kane soon developed his own network. He bought drugs directly from Lambert and sold them in bars situated between the ones his boss had already cultivated. His take jumped from $700 to $3,000 a week very quickly. But drug sales are a dangerous game built on fear-based respect, and many dealers didn't fear or respect the slight 21-year-old who arrived with his wife and baby in a beat-up old Pony. Although he nominally worked for Lambert, the point-of-sale dealers knew Kane couldn't call in the Condors' muscle, and they started stringing him along on their debts and haggling over previously set prices. Some even refused to pay altogether. Kane knew it was time to get tough.

First, he approached a Condor who owned a South Shore gym and bought steroids and weights from him. In months, the pills and workout routine transformed the scrawny punk into a thickly muscled tough who was prone to bouts of hysteric violence. Any questions about payments were answered with a punch or kick from the newly strong Kane; and debts started clearing up rapidly. The Condors helped him achieve the second half of his transformation when they drove him to the Kahnawake Mohawk territory and made some introductions. Kane left with the first of many handguns. He immediately started to carry his gun on his rounds and made a point of showing it to his business associates. He even shoved it into the mouth of one reluctant debtor, emulating something he'd seen on TV, before getting paid. Astutely recognizing another revenue stream, Kane started selling handguns and submachine guns he acquired from the Mohawks to bikers and other underworld types.

By the spring of 1992, Kane had gained a great deal of respect on the South Shore. In just a few short years, he'd evolved from skinny, unemployed thread-maker to a feared and successful drug and arms dealer who had the muscle and will to back up his promises. It was time, the Condors decided, to put him to the test. One of their dealers had been turfed from the Bar Delphis in St-Luc. Since the dealer was also a member, the Condors weren't just losing revenue; they were losing face in the community. They decided to blow up the bar, and they wanted Kane to do it for them. No problem. On the night of May 2, the empty Bar Delphis exploded and burned to the ground. Its owner, Réal "Tintin" Dupont, understood the message and left the area (he later emerged as a member of the Rock Machine). For his part, Kane gained respect, experience and a contact at the Canadian Armed Forces base in Valcartier who sold him 4.5 kg of C4 plastic explosive—enough to bring down a large apartment building—for $5,000.

A few days later, Kane and Josée started living apart. He reasoned that she could get a bigger welfare payment as a single mother (she was also working under the table as superintendent of her building in exchange for a rent-free apartment) and that his business might be too dangerous for her and Benjamin to be too close to him. He moved into a house in nearby L'Acadie with two Condors and a career criminal named Robert Grimard. In July, Kane took two new friends, local street punks Martin Giroux and Eric Baker, back to the house for a few beers and some pot. After they got good and stoned, Kane took the two skinny 19-year-olds to a closet under the stairs to show off his pride and joy. When Kane pulled out the hockey bag, Baker later told police, they thought it would be full of drugs. They were shocked to see it was full of guns, which they recognized immediately as both illegal and highly desirable. As stupid as it may sound to anyone who isn't a 19-year-old criminal, they decided there and then to steal them. Two days later, the boys watched the house. When they were sure nobody was home, they broke in through a back window and made off with the hockey bag.

Compounding their predicament, they immediately drove to the seedy bars of St-Jean, deep in the heart of Condors territory, and tried to sell their booty. Their intended customers, all of whom immediately realized that the guns were Kane's, laughed at the boys and told them to get lost for their own good. Realizing that they weren't going to sell any of the guns, Giroux and Baker raced back to the house in L'Acadie, planning to return the bag to the closet in hopes that Kane would never find out about the theft. But Kane, Grimard and two Condors had been tipped off and were already inside the house, waiting for the boys. They grabbed Giroux, but Baker managed to elude them by running through a cornfield. They beat Giroux until he was a bloody pulp and told him that he'd suffer a lot more if he didn't help them find Baker.

Five days later, in the town of La Prairie, Baker was thrown into the backseat of Grimard's car next to Giroux. Oddly, officers from the Sûreté du Québec who had been tailing Grimard that day saw the incident but lost the car as it weaved through the town and got on the highway, and they gave up the chase. The boys were taken to an abandoned quarry just outside Napierville, where Giroux was released. Kane took out a handgun and, with one shot, put holes in both of Baker's legs. Another car showed up and two Condors, Louis David and Richard Proulx, and an associate named Daniel Audet came out. David announced his presence by twisting Baker's right arm until it fractured. After about two hours of torture—including being cut with a stick, having his face urinated on and then pushed into a fire, having a bullet graze his skull and having cars speed at him only to brake at the last second, with Kane threatening to kill him all the while—Baker was surprised that he was still alive when Kane and his men drove off. Not sure if it was another trick, but unwilling to die alone in a giant pit, Baker crawled away in a random direction using his unbroken arm. He later estimated that it took him more than an hour before he arrived at a nearby farmhouse. Although Baker begged him not to call the cops, the farmer was talking to the SQ as soon as the boy was in his house. Baker was promised police protection if he'd testify against whoever tortured him. He agreed.

Kane, Grimard, David, Proulx and Audet were arrested. A search of Grimard's house netted the SQ the guns and bomb-making equipment, but Kane's C4, drugs and drug paraphernalia were safely stashed in Josée's apartment. While the kidnappers and torturers were in jail, their lawyers made a deal with prosecutors: they'd plead guilty to all charges as long as the attempted murder charge was dropped. Kane, who was identified as the leader of the group, got the worst sentence, two years less a day plus three years probation. Just before he left for prison, Kane learned Josée was pregnant again.

Inside Montreal's notorious Bordeaux prison Kane met someone who changed his life. Every prison has at least some inmates like
Tamara, men who behave with excessive, stylized femininity and exchange sex and other favors for protection and companionship. And
Tamara himself attached to Kane, who began to realize he liked sex
with men as much as with women.

Things changed on the outside, too. Josée gave birth to a daughter,
Nathalie, and the Condors ceased to exist. Seeking to consolidate operations on the South Shore, Stadnick decided to have the Evil Ones
absorb the best of the Condors and force the others into retirement.
Pat Lambert was welcome to join, but decided instead to operate his
drug sales and stripper booking/escort agency independently. When
he was released from prison, Kane was approached by the Evil Ones
to be a hangaround, but he chose to stick with Lambert. In return,
Lambert introduced Kane to David Carroll, who immediately liked
him, and Carroll introduced him to Stadnick. The biker chieftain was
impressed by Kane's physique and his resumé—he was an expert biker
who'd sold drugs and guns with visible success, he'd blown up a bar,
gone to Bordeaux and not told on anyone. Rather than slowly working his way through the Evil Ones' ranks, Kane became a Hells Angels
prospect almost as soon as he showed up.

And he was Stadnick's first choice to be in charge of the Hells Angels'
puppet gang in Ontario. He even named it—the Demon Keepers—using
his own initials. The plan was simple and decidedly corporate: the Demon
Keepers would move into Ontario towns and offer high-quality drugs at
lower prices than existing gangs, with better delivery. Kane worked hard to
get things ready and on January 29, 1994, at a party in Sorel to inaugurate
the new gang, he showed off his hand-designed colors.

With an eye to expanding, the Demon Keepers set up shop in
Ottawa, Cornwall (at the narrow part of the St. Lawrence across the
river from where Quebec and New York State meet) and Toronto, the
richest drug market in Canada. There were significant problems from
the start. Instead of an easily defended industrial or commercial space,
Kane chose a luxurious third-floor apartment in the trendy Yonge–
Eglinton area of Toronto to be the Demon Keepers' headquarters, a
move local police found hilarious.

A bigger problem than Kane's taste in clubhouse was his staff. Culled from puppet gangs on the South Shore, the Demon Keepers were recruited for their size and toughness, not their intellect. Years later, Kane would describe the men at his disposal as "no-talent imbeciles." Worse than their stupidity was their inability to speak English, their lack of underworld contacts and understanding of the Ontario drug culture. Under Kane's direction, the Demon Keepers approached bikers, toughs, strippers, bouncers, bartenders and other potential customers from Ottawa to Niagara Falls. But their awkward, unsubtle style and their broken English were met with little but confusion and scorn. With virtually no sales, they did very little but keep an eye on local Outlaws and plot to kill them, although no shots were fired. The only success Kane had was to find an office where Lambert could import fresh Quebec strippers to more lucrative gigs in Toronto. Looking for help, Kane repeatedly called Carroll, but he was always too drunk or hungover to be of much help. Frustrated, he resorted to calling Stadnick, who was busy taking care of business in Winnipeg and Montreal. The exasperated, distracted president told him he wasn't being aggressive enough and suggested that the Demon Keepers start wearing their colors more prominently. That idea backfired almost immediately. Within two weeks, 11 of the 18 Toronto Demon Keepers were arrested on minor infractions. The Toronto police, who'd been tipped off by the SQ and OPP that the Demon Keepers were representing the Hells Angels, made them a deal—no charges if they would get out of Ontario and stay out. All of them took it. Despite the difficulty, Kane soldiered on, although he told police later that he often wondered if Stadnick had set him up to fail.

On the afternoon of April 1, 1994—April Fool's Day—Denis Cournoyer, the Demon Keepers' second in command, dropped by the Sorel headquarters to pick up Kane. They could hardly have been more inconspicuous in Cournoyer's 1992 Chevrolet Corsica, but they were tailed by the SQ as they drove down Autoroute 20 at exactly the speed limit. They stopped in Montreal to pick up another Demon Keeper, Michel Scheffer, at his girlfriend's place, and then drove towards Ontario. But, thanks to an informant embedded within the new gang, the SQ knew where they were going and alerted the OPP. When

Kane and Cournoyer crossed the border into Ontario where Autoroute 20 becomes Highway 401, the OPP, who were waiting on Roy's Road, took over the chase. A series of unmarked cars followed the Corsica to Belleville and down the Front Street exit to the parking lot of a Wendy's fast food restaurant patronized mainly by truckers and travelers on the 401.

Kane, Cournoyer and Scheffer planned to meet more Demon Keepers there, drive to Toronto and reinforce the chapter. Cournoyer was told to look for a yellow Mustang, which would contain his gang members. They were there, and so were the OPP. At 10:05, Cournoyer parked the Corsica next to the Mustang and opened the door. Before he was out the car, he heard it. "Freeze! You're under arrest!" His English wasn't very good, but he knew what was up. His first thought was to get back into the Corsica and speed away, but the OPP had blocked both cars. Kane, Cournoyer, Scheffer and the Demon Keepers in the Mustang surrendered without incident. In fact, the OPP was so proud of how easy the bust was, they used footage of it in instructional and promotional videos. An intensive search of the Mustang revealed nothing, and its occupants were free to go.

The guys in the Corsica would have to stick around. The police found a .357 Magnum under Kane's seat and a green Hefty bag with a nickel-plated .32 under the back seat, where Scheffer was sitting. In the trunk, they uncovered three jackets with Demon Keepers colors, a hunting rifle, ammunition for all three guns and gloves with lead sewn into the fingers. Kane tensed up when he saw Dillon, the OPP's German Shepherd, arrive. Within seconds, Dillon found a gram of hash between the front seats.

Kane, Cournoyer and Scheffer were locked up. A couple of simple computer checks put things in perspective for the police. Cournoyer and Scheffer had relatively clean records but the torture session at the quarry showed up on Kane's, and the OPP correctly determined that he was the boss. Worse yet, the Magnum showed up as stolen, and since it was under his seat, the police linked it to Kane. The three accused were allowed to confer with Peter Girard, a Belleville criminal lawyer. Since Kane's record meant that he'd end up behind bars no matter what, he'd take the bulk of the blame; and since Cournoyer was one of the few bikers under Hells Angels' control who knew how to make PCP and crystal meth, he'd be portrayed as an unwitting driver. The OPP accepted their terms. Cournoyer was released, Scheffer got two months on a restricted weapons charge and Kane was sentenced to four months for possession of a restricted weapon and another four (to be served concurrently) for possession of stolen property. The gram of hash was forgiven.

Barely two months after their inception, Stadnick disbanded the Demon Keepers, telling all but three of them to get lost and stay lost. His bold, but poorly executed, plan was an abject failure and he wanted to put what had become a humiliating chapter in Hells Angels history behind him. Stadnick also sent a message to Kane in Quinte Correctional Centre that the Hells Angels held no grudge against him and that he was welcome at Sorel when he was freed.

What happened next is a matter of disagreement. The RCMP claim that Kane called Interpol's Ottawa office, and they transferred his call to them. Other officers maintain that Kane asked a prison guard at Quinte to get him in touch with the RCMP. Either way, Kane agreed to become what the RCMP call an "agent-source"—a paid informant—embedded within the Hells Angels. He'd have plenty to talk about.

When Kane got out of prison, he visited Sorel to feel out his standing. He spoke with Carroll, who'd been his strongest supporter in the past. Drunk again, he seemed genuinely happy to see Kane, but advised him that his best course of action would be to join the Evil Ones as a prospect and work his way up the ladder. Disappointed, Kane cautiously approached Stadnick. Although Stadnick had little time for Kane, he didn't seem angry over the Demon Keepers fiasco, just distracted. He'd stepped down from the office of national president on June 30 for a secret project with Boucher and neither appeared interested in anything else.

Stadnick's replacement as national president, Robert "Ti-Maigre" Richard, didn't exactly strike Kane as someone he could get close to. Like many bikers, Richard's nickname was a joke. "Ti-Maigre," which is often translated as "Tiny" in English, is actually closer to "Li'l Skinny," hardly an accurate description of the 300-pound mammoth.

A veteran sergeant-at-arms for the Sorel chapter, Richard is said by many to have been an instrumental player in the Lennoxville Massacre, despite his acquittal.

A quiet man who emanated strength and malice, he was unapproachable by all but the most courageous. One young biker managed to penetrate Richard's tough exterior and become not only his protégé, but his trusted friend: Scott Steinert was a tall, handsome American who, even police admitted, could be utterly charming. He was so charming that, under Richard's massive influence, Steinert became a Sorel prospect without having to apprentice in a puppet gang or even serve as a hangaround. Life as a prospect for him was easy, as many full-patch members treated him with undue respect for fear of angering the volatile Richard.

Kane immediately attached himself to the rising star and the two became good friends very quickly, with Steinert serving as godfather at the christening of Guillaume, the son Josée gave birth to while Kane was in Quinte. What impressed Kane most was Steinert's plan to start his own puppet gang in the Belleville/Kingston area, which would import drugs from the United States across the St. Lawrence and sell them to the huge prison population in the area. It couldn't happen until he was a full-patch member, but Kane was sure that wouldn't take long and that Steinert—aggressive, confident and bilingual—could succeed where Stadnick had failed. Kane considered him to be the future of the club, and an alliance would allow him the flexibility to choose his loyalty—to the Hells Angels or the RCMP—whenever he wanted.

One reason Stadnick and Boucher were too busy for the presidency and Kane was that they smelled blood. With the Outlaws virtually extirpated from Quebec, the only gang that stood in the way of the Hells Angels' total domination of the province was the rapidly growing Rock Machine. With 51 full-patch members and many associates in the Montreal underworld, the Rock Machine was beginning to represent a serious threat. But when founders Salvatore and Giovanni Cazzetta both went to prison in separate drug-smuggling incidents that year, Boucher tried to convince Stadnick that it was the time to strike. Without their leaders, he argued, the Rock Machine would fall apart under even a small amount of pressure. After much thought, Stadnick agreed.

With that decision Stadnick launched a plan that would change Canadian organized crime forever and give him power far beyond what he held as national president of the Hells Angels. He would create an elite super-gang that was almost impervious to prosecution. He would also unleash a gang war that would take the lives of almost 200 people, including an 11-year-old boy, and imperil the very government of Quebec.

Chapter 7

It didn't start with a bang. Or a boom. Instead, the Hells Angels' war against the Rock Machine began with a politely worded letter. On a pretty, almost cloudless August afternoon in 1994, Hells Angels national president Robert "Ti-Maigre" Richard walked over to the Rock Machine clubhouse in Montreal and dropped an envelope on the steps. It was a typically bold move by the one-eyed, 300-pound Richard, who wore his colors into enemy territory for the event.

In the note, the Hells Angels simply asked the Rock Machine to stop calling themselves a motorcycle club. They had a point, since almost none of the Rock Machine members, especially after the Cazzettas were incarcerated, owned or even rode motorcycles. But it was not a mere lesson in semantics. The members of the Rock Machine understood what the note really meant—Quebec is Hells Angels turf; your presence is not welcome here.

But it was too late for mere intimidation. As the Hells Angels and their puppet gangs swallowed up more and more of the Montreal drug market, many street-level dealers became disenchanted with their tactics. If a dealer wanted to sell drugs in a Hells Angels neighborhood, he had to sell Hells Angels' drugs at Hells Angels' prices. If that dealer went to a different source, he would have to pay a Hells Angels' penalty—perhaps his life. Since no single group had the manpower or will to stand up to the Hells Angels, many turned to the No. 2 gang, the Rock Machine. Since they had also seen their bottom line suffer, the Rock Machine gladly accepted them and moved to establish a new force to fight the Hells Angels.

Simply called the Alliance, the new group consisted of the Rock Machine, Montreal's few remaining Outlaws, some independent dealers and a number of bar owners who sold drugs in their establishments and referred to themselves as the Dark Circle. Identified by a ring with an engraved eagle's claw, the Dark Circle was very effective in recruiting young soldiers, even those with no criminal record, to fight for their right to sell cocaine. Their presence swelled the ranks of the otherwise small Rock Machine to a size and confidence that allowed them to take on the Hells Angels in Quebec in a way the Outlaws couldn't.

Of course, even before Richard declared war in earnest, there had been some skirmishes. Pierre Daoust was one of those guys Stadnick found very useful. He wasn't a member or prospect, but he was a close friend of the gang and was a particularly valuable asset to the club because he owned and operated the biggest Harley-Davidson repair shop in Montreal's East End. The Hells Angels prize Harley shops, not only because they can have their bikes repaired and customized, but because they can also conduct club business away from their clubhouses, which run the risk of being bugged.

Although Daoust had never been in trouble for anything that had happened at his shop, he was well known to be a close associate of the Montreal Hells Angels and had often been seen riding with them. On the afternoon of June 13, 1994, two young men walked into his shop. It wasn't uncommon for wannabes to approach him looking for a job or a deal on a bike, and these two looked like the kind he'd get rid of with a few brief words. As Daoust stood up and started to walk towards them, one of the men pulled a revolver from under his denim jacket and shot him. Although nobody was ever charged with Daoust's murder, many within the Hells Angels suspected that the Rock Machine was involved.

The very next day saw more violence. As part of the master plan to insulate the important decision makers within the Hells Angels,

Stadnick and his men had established or taken a number of smaller clubs—like the Evil Ones and the Condors—and provided them with drugs and protection in exchange for various illegal services. The reasoning is simple: if a member of a puppet club is caught carrying out a task given to him by a Hells Angel, he keeps quiet, takes his punishment and is handsomely rewarded with cash, drugs or even a Hells Angels prospective membership when he gets out of jail. And it worked very well. The puppet club in Montreal, the Rockers, specialized in intimidating street-level dealers into working only with Hells Angels. One of their leaders, a tough guy named Normand Robitaille who was already a good friend of Maurice "Mom" Boucher, was on his way home on June 14 when he was shot by two masked men who ran away. He was seriously hurt, and the statement was clear.

Later that same day, the Montreal police, acting on an anonymous tip that the Rock Machine was planning to blow up the headquarters of the Evil Ones, searched the hotel rooms of five members of the Rock Machine. They found three remote-controlled bombs, 12 sticks of dynamite and two handguns. Of the five men arrested, two—Fred Faucher and Martin "Blue" Blouin—belonged to the gang's Quebec City chapter.

Three days later, two men known to be friendly to the Rock Machine were arrested in East End Montreal. They were wearing masks and body armor and had dynamite and detonators with them. Word quickly spread that they were a team sent out to assassinate Boucher. According to Vincent, the informant who claimed to be close to Stadnick and Boucher, the Hells Angels considered the attacks more of a nuisance than a war. "It's true that Robitaille got hurt, but they went to a lot of effort for very little results and a bunch of them got arrested," he said. "It was obvious they were trying to cause some damage, but it was also clear that they had a rat in there—the cops always seemed to catch them just before they could get anything done."

But the Hells Angels couldn't stand to let even a minor insurrection go unpunished, and they decided to hit the Alliance hard. The first target was a natural. Sylvain Pelletier, along with his two brothers, ran Montreal's biggest drug ring not affiliated with the Hells Angels. In fact, they ran much of the cocaine trade in Maisonneuve–Hochelaga,

Boucher's home neighborhood. A few miles down river, on the tree-lined streets of Repentigny, on the morning of October 26, 1994, Pelletier got into his brand new Jeep Grand Cherokee and turned the key. Before he could shift from park to reverse, he was engulfed in flame and molten metal and plastic. His body was later positively identified by dental records.

Two weeks later, Daniel Bertrand, a well-known Rock Machine associate and drug dealer, was relaxing with some friends in Sainte-4, a popular bar in Montreal's gay village, a district the Hells Angels' Scott Steinert hoped to control. Bertrand had just sent a young friend to go get another round of drinks when two men walked up to his table and pulled out a pair of submachine guns. In what looked like a scene out of *Scarface*, the men showered the club with gunfire, then fled. Bertrand died and three of his friends were seriously injured. The gunmen were never tracked down.

But to the men in the Sorel clubhouse, the unpleasantness with the upstart Rock Machine was a sideshow to the real news. On December 4, the Hells Angels threw a party at the Sherbrooke clubhouse—site of the Lennoxville Massacre—to celebrate the 10th anniversary of the Sherbrooke and Halifax chapters and to honor Stadnick for his work as national president. Every Hells Angel in Canada was invited and nearly all of them showed. But it wasn't just a massive drunk; there was business to attend to. Topping the agenda was a tribute to Stadnick. After a series of speeches from members, prospects and invited guests from all over Canada, the former president was presented with a gift perfectly tailored to his unique sense of style. It was a gold-plated belt buckle, as big as a bread plate and as heavy as a brick, emblazoned with the familiar winged skull of the club.

When Stadnick got up to make his speech, he announced something that would change the course of biker culture and organized crime forever. The reason he gave up the presidency, he said, was that he was joining a new club. The partiers, who had been pretty relaxed up to that point, fell absolutely silent. Stadnick laughed and then announced his brilliant plan. This new club, something more than a chapter, would be made up of veteran Hells Angels who had proven their value over years of service. They'd be part of no chapter, but would work with Hells Angels and puppet clubs throughout the country.

Hells Angels form a funeral cortege near Drummondville, QC in tribute to slain leader Yves Buteau in 1983. (CP)

(*left*) Yves "Apache" Trudeau was a prolific killer, admitting to 43 murders. Most of his victims were other bikers. (CP)

(*below*) Stadnick's attention was always sought after. Here, he's listening intently to Andre Wateel, former president of Satan's Choice Kitchener Chapter. (*The Toronto Sun*)

(*opposite page, top left*) Serge Quesnel was a paid assassin for the Hells Angels. He agreed to testify against his former employers for a lighter sentence. (CP)

(*opposite page, top right*) Sgt. John Harris was a Hamilton biker cop from 1980-1990 and followed Stadnick's career intently. (Jerry Langton)

For much of his term in office, Quebec Public Security Minister Serge Ménard denied the existence of a biker war in his province. Few agreed with him. (Jacques Boissinot/CP)

The death of 11-year-old Daniel Desrosiers in Montreal turned public opinion against the bikers. Thousands attended his funeral. (Robert Galbraith/CP)

(*top left*) Maurice "Mom" Boucher was one of the original Nomads and the most famous biker in Canadian history. (John Mahoney/CP)

(*top right*) Stadnick frequently displayed his colors and insignia in public. Police monitored his rise to prominence by noting which patches he wore. (*The Toronto Sun*)

After Paul "Sasquatch" Porter defected to the Hells Angels, the Rock Machine had little fight left in them. (John Mahoney/CP)

As national president, Stadnick was often present at events throughout the country. Here, attending a funeral in Winnipeg, he is flanked by bodyguards from British Columbia. (CP)

Stadnick made many friends. In this photo he poses with Stockford and Pat Burns, former NHL player and coach. (CP)

Fred Faucher became president of the Rock Machine as other leaders of the biker gang were imprisoned or murdered. He made overtures toward a merger with the Outlaws. (Jacques Boissinot/CP)

When Hamilton police searched Stadnick's house, they found evidence, but no drugs.
(Cathie Coward, *The Hamilton Spectator*)

Among Stadnick's possessions seized by police, his beloved Harley-Davidson was later auctioned off.
(John Rennison/*The Hamilton Spectator*)

He didn't announce it that night, but the Nomads existed to insulate Stadnick and his allies from prosecution. It was too dangerous to do business at any of the existing clubhouses. Instead, the Nomads would get members of the Hells Angels or puppet clubs like the Rockers to do their bidding and, if necessary, take the fall. As the Hells Angels sought to control the Canadian drug market, the Nomads were formed to control the Hells Angels—and it soon became apparent that Hells Angels and puppet clubs could buy drugs from nobody else.

Dany "Danny Boy" Kane was by this time a trusted confidante of many of the most prominent Hells Angels (he was also an informant for the Royal Canadian Mounted Police). The day after the party he told the police what had transpired, letting them know the details of the Nomads more than two months before their patches arrived from the Austrian factory that makes all Hells Angels colors. After a look at the members of the new club, the RCMP labeled the Nomads as a Hells Angels "dream team." Indeed, it did feature a roster of all-stars. Besides Stadnick and his trusted friend Don "Pup" Stockford, the original incarnation of the Nomads featured Boucher, Halifax president David "Wolf" Carroll, former Trois-Rivières president Louis "Mèlou" Roy and his best friend Richard "Rick" Vallée, Gilles "Trooper" Matthieu, Denis "Pas Fiable" Houle and Normand "Biff" Hamel, leader of a North Shore puppet club called the Death Riders. According to police, all were well known to be heavyweights in the drug trade, and none of them would hesitate to use violence. Kane told them that, although Boucher was nominally president, the roles of the three biggest players wouldn't change. Boucher would control Quebec, Carroll the East Coast and Stadnick the rest of Canada, with an eye on taking over Ontario.

Although the plan was to eventually have no clubhouse—they were magnets for police and media surveillance and, consequently, dangerous places to do business—Boucher set up a temporary headquarters on Rue Bennett, in the center of the Maisonneuve–Hochelaga neighborhood where he grew up.

While the top of the Canadian Hells Angels was busy morphing into a new club, the task of dealing with the Rock Machine fell to lowerlevel members. One man, in particular, jumped at the chance.

Scott Steinert was in many ways unlike the other Montreal Hells Angels. Born in Beloit, Wisconsin, Steinert moved to Sorel as an eight-year-old in 1970 when the Beloit Corporation—the world's largest manufacturer of paper-making machinery—transferred his father there. His family was well off, and he attended an exclusive English-language school. Although he was intelligent and sociable, Steinert got poor marks, was frequently in trouble with teachers (sometimes coming to blows) and was a regular in juvenile court. By the time he was 18, he'd dropped out of high school and moved to Vancouver, where he worked as an amusement park ride operator and small-time drug dealer. While there, he got involved with a bunch of would-be bikers and bought a Harley.

When his high school girlfriend, Louise, called to tell him his parents had moved back to Wisconsin, Steinert came back to Sorel. He returned a different man. Always big, Steinert had been working out religiously and had grown huge and muscular. He rode a Harley and was an experienced drug dealer and enforcer. Fluently bilingual, he used connections with old friends to set himself up with jobs ranging from beating up recalcitrant debtors to trafficking stolen goods and drugs. He was making a name for himself, until October 1985, when he sold two pounds of PCP to an undercover RCMP officer. He pleaded guilty and was sentenced to five years in prison. But Corrections Canada was not prepared for his intellect and charm. Claiming that he never sold drugs to minors and had no connections to any organized crime figures, Steinert managed to get a parole hearing. Prison officials referred to him as having "interesting qualities" and "higher than average potential." After Louise testified that his parents had loaned him money to set up an insulation business and that they had a circle of non-criminal friends, Steinert was released after just over two years in prison.

Less than a year later, Steinert was brought before a judge again. He'd been caught beating up a man who'd borrowed $300 from a loan shark. The man, who was on welfare, couldn't come up with the $2,000 the loan shark demanded, so Steinert was sent to make an example of him. Though caught in the act and clearly working on behalf of organized crime, Steinert was sentenced to a single month in prison. While behind bars, Steinert made many friends and valuable connections. In fact, he was aggressively courted by a number of groups and decided to join the Hells Angels. And, before long, he became a favorite of Richard, the new national president.

Steinert's bomb-making crew, which included Pat Lambert, had set bombs in two East End bars at the start of December 1994 in an effort to intimidate the Rock Machine. Kane told the RCMP. The police found the explosives, which had been triggered but—thanks to poor build quality—had failed to ignite. The first of Steinert's successful bombs went off on December 5, when Rock Machine prospect Bruno Bandiera started his Plymouth minivan and was blown to pieces. Steinert planned another remote-controlled explosion, this time at a Rock Machine clubhouse, but had to call it off because children were playing in what could become the blast area. According to Kane, Hells Angels would never endanger children, even those of their worst enemies.

On December 16, a pickup truck was parked in front of a restaurant Mom Boucher liked to visit for lunch. Luckily for him and the other patrons, he came late that day. The pickup, which had been parked on the busy street since 8 a.m., was towed away before Boucher arrived. The guys at the pound were surprised when they found sticks of dynamite and a remote detonator under the tonneau cover. Realizing he was the target, Boucher put bullet-proof windows in his home and started wearing body armor when he was away from safe areas. More important, though, he realized that the Rock Machine was a big enough threat that the Nomads had to become involved.

* * *

Normand Baker, a prominent member of the Rock Machine who had once been arrested for possession of explosives, decided to escape the snow and violence of Montreal with a vacation in Acapulco. Whether he knew it or not, he had actually flown into Hells Angels territory. The Pacific side of Mexico had become very popular with Montreal Hells Angels after Boucher, who was barred from entering the United States, started vacationing there and eventually bought half-ownership of a hotel in nearby Ixtapa. The day after Baker left for Acapulco, so did six members and two prospects from the Hells Angels Trois-Rivières Chapter.

On January 4, 1995, Baker was eating lunch with his girlfriend at the Hard Rock Café in Acapulco. He was approached by a nervous-looking man wearing a bathing suit and sneakers. Baker, annoyed, asked him in English "what the fuck" he wanted. The man said "Happy New Year" in French, then pulled a gun out of a bag and shot him in the face. At first, the other patrons thought it was a joke, but they stopped laughing when blood started spurting everywhere. The gunman tried to flee, but bouncers barred the door. Desperate, he crashed through the plate-glass window and started running down Avenida Casiera Miguel Aleman. He didn't get far. A combination of bouncers, patrons and passers-by managed to tackle, subdue and detain him until police arrived. He was identified as François Hinse, a Hells Angels prospect from Trois Rivières. A day earlier, Kane had told his RCMP handlers that Baker was Steinert's No. 1 target.

Hinse attended an initial hearing on January 14 and prosecutor José Vélez Zapata asked for a 40-year sentence. Despite detailed descriptions by dozens of eyewitnesses, many of whom extended their Mexican vacations just to testify, and gunpowder burns on Hinse's hands, judge Edmundo Román Pinzón decided there was insufficient evidence to charge him and released him to immigration officials, who sent him back to Canada. The RCMP were convinced it was "a flagrant case of corruption," with the equivalent of $270,000 being paid by the Hells Angels. Kane later told the RCMP that a Mexican police officer told Boucher that he'd have taken care of Baker for $5,000 and saved him all the trouble with the courts.

In fact, Boucher had also formed alliances with police at home. Through corrupt officers in suburban police forces, the Hells Angels had managed to obtain photographs and home addresses of a number of Rock Machine members and associates. Kane also recalled how Boucher once met with a man in a black Mustang and returned saying "that's my pig."

Back home, the war raged on. The day Hinse was released, Rock Machine member Daniel "Dada" Senesac carefully put a home-made bomb into the trunk of his Corsica and surrounded it with towels and blankets to cushion the bumpy ride. On his way to a Sorel bar known to be a Hells Angels hangout, Senesac hit a fatal pothole. Although he had been smart enough to invest in body armor, his head and arms were never found and his body was identified by tattoos on his back.

With bombs going off regularly in the streets of Montreal, the public was anxious for government intervention. It was one thing for a biker to shoot another biker in a biker bar, but the war had become entirely different.

The use of bombs, especially poorly made ones that exploded haphazardly, put everyone in danger. Serge Ménard, Quebec's minister of public security, denied on January 19 that the bombs were part of a biker war. Through a spokesman, he said that they were "isolated incidents" and that he didn't think it was necessary to set up a task force, choosing instead to let the Sûreté du Quebec (SQ) and local police forces handle the problem.

Less than two weeks later, three "isolated incidents" involving bombs and bikers occurred on the same day. On the snowy morning of January 31, members of Montreal police anti-gang squad found 200 sticks of dynamite (the same kind used in Steinert's unsuccessful bombs two months earlier) in a car and 50 remote-controlled detonators in a nearby house. That night, Simon Bedard, a member of the Hells Angels Quebec City puppet club, the Mercenaires, hopped into his Chevy S-10 pickup and lost a leg when it exploded. Three days later, Claude "Le Pic" Rivard, a member of the Pelletier gang and a noted drug salesman for the Alliance, was stopped at a red light when another S-10 pulled up beside him. The man in the passenger seat, Serge Quesnel, rolled down his window and shot Rivard in the face. A uniformed officer on routine patrol happened to witness the murder and gave chase. After six blocks, the stolen S-10 wound up in a ditch and its two occupants took off on foot in different directions. Quesnel left the gun behind. Both men got away.

As the level of violence escalated on the streets of Montreal, more and more bikers found themselves behind bars, where they continued the war. One such soldier was Stéphane "Godasse" Gagné, a constantly stoned thug with a seventh-grade education, who had somehow managed to mastermind a drug-trafficking network in the East End that netted him about $250,000 a year. At least it did until he got a phone call in the summer of 1994 from Paul "Fonfon" Fontaine, a full-patch Hells Angel. Fontaine told Gagné to shut down his operation and Gagné complied without argument. He did, however, set up a meeting with Boucher through a common friend who owned a Hells Angels–associated cell phone store. Impressed by Gagné's ambition and the fact that he'd named his son Harley-David, Boucher told him that he could go back to selling drugs in the East End, but he would have to get them from Fontaine and give him a portion of the proceeds. That arrangement worked out well until Gagné sold 1.5 kg of cocaine to an undercover member of the SQ. Knowing better than to rat out the Hells Angels, Gagné took his punishment in hopes it would gain him prospect status when he got out.

Like many Montrealers convicted of drug offenses, he was sent to Bordeaux prison in the city's north end. By early 1995, the notorious prison had become the most intensely fought-over chunk of real estate in Quebec. With an interior drug trade that police estimated as worth more than $7 million a year and supplied in part by paper bags and even tennis balls full of narcotics thrown over the prison walls during recreation time, Bordeaux was deteriorating into an uncontrollable war zone. Inside, members of the Hells Angels and Rock Machine recruited other prisoners with drugs, cash or threats of violence. By February, all but 20 inmates had chosen up sides. When, by mutual consent, the two sides severely beat the 20 nonaligned prisoners, the guards finally stepped in. From that point forward, half the prison would be reserved for the Hells Angels and their associates and the other half would house the Rock Machine and their allies. The two groups would never meet without intense supervision and nonaligned inmates would be forced to fend for themselves against whichever group controlled their wing.

On his way into Bordeaux, Gagné told the guards that he had some friends in the Hells Angels. They pulled his arrest record and, finding no connection to either gang, tossed him into C Block, the heart of Rock Machine territory. On his first day in his new cell, he was surrounded by six inmates. They didn't know who he was, so they put him through the standard test. One of the men, Jean Duquaire, pulled out a photo of Mom Boucher and told Gagné to spit on it. When he refused, the other men pummeled him, breaking three of his ribs and knocking out two of his teeth. While recovering in the prison hospital, he met up with some Hells Angels associates who provided him with a metal rod (which he smuggled out in his pant leg) and a sharpened spoon that could be used as a knife. On his first day back in CBlock, he found Duquaire alone and bludgeoned him with the metal rod. After two whacks, Gagné noticed someone behind him. The witness, a nonaligned inmate about half Gagné's size, was then forced to stab Duquaire's unconscious body. That involuntary involvement would, Gagné hoped, prevent him from ratting. His job done, Gagné retreated to his cell and pretended to sleep. Less than an hour later, he was taken into protective custody without explanation and eventually transferred to a Hells Angels-dominated prison in Sorel.

When he arrived, he was surprised and delighted to see Boucher. Just a few days earlier, March 24, 1995, Boucher and his right-hand man André "Toots" Tousignant had been on their way to a Sherbrooke motorcycle show when they were stopped by police for failing to signal a lane change. Aware of who they'd stopped, the officers asked both men to get out of the car. A quick frisk revealed an unlicensed, unregistered 9-mm handgun tucked into Boucher's belt. The serial numbers had been filed off. Boucher pleaded guilty to possession of a restricted weapon and was sentenced to six months in prison. But things were very different in Sorel than they were in Bordeaux. The Hells Angels ran the facility and lived in a relaxed atmosphere rich in drugs and free from the threat of the Rock Machine, or even the guards. They were so bold in Sorel prison that when the warden refused to grant day passes to Boucher and two friends, her house was fire bombed the same night. Boucher had heard about what happened in Bordeaux and assured Gagné that his loyalty and courage would be rewarded.

* * *

Outside the prison walls, the war had been growing more dangerous. On February 12, Rock Machine associates stole 2,500 sticks of dynamite that were mysteriously left unguarded from a construction site in Joliette. A week later, police acting on an anonymous tip found something even more chilling. In an East End garage frequently used by Hells Angels and their associates, they discovered two vans full of explosives and detonators. One of them contained a bomb in which four sticks of dynamite were surrounded by hundreds of nails. This was the first time police had found evidence of a shrapnel bomb. While dynamite may cause absolute devastation in a contained area, a nail bomb sends a shower of sharp, white-hot metal over a much larger, less defined area. Anyone in the vicinity of the explosion is likely to be killed or severely wounded by the shrapnel. Its discovery led the police to the frightening conclusion that the bikers were now using public terror as a weapon in their war. "Many people would have been killed or maimed if this bomb had exploded in a public area," said Detective Michel Gagné of Montreal's anti-gang squad. "It is no longer a war just between gangs."

The next day, February 21, Montreal police transfered 15 more officers to its anti-gang squad. They had been on duty just a few hours when the next bomb went off. Bar L'Energie was a nightclub frequently visited by Hells Angels and their associates, and it had already survived one small explosion in 1993. This time, though, a bomb containing 5 kg of high explosive and surrounded by 9-mm bullets, which ignited simultaneously and shot off in wild directions, took the club's facade off. Since it was a Tuesday night, L'Energie was empty. The explosion didn't kill anyone, but it served its purpose. The Rock Machine had shown that they had large-scale, anti-personnel weapons too, and they were not afraid to use them. The Hells Angels responded by firing three bullets into the head of Claude Cossette, one of the oldest and most influential Alliance drug dealers, as he left his house in Chateauguay. A week later, two Rockers found a cardboard box on the doorstep of their clubhouse and opened it gently. Not surprisingly, there was a bomb inside. Frightened and confused, they called Boucher. He sent over Tousignant, who calmly ripped the detonator off the dynamite and threw it down an alley. It exploded with a loud pop. That night, police found another bomb in a bar owned by a man alleged to be a member of the Dark Circle.

While Boucher was on vacation in Ixtapa, the violence diminished and the Hells Angels went back to business. Although he was still just a prospect, the ever-ambitious Steinert started flexing his muscles. In open defiance of club rules, Steinert started a puppet club called the Group of Five, which approached bars in trendy, more wealthy parts of Montreal and Ottawa—places that had previously received little attention from either the Hells Angels or the Rock Machine—to supply cocaine and ecstasy. Steinert was already getting rich with his stripper/escort agency Sensations, when he made a separate deal with a New York City mafia lieutenant to supply strippers to a resort in the Dominican Republic. After that, he openly bragged about how he intended to control every other agency in the province—by force if necessary. It was an astute plan; the sex industry may not be as lucrative as the drug industry, but the money is easier to make and harder to trace. And Montreal, which a recent study by the Quebec Conseil du Statut de la Femme declared the "Bangkok of the West," is the place to make it. But it was a direct threat to Carroll, who had taken over Aventure, Lambert's company that supplied girls from the East Coast and Quebec for jobs in Ontario.

Even worse, the boastful Steinert told anyone who would listen about his plan to start a new and better gang in the Kingston/Belleville region. Making an enemy of the alcoholic, often penniless Carroll was one thing, but stepping on Stadnick's toes was quite another. It was bad enough that Steinert was openly planning to start a gang in Ontario, an area the club had reserved for Stadnick alone, but to constantly point out how and why Stadnick's Demon Keepers had failed was particularly annoying. For the moment, Stadnick would let Steinert mouth off.

On March 14, Rock Machine associate Denis Marcoux was driving to his job at a Quebec City bar when a remote-controlled bomb exploded in his pickup. Unlike previous bombs, which had been placed in the vehicle's dashboard or console in an effort to kill the driver or passenger, this one was embedded in the driver's side door. When it exploded, Marcoux's left leg was severed, while the truck's running board detached and flew threw the window of an apartment across the street. It came to rest on the floor of a room beside an 18-month-old baby. Although he and his ten-year-old brother were covered in their own blood and shattered glass, neither was seriously hurt.

Innocent bystanders had been caught in the crossfire before, but this was the first time children had been harmed. Public fear turned to outrage. The following day, Quebec public security minister Serge Ménard met with the cabinet in an effort to form a plan. When he eventually emerged from the meeting and was mobbed by the press, Ménard finally admitted what the people of Quebec had known for a long time: "It's a war between the Hells Angels and the Rock Machine for the control of drug sales."

Sensing an opportunity, the Hells Angels began an aggressive PR campaign. Some sources say the orders came down from Stadnick himself. The Hells Angels were allegedly behind a campaign that distributed hundreds of thousands of leaflets throughout Quebec disclaiming any responsibility for the violence and placing the blame on the SQ. The most popular of them stirred up old hatreds by telling readers that the SQ had blown up bars during the Front de Libération du Québec (FLQ) crisis and they were not above doing it now to discredit the bikers. In response, the SQ issued an unsigned press release claiming to have negotiated a peace treaty between the Hells Angels and the Rock Machine.

In all likelihood the truce never actually existed, but the violence did subside in April 1995, while Boucher was in prison and Stadnick was on the road. A couple of uniformed cops in downtown Hamilton saw Stadnick's Jaguar and decided to stop him. They followed him until he failed to signal a lane change, then pulled him over. As usual, he was polite and cooperative, if not exactly friendly. As he stepped out of the car, one of the officers (now retired) noticed his monstrous gold belt buckle. After a few questions, the police confiscated it as a potentially dangerous weapon, gave Stadnick a ticket and let him go. After a night at home and a morning in church with his parents, he went to Hamilton airport and boarded a plane for Winnipeg.

* * *

The prairie city had become something of a third home for Stadnick. According to police who were familiar with him, he bought a condo there and gave it to his local girlfriend Tiffani and their son Damon (Nomad spelled backwards). He stayed with them when he was in town. And in April 1995, he was there on business. Meeting with a number of Spartans who were growing dismayed by Darwin Sylvester's bizarrely violent leadership, Stadnick formed them into a new club. Typical of his operations, the plan was large in scope and meticulous in its execution. Called the Redliners, Winnipeg's newest gang was a puppet of the Rockers, which was itself a puppet of the Nomads, which was an elite subset of the Hells Angels. Although Stadnick had created the Redliners, the police said the connection to him was too complicated to be proven in court. And unlike the Spartans and Los Brovos, who operated out of members' homes or storefronts, the Redliners clubhouse was the first fortified biker bunker in the Canadian prairies. Situated between the airport and massive rail-yards and equipped with armor plating, automatically locking doors, an emergency generator and the latest in audio and video surveillance equipment, the Redliners' clubhouse impressed Winnipeg police as a harbinger of a war to come.

Stadnick spent much of the spring and summer of 1995 in Winnipeg overseeing the Redliners, although he was never seen at or even near the clubhouse. He met with them frequently at bars and restaurants, inspected their appearance and listened to their progress reports. The discipline he enforced surprised police. Unlike the other bikers in Winnipeg (or the original Hells Angels for that matter), Stadnick forced the Redliners to have short, well-groomed hair and to dress neatly and appropriately at all times. Rick Lobban, biker cop for the Winnipeg police, later told reporters that "the Redliners were his attempt to create a group and give it a pedigree that could become a Hells Angels chapter."

According to Kane, Stadnick had even more to do in Winnipeg. His reports to the RCMP allege that Stadnick, who was still dealing with Los Brovos and the Spartans, arranged for a series of drug couriers to get on a Via Rail train in Montreal with up to 7 kilos of cocaine in two suitcases. The plan was to stop at Toronto's Union Station, rendezvous with an anonymous contact and exchange one suitcase with drugs hidden inside for one full of cash. When the courier arrived in

Winnipeg, he was to call a pager number and leave a code indicating his hotel and room number. Before long, another man unknown to the courier traded another suitcase full of cash for the remaining drugs. The courier then gave the suitcases full of money to a third contact in Montreal. It was a system that worked perfectly and repeatedly.

With Stadnick back in town and Boucher out of prison, the war resumed in Montreal. On July 3, tipped-off SQ officers recovered a white cargo van in Lachine that had been stolen from the McGill University maintenance department in January. What they found inside—an arsenal worthy of a large-scale military assault—sent a shockwave through the province. Welded to the van's floor was a tripod mount and a 7.62 mm FN machine gun (the kind used by many NATO armies as an anti-personnel weapon) with a two-meter-long belt of ammunition. Beside it were four Mac-10 submachine guns, two sawed-off shotguns and a U.S. military issue .30-caliber M-1 semiautomatic carbine. Farther back were 122 sticks of dynamite, 50 detonators and a seven-pound nail bomb. Although the munitions were terrifying enough, the police found something that could have had an even more profound impact on the already critical situation—stolen SQ insignia. If the stick-on labels had been affixed to the outside of the van, any attack it was involved in would have been blamed on police. Although they never took credit for the van, some Hells Angels later claimed that the SQ had planted the decals there to further discredit bikers.

The origin of the insignia notwithstanding, the SQ managed to turn a huge victory into a PR disaster bigger than the Hells Angels could have imagined. It was the middle of the night when the Montreal police delivered their bomb-disarming robot. Rather than evacuate the area, the police hid behind a blast shield and sent the robot in by remote control. Normally a flood of water from its high-pressure hose is enough to neutralize any bomb, but something went wrong in the parking lot in Lachine that night. For some reason, the spray ignited the explosives and turned the van into millions of pieces of flying metal. Debris was scattered over a half mile of apartment buildings and stores, with some of it coming agonizingly close to an old chlorine storage tank at a water treatment plant. Although the residents of the area didn't wake up to a cloud of poisonous gas, they did find their windows shattered and their floors covered in pieces of glass, metal, brick and asphalt. Miraculously, nobody was hurt. But the SQ was widely accused of knowingly and unnecessarily putting a huge number of innocent people into mortal danger. And they owed the Montreal police a new bomb-disarming robot.

The SQ thought they had caught a break when they arrested a small-time Quebec City hood and former Mercenaire named Michel "Pit" Caron. It became clear under questioning that Caron was more deeply involved in the war than police had originally thought and, when talk turned to murders, they were willing to deal. In exchange for some dropped charges, Caron told the SQ about his old friend and sometime partner, Serge Quesnel.

A high-school dropout from suburban Trois-Rivières, Quesnel had only once held a legitimate job—as a fast-food cook for two weeks. Instead, he used his muscles to make a very successful living as an enforcer and debt collector for area drug dealers. He moved up in the eyes of the underworld in 1988 when he bludgeoned a small-time dealer named Richard Jobin to death. It was an effort to impress potential employers, and it paid off—Quesnel started getting more work than ever and getting paid more for his services. When another dealer, Martin Naud, let it slip that he knew enough details of the Jobin murder to endanger him, Quesnel stabbed him in the eye with a pair of scissors, then cut his throat before burning his body.

Quesnel spent a short stint in Donnacona prison on an unrelated offense, during which he made money and connections by beating and stabbing fellow prisoners. He later claimed that his lawyer offered to introduce him to Louis "Mèlou" Roy, president of the Hells Angels Trois-Rivières Chapter and one of the original Nomads. Impressed by Quesnel's résumé, Roy offered him a job as professional murderer. In case he wasn't sold by the offer of $500 a week and anywhere from $10,000 to $25,000 for each murder (depending on the risk), Roy told him "there'll be a lot of work." Quesnel quickly agreed. To start him off, Roy gave him a handgun and $2,000 in cash, got him a haircut and bought him $800-worth of clothes.

On December 14, 1994, Quesnel received a call from Sylvain "Baptiste" Thiffault, the second most powerful and influential member of the Trois-Rivières chapter. He gave Quesnel his first assignment. Jacques Ferland was a PCP cook and sometime dealer from Grondines, a suburb of Quebec City, who occasionally sold to members and associates of the Rock Machine. Thiffault told Quesnel as much as he could about Ferland, including his home address, favorite restaurants and other habits. Since it was an easy hit—Ferland was a small-timer with no heavyweight friends or security plan—the fee was $10,000. Excited and a little nervous about his first contract, Quesnel called his old friend Caron and offered him $4,500 if he'd help. On the evening of January 29, 1995, Caron drove Quesnel to Ferland's house and waited in the car. Quesnel ran into a friend of Ferland's, André Bédard, on the sidewalk and the two men walked into the house together. Bédard shouted that Ferland had a visitor and left. When Ferland walked down the stairs, Quesnel shot him twice in the head. Ferland's wife, still upstairs, heard the gunfire and hid. She needn't have worried; Quesnel was under strict orders to spare her life. As they'd planned, Caron and Quesnel dumped the stolen car and snowmobiled back home.

Satisfied with the Ferland job, the Hells Angels, again through Thiffault, offered Quesnel another opportunity. They even supplied him with a driver, Mario Lussier—a member of the Rowdy Crew, a puppet gang who sold Hells Angels drugs in nearby Lanaudière. The murder of Claude "Le Pic" Rivard almost went bad as a cop happened to see the killing, but the Hells Angels were impressed by the fact that both Quesnel and Lussier managed to get away and the police didn't have anything but a wrecked stolen pickup truck. The Hells Angels gave Quesnel $15,000 and the promise of more work.

Richard "Chico" Delcourt thought he was pretty smart. He'd successfully managed to sell drugs without dealing with the Hells Angels or the Alliance and was getting away with it. When word of his independent operation made it to the Hells Angels, they offered Quesnel $10,000 to murder him. Quesnel assumed that, like many drug dealers in Quebec at the time, Delcourt dreamed of someday joining the Hells Angels. On the pretext of taking him to a Quebec City Hells Angels party at which, he hinted, they would be auditioning new members, Quesnel offered Delcourt a ride. Delcourt was understandably cautious, but Quesnel laughed and said, "If we wanted to kill you, we would have done it long ago." Delcourt agreed to go with him.

Quesnel originally planned to have his old partner drive, but Caron was avoiding his former partner because he was afraid he might become his next victim. When another driver also failed to show, Quesnel stole a car and picked up Delcourt alone. After explaining that he always took back roads to avoid the police, Quesnel parked the car on a snow-covered gravel road and told Delcourt he had a confession to make: "I don't have a driver's license." Not wanting his new friend to get in trouble, Delcourt offered to drive. As they got out of the car to exchange seats, Quesnel shot him three times, then sped away.

Things were going well for Quesnel until Caron fingered him. On April 1, 1995, the SQ stopped his car, charged him with the murders of Ferland and Delcourt and took him to jail. Much to Quesnel's relief, the police were willing, even anxious, to deal. In exchange for his testimony against Roy and other Hells Angels and confessing to five murders and 13 other crimes, the SQ offered Quesnel a 20-year sentence with a chance at parole after 12. Quesnel was ready to take the deal, but when he paused before answering, the SQ sweetened it to a ridiculous degree. Realizing that Quesnel's primary concern was his own protection, they offered him a new identity and even promised to pay to remove his tattoos, including the blue teardrops etched under his eyes. Sensing their desperation, Quesnel held out and indicated he'd appreciate some financial reward for his efforts. Without even faking reluctance, they put the money on the table. For his cooperation, they'd pay him $500 a week for 15 years. Quesnel did the math in his head—that was a total of $390,000. Even if the money was just dumped into a savings account, he'd come out of prison a millionaire. Not bad for a guy who just admitted to killing five people. Stifling his laughter, Quesnel agreed to testify.

Within days, the police rounded up a dozen Hells Angels and associates, including Roy and Thiffault. But the SQ let another potential victory slip through their fingers. Considering Quesnel far too valuable to expose in any prison, the SQ kept him in a cell in their Quebec City headquarters. While there, he was frequently visited by his girlfriend, a 21-year-old stripper named Sandra Beaulieu. Officers began to look forward to her visits and two of them even convinced her to pose for some risqué photographs, as long as she was allowed to retain copies.

As the Crown was preparing for a preliminary hearing against Lussier, the first of the men Quesnel was to testify against, Martin Tremblay, a lawyer who defended many Hells Angels, put a bold plan into action. He sent copies of the photographs the police had taken of Beaulieu, along with another of her sitting in Quesnel's lap in an SQ office, to local newspapers. He also sent along an affidavit in which Beaulieu swore that she'd had sex, alcohol and PCP with Quesnel in SQ offices. He then released some details of the deal SQ had made in exchange for Quesnel's testimony. And he noted that since Quesnel had convinced Beaulieu to smuggle PCP into the police station, he had committed conspiracy to distribute illegal drugs, a crime that should have voided his deal with the SQ. Public reaction was predictably negative. Quesnel fired back by accusing Tremblay of plotting to kill Roger Aubin, a former client. When investigators found no evidence to support his claim, Quesnel's credibility sank even lower.

* * *

If the bikers had any support in the public, if their mystique had any currency with the people of Quebec, it died on the afternoon of August 9, 1995. At the corner of Boulevard Pie-Ix and Rue Adam in the heart of Montreal's rough Maisonneuve–Hochelaga district, two men got into a Jeep Wrangler. Six other men were watching. Just as the driver turned the ignition key, one of the six others detonated a bomb under his seat. The blast was powerful enough to send the driver's suddenly legless body flying 12 feet into the air and shower the quiet, tree-lined streets with shrapnel. But this time, there was no miracle. Across Rue Adam from the explosion, two boys were playing on the lawn in front of Saint-Nom-de-Jésus School. When the blast occurred at 12:40 p.m., Yan Villeneuve and Daniel Desrosiers fell to the ground. Desrosiers never got up again. As the wall of debris from the explosion showered them, a piece of hot metal—about the size of a roll of dimes—seared its way through the boy's skull and lodged in his brain. The 11-year-old boy went into a coma and died four days later.

When news of the incident broke, Montrealers were sick and angry. Although many just hated all bikers—even if it proved to be a Rock Machine bomb, it could have just as easily have been a Hells Angels bomb—everybody wanted to know the identity of whoever had pulled the trigger. The type of remote-control device used in such bombs has a very short range, and the detonator must see his intended victim get into the car in order to ignite the bomb at just the right moment. For the bomber to be able to see the driver, he almost certainly also had to be able to see the boys. Of course, neither side wanted to be labeled child-killers, so both denied involvement. Not wanting to see the public choose one side as the bad guys (making the other appear good by comparison), the police denied that the Jeep's driver, Marc Dubé, or passenger, Jean Côté, had any connection to either gang. Some more gullible members of the media bought a story that Dubé was just an honest citizen who happened to bear a resemblance to Alliance drug dealer Normand "Bouboule" Tremblay and coincidentally drove the same kind of car. Of course, the idea of someone as high-profile as Tremblay cruising around Maisonneuve–Hochelaga on foot and in an open-topped car, just four blocks from Boucher's headquarters, was ridiculous. And even if the cops' scenario was true, the Hells Angels would still have been responsible for the bomb and Desrosier's death.

Realizing there was little they could do to assuage the public's anger, the Hells Angels repeatedly denied any involvement with the bomb, but offered Daniel's mother an undisclosed amount of cash "in a gesture of sympathy." Predictably, she was outraged. "It disgusts me; I'll never forgive this act," said Josée-Anne Desrosiers, who, like the public, turned much of her anger on the police. "This has been going on for five years, and the government has done nothing." Aware of the PR opportunity, but underestimating her defiance, the Rock Machine also extended her an offer of cash.

As images of Daniel Desrosiers, his funeral and processions of crying school children flooded the Montreal media, the police were overwhelmed by angry citizens demanding to know what their protectors could do against the obvious menace. For the moment, at least, they could do little more than sympathize. "People are asking why this is happening," said Jacques Duchesneau, chief of the Montreal Urban Community Police

Service. "It's not like they are living in Beirut." All he could offer for the time being was a 24-hour toll-free anonymous hotline for tips.

But the police were also fudging the truth. Dubé was a small-time drug courier who worked exclusively with associates of the Hells Angels. Police later learned though informants, primarily Kane, that the Hells Angels sacrificed Dubé in an effort to make it appear as though the Alliance was endangering the public by openly striking in residential areas. Although nobody ever came forward to say that he or anyone else had knowingly exposed the Desrosiers and Villeneuve boys to danger, the identities of the men ultimately responsible for the blast became clear. Before the incident, the ever-boastful Steinert was talking nonstop, if cryptically, about a plan he and Boucher had that was *plus rock 'n' roll* (Quebecois slang for "more impressive") than anything that either gang had done before. He was reportedly giddy and nervous when he ordered three remote control detonators from Pat Lambert on August 8. Two days earlier, an explosion in a northern suburb of St-Lin that nearly injured some innocent children (young nephews of the intended target) had drawn harsh criticism within the club from Stadnick and Carroll. Carroll reportedly even suggested that the bomber pay for such a mistake with his life. Nothing they said slowed down Steinert in his anxious bid to impress Boucher, the man he saw as the club's real power.

After the Desrosiers bombing, Steinert fell uncharacteristically silent. He stopped his barrage of self-promotion and even refused to answer questions about the detonators he had bought from Lambert. When he finally started talking, he solemnly discussed the incident with his friends in the chapter, quizzing them about what they thought of it, while never accepting a shred of responsibility. When he asked them if they thought the bomber, if he was ever tracked down, should be executed by the club for killing a child, the answer was a resounding and unanimous *yes*. Much of that information came to the RCMP through Kane, but his contacts noticed that he was reluctant to talk about the incident and gave few details. At least some wondered aloud if Kane, who had a great deal of experience as a bomber and was a close friend and associate of Steinert's, was feeling guilty because he was involved. Others countered that Kane, a father of three, may have been suffering from the same grief as the rest of the city and shame at what he assumed was his friend's horrible blunder.

When Desrosiers died on August 13, Montreal mayor Pierre Bourque asked the federal and provincial governments for stronger anti-gang laws. Ménard and Allan Rock, the federal justice minister, refused, citing how such laws would compromise the civil liberties not just of bikers, but of the entire public.

With the force of public anger aimed squarely at police and government, the gangs resumed their bombing campaign. The first attack was a dud. Someone threw a hand grenade (which was later traced to a theft from the Canadian Armed Forces) at Bob Chopper, which had formerly been owned by Hells Angels' national president Robert "Ti-Maigre" Richard and was still the club's favorite Harley repair and customization shop in the Montreal area. The grenade failed to explode, leaving just a long crack in the front window of the Longueuil shop. Three days later, a homemade bomb exploded in front of the Rowdy Crew's clubhouse in Le Gardeur. Although the explosion was large and loud, it did little damage to the heavily fortified house, other than kill the club's pit bull.

Police received an anonymous phone tip just after midnight on August 26 that a car bomb was parked in the East End. When they got there, they found a light blue Chevy Lumina—just as the caller had described—with a rather prominent wire sticking out of the engine compartment. At about 2 a.m., just as the police were beginning to realize there were no explosives in the car, across the river a bomb with almost 10 pounds of C4 tore the back wall off Bob Chopper. By the time the police arrived at the actual bombing, they were greeted by a lawyer (known to have defended Hells Angels in the past) who demanded they return with a search warrant if they wanted into what remained of the building. By the time they returned, witnesses said that some men had walked into the smoking building and rushed out carrying some cartons that they threw into cars. The next night, a tattoo parlor frequented by Rock Machine members and associates was destroyed by gasoline bombs.

Emboldened by the lack of arrests despite public outrage, the Alliance stepped up the violence even further, targeting people instead of property. On September 11, one of their men exploded a bomb on the patio of Bar Le Harley in a suburb north of the city, waiting until the waitress went inside before pulling the trigger. All nine of the injured had strong ties to the Death Riders, a North Shore Hells Angels puppet gang. Among them was Mario Lepore, reportedly Boucher's favorite accountant, who lost a leg.

Four days later, the Alliance escalated the war with a truly bold assassination—the first time a full-patch Hells Angel had been hit. A former Missile and one of the founders of the Hells Angels Trois-Rivières chapter, Richard "Crow" Émond and his girlfriend were returning to their car after shopping at an East End strip mall when somebody called out his name. When Émond turned around to see who it was, a masked man fired six times. Three of the shells hit him and, when the police arrived, they found Émond's dead body lying half in and half out of his white Pontiac Bonneville. They also found a loaded handgun under the driver's seat. Émond's death hit the underworld in much the same way that Desrosiers' affected the public.

Flags flew at half-staff at Hells Angels' clubhouses across Quebec, and the police began to get nervous. They made the natural assumption that the Hells Angels wouldn't tolerate the murder of an influential member. The days of bombs in empty bars appeared to be over; the era of murder had begun.

Finally, the government stepped in. Montreal's overwhelmed police got some help at long last. On September 23, 1995, Ménard, who had repeatedly denied the existence of a biker war, announced the creation of an anti-gang police task force. With a huge budget, 30 officers from the SQ joined 30 more from the Montreal police (ten more were later added from the RCMP and total membership would eventually top 100 officers). The task force was solely devoted to bringing down the bikers. It was a perfectly timed event and the government knew how to play to an audience starved for any effort from a government they were sure had forsaken them. They called the new group "Carcajou," French for Wolverine, an animal with legendary status in Quebecois culture. The largest member of the weasel family, the wolverine is an animal with enormous strength and courage; they have even been known to scare grizzly bears away from a kill. The name resonated so well in Quebec that an old hunter actually pulled the stuffed carcass of a wolverine out of his attic and sent it to the Montreal police. But what the police didn't mention was that, despite all its ferocity, the wolverine was an endangered species. In fact, nobody had seen a live one in Quebec since 1978.

Chapter 8

After the Hamilton police realized there was no way they could prove in court that Stadnick's belt buckle was a dangerous weapon, they returned it to him. He was shocked to see what condition it was in. It looked as though it had been kicked around the floor of the evidence room. Stadnick was not going to stand for it. The Hamilton police were trying to push him around based solely on his reputation. He'd never gotten in trouble there, and he'd never been convicted of anything anywhere. He called the police to complain. Eventually, he was connected to Sergeant John Harris.

Although Harris had been out of the biker business for a few years, he was supervising staff sergeant for Central Division, which made him, in effect, the boss of the officers who had arrested Stadnick. "At first I didn't believe it was him on the phone; I thought someone was playing a joke," said Harris. "When I realized it was him, I was truly surprised about what he was calling about." Obviously the belt buckle meant a great deal to Stadnick. Harris invited him down to talk; maybe he had a holding cell free. Unamused, Stadnick hung up. Harris later got a letter from Stadnick's lawyer, Stephan Frankel, informing him that he and the arresting officers were being sued for $500 to cover the belt buckle's repairs and Stadnick's mental anguish. Harris laughed;

there was no way he was going to pay. The case actually made it to small-claims court. "We lost the case, but Walter, I think, considered it a moral victory," said Frankel. "And I have been told that at least some parties were pleased that those three officers were obliged to spend a day in court."

About an hour's drive away, small events were taking place that would precipitate major changes in Ontario's biker détente. Frank Lenti, the moody biker Stadnick had found wanting at his Wasaga Beach recruiting drive, was dumped as president of the Loners. Immediately, he and some Woodbridge-area friends formed a new club, the Diablos, in Lenti's house across the street from the Loners' clubhouse. Far outnumbered, the Diablos generally stayed out of the Loners' way and arrived for meetings through Lenti's backyard. Although they were familiar with Lenti's mood swings and temper tantrums, the Toronto members of Satan's Choice saw some value in the Diablos. Lenti owned a stripper/escort agency and a towing business and, with Bernie Guindon back in charge, the leadership of Satan's Choice was looking to expand, especially into an area as important to the drug trade as Woodbridge.

To the surprise of many Toronto police officers, Satan's Choice extended prospective membership to the Diablos on July 6, 1995. "It was strange; they knew Lenti, they knew he'd been thrown out of the Loners, and they still invited him in," said Tony, a veteran Toronto cop who'd rather not identify himself. "It was like they were desperate." Tensions that had been limited to insults shouted across the street escalated into violence once the Diablos' confidence was boosted by their new status. A few days after they received the news, two Diablos took it upon themselves to throw a Molotov cocktail at a tow truck owned by a member of the Loners. Already angry, the Loners were enraged that the Diablos, who they considered lowlifes no matter what Guindon thought, would be so bold, and they upped the ante in an effort to frighten them off.

On July 22, a couple of Diablos were sitting in a car trying to decide what to do that night. They eventually went to a hospital emergency room. Five bullets crashed through the car's back window, and both men were hit once. Although neither man was seriously hurt, war was undeniably declared. In a less-than-courageous response, the Diablos convinced a pair of underage girls to pour gasoline all over the cars at a used-car lot owned by a Loners associate. They chickened out before either could light a match and were arrested about a block away.

At that point, local police stepped in. They held a meeting with some representatives of both the Diablos and the Loners and warned them against using minors and bombs to solve their differences. The cops pointed to what was happening in Montreal as an example of how a biker war could get out of hand. "In retrospect, it was a bad idea," said Tony, pointing out that neither the Diablos nor the Loners struck him as exceedingly intelligent. "It's almost like we gave them the idea."

Appalled at how low the Diablos would stoop, the Loners brought the war downtown. On the night of August 1, Toronto suffered its first biker bombing when an explosive device took off the front door of the Satan's Choice headquarters, not far from the Don Jail in the rapidly gentrifying industrial part of old Toronto. The bomb was big enough to shatter windows on houses and cars around the block, but did little to damage the heavily fortified building. None of the five bikers inside were hurt, but they were angry. Less than four hours later, somebody threw a firebomb through the front window of Pluto's Place, a tattoo parlor in the same neighborhood that was frequented by Loners. A little more than 24 hours later, three Molotov cocktails crashed through the windows of Bazooka Joe's, a bar north of the city frequented by members of Satan's Choice. As was the case at the beginning of the war in Montreal, the bombing took place in the middle of the night and the bar was empty at the time. The next explosion happened at a machine shop owned by a Diablos associate just after sunrise.

Desperate not to turn into another Montreal, Toronto city council set up a committee to find a way to get the clubs into legal trouble. They pored over thousands of documents until they found out that recent renovations—bomb- and bullet-proofing—done to the Satan's Choice Kintyre Avenue clubhouse violated an earlier agreement and reverted the building's zoning to residential. When the city informed the bikers they'd have to give up their building, they responded by moving in a club member, making the clubhouse an official residence.

The police actually made the next move in the war. On August 15, two cops saw Loners president Pietro Barilla's white Lincoln Town Car in a Harvey's parking lot. As two of his associates brought back the burgers and fries, the cops stopped them. A quick search of the car found a pair of .380 caliber handguns under the front seats. The following day a bomb planted in the alley behind a Loners clubhouse in Markham, north of the city, blew off a portion of the building's back wall.

Just as the assassination of Émond in Montreal gave police fears of massive reprisals from the Hells Angels, the cops in Ontario saw the Loners make a move they felt would require a crushing response by Satan's Choice. In broad daylight, a car drove past the house of Andre Wateel, president of the Satan's Choice Kitchener chapter, and threw a firebomb through the front bay window. The drapes immediately ignited and, if not for the quick reaction of the fire department, the house would have burned down. Wateel wasn't home at the time, but a woman and child were upstairs. They escaped unhurt. Not only had the Loners taken the war outside of Toronto, they picked the wrong guy. A close friend of both Guindon and Stadnick, Wateel was seen within the club as a rising star and by police as a rare biker with both leadership skills and the will to fight when he had to. Hoping to put at least some fear into the bikers before they struck back, a group of high-profile Ontario police officers asked federal justice minister Allan Rock for stronger anti-gang laws. He refused.

The final blow of the war was struck the following day. At 10 a.m., Frank Lenti was halfway into his Ford Explorer when a Loner across the street detonated a bomb. The Diablos president lost his right leg. When police searched his house, they found an unlicensed handgun and a Mac-10 submachine gun. "I know he was officially aligned with Satan's Choice, but it seemed like both sides were relieved he was out of the picture," said Tony. "With Lenti gone, they all stopped fighting." Without their president, the Diablos quickly folded. Without an enemy in North Toronto, the Loners decided to make peace with Satan's Choice. After feeling out the situation with some go-betweens, the Loners went to a Satan's Choice party and forged an informal alliance, hinting that they might even be willing to take the Diablos' place as a North Toronto chapter.

Lacking any intelligence on the peace treaty, Toronto city council was still panicking. With news of Desrosier's death still fresh, they were desperate to stave off a full-scale war. Desperate enough that frustrated Toronto mayor Barbara Hall decided to deal with the bikers. On September 20, she called the Satan's Choice lawyer and told him the city was willing to buy their clubhouse. The next day he called back and said his client, former chapter president and owner of the house, Larry McIlroy, was willing to sell for $350,000. Although the building had been recently appraised at $190,000, Hall agreed and told them to draw up the papers. When the media, who had been largely supportive of Hall up until then, heard, they reacted in a huge way. The item became front-page news and Hall was saddled with the nickname "Biker Barb." Despite a large public outcry—one that did not include the clubhouse's neighbors—city council pushed through the plan. After many concessions were made, all on the city's side, the plan finally came to a humiliating end on October 20, when the club refused to include a clause that would prevent them from acquiring a new clubhouse in the same area. In a futile attempt to mitigate the disaster, city council hired a lawyer to help a neighborhood association search for more zoning violations.

A week later, the police mounted a massive raid on the Loners' Woodbridge clubhouse. Although they found three restricted weapons—a submachine gun, an assault rife and a spray can of mace—they failed to close it down and made no significant arrests. Far more effective was the owner of a farm in Milton, which the Loners were planning to use to serve the Hamilton area. When he read in *The Hamilton Spectator* about the Loners' war with Satan's Choice, he threw them out and suffered no repercussions.

* * *

While bikers and their supporters were laughing at the authorities in Toronto, the war-weary people of Montreal finally saw faint glimmers of hope. Carcajou paid almost instant dividends when Mom Boucher made a surprising slip on September 25. An old friend, low-level cocaine trafficker Steven Bertrand, called him looking for advice. A few days earlier, Bertrand had seen a man flirt with his girlfriend and attacked him. The two men were rolling around on the bar floor when the interloper's friends pulled Bertrand off and showed him their handguns. Bertrand and his girlfriend had slunk out of the club threatening revenge. Eavesdropping police heard Boucher laugh as he counseled Bertrand. On tape, he told Bertrand to collect a few friends, grab some baseball bats, go back to the bar and get his manhood back. Counseling violence is a major violation for someone on probation, and the police issued a warrant for Boucher's arrest. When he found out, Boucher fled. Carcajou officers anticipated this and got warrants to search clubhouses. On October 23, 1995, the cops raided the headquarters of three puppet clubs. Realizing he wasn't going to avoid the police forever and that the more they searched the more chance there was that he would get into much bigger trouble, Boucher surrendered the next day.

The public, many of whom considered Boucher responsible for the war, celebrated. Although he had been convicted 14 times in Quebec courts—including once for sexual assault with a weapon—and he was on probation for two different crimes at the time, Boucher was freed on bail. His lawyer, Léo-Réne Maranda, told the press, "it's not against the law to be a Hells Angel." The judge may have disagreed. Among the many conditions of Boucher's bail was a stricture against communicating with any other members of the club.

After that small success, Carcajou declared all-out war. In a raid on the Rockers' Lachine clubhouse, the squad came up with automatic weapons, shotguns, detonators and drugs. Six bikers were arrested. A few days later, an Evil Ones associate named Patrick Dupuis was arrested with four sticks of dynamite in the trunk of his Ford Tempo. With information gleaned during the search for Boucher, Carcajou officers conducted a raid of eight buildings, including the houses of six Hells Angels associates. The October 26 assault led to the arrest of two Death Riders and 13 others, the confiscation of illegal weapons ranging from an assault rifle to a hand grenade and enough marijuana and cocaine to bring distribution charges. Then Carcajou officers proved they weren't playing favorites when, on November 9, they raided 25 locations associated with the Rock Machine and made 22 arrests on weapons and drug offenses. Three weeks later, a raid on the Jokers' clubhouse yielded the usual weapons and drugs, but also something more grisly. In September, three Rock Machine associates had attempted to blow up the Jokers' headquarters when their home-made bomb exploded as they were planting it. In a macabre twist, the Jokers were found to have been collecting souvenirs. When the police found dozens of pieces of human remains in jars of preservative and in food storage bags in the clubhouse freezer, they identified many of them by their still-legible tattoos.

Despite the arrests, there was no decline in biker-related violence. Bombings were still commonplace. The house of the warden of Sorel prison was set on fire again, and Rock Machine snipers had taken pot shots at some Hells Angels as they walked around the exercise yard of Leclerc Prison in Laval. It seemed like the bikers were running out of ideas when Bob Chopper was bombed again. Marcel Blondeau, a mild-mannered father of two who lived next door to the biker hang-out, couldn't take it anymore. He'd tried to sell his house, but nobody in the Montreal area would consider it at any price. Finally, he begged Longueuil mayor, Claude Gladu, to do something. At the same time Barbara Hall was trying to pay the Hells Angels to leave Toronto, Gladu convinced the city of Longueuil to rent the Blondeaus a house on the other side of town until they could sell theirs. Both acts showed that the authorities understood the biker problem, but also underlined the fact that neither could do anything about it.

Tired of dragging Serge Quesnel out to biker trials only to have his testimony discredited every time, the police were desperate for another, more impressive witness. They found him—a man so bad the other bikers called him "Satan"—in a cell awaiting trial for drug offenses stemming from the October 26 raid. In exchange for dropped charges, Martin "Satan" Lacroix agreed to testify against his boss. Michael "L'Animal" Lajoie-Smith was a big strong man with a hair-trigger temper. After the members of Sorel eliminated the Laval chapter, they set up a puppet club, the Death Riders, to operate their business in the city just north of Montreal. They sent full-patch member Lajoie-Smith to oversee the gang and make sure they did as they were told and that they commanded respect in the area. When he got there, he showed up at La Marsolaise bar, where the owner had refused to pay protection. Lajoie-Smith didn't negotiate; he simply picked a bar patron at random and beat the hell out of him. He was very thorough. The victim, 32-year-old Alain Cadieux, hasn't left his wheelchair or institutional care since.

Two months later, Lajoie-Smith gave Lacroix $400 to deliver a bomb to Le Gascon, a strip club popular with Alliance members in nearby Berthiersville. It didn't explode, but it and the Cadieux beating were enough to put Lajoie-Smith away for a long time, and Lacroix told the police everything he knew. The officers of Carcajou had learned from the Sûreté du Québec's mistakes with Quesnel. They didn't give Lacroix any cash and, although they put him in protective custody, kept him in prison. When police told Lajoie-Smith about the charges, he was already in jail on unrelated weapons charges. He didn't show much emotion, but asked that he not be sent to Bordeaux prison, which was now Rock Machine territory.

Overwhelmed by the amount of evidence against him, Lajoie-Smith later pleaded guilty to the Cadieux beating. Using the proceeds-of-crime law, Carcajou seized his residence, Cadillac and two Harleys. A week before the government was to auction off his 13-room house, it mysteriously caught fire and burned to the ground. With Lajoie-Smith out of commission, the Hells Angels sent the still-ambitious Steinert north to act as the Death Riders' godfather.

* * *

While Carcajou was seeing some success putting Hells Angels and members of the Alliance behind bars, three men had managed to remain remarkably unscathed. Perhaps not coincidentally, they also happened to be the three highest-ranking Anglophone Hells Angels in Quebec, all of them Nomads. Stadnick, who had never been convicted, and Stockford, who had never even been arrested, approached their old friend Carroll to help them with their ultimate goal: Ontario. On February 20, 1996, Stockford met Carroll at a chalet in the Laurentian ski resort town of St-Sauveur. Despite the hospitable surroundings, it was primarily a business meeting. Under what Kane told police was Stadnick's direction, Stockford purchased a large quantity of drugs from Carroll and arranged for them to be shipped back to Montreal. From there a courier took 4 kilos of hash to a contact at Toronto's Union Station and then rented a car for the big deal.

A little more than halfway down the Queen Elizabeth Way from Toronto to Hamilton, the courier turned off onto Bronte Road and stopped at a Tim Horton's. Once inside the familiar brown-on-brown doughnut shop, he met a contact: Stockford's cousin. The two men then walked out to the parking lot and, in the rental car, they exchanged a bag full of cash for a bag containing a kilogram of cocaine and 1,000 hits of ecstasy destined for the Hamilton market. According to what Kane told the RCMP, it was the first of many such shipments to the area. Although the Hells Angels had no official presence in Ontario, they didn't have any problem selling drugs there.

Just a few miles away, a fledgling biker gang got a big break and helped contribute to the anti-Hells Angels forces in Ontario. When Johnny Sombrero took over the presidency of the Black Diamond Riders, a small but well-established Toronto gang, he threw out all the members with criminal records. He just wasn't interested in going to prison when one of his men slipped up. There was no argument. None of the exiled members would challenge Sombrero, an all-time tough guy, and they left without incident. Instead, six of them formed a new club in Milton, the hometown of two of them. They gave it a rather defeatist name: The Lost Souls.

Just north of Burlington, Milton had been a sleepy farm town until people started moving out of Hamilton in droves. As the standard of life rapidly declined in the city, those who could afford it moved to suburbs like Milton, Waterdown and Ancaster. With their rapidly swelling populations of displaced urbanites, the towns surrounding Hamilton became very profitable markets for drugs like cocaine and ecstasy. On April 13, 1996, Satan's Choice, clearly not as choosy as Sombrero and the Black Diamond Riders, approached the Lost Souls with an offer. If they would sell Satan's Choice drugs in the area and kick 10 percent of proceeds back to the nearby Kitchener chapter, they would become a prospective chapter.

The imbalance didn't last long. On May 4, all 20 members of the Loners showed up at the headquarters of the Para-Dice Riders,

Toronto's biggest independent club. Despite having flirted with Satan's Choice after the Diablos went down, the Loners showed up with an offer: they wanted to be a Para-Dice Riders chapter. The Loners offered the bigger club a presence in North Toronto and access to some of the Italian mafia's biggest names. The reason they wanted to join, they said, was that Satan's Choice, particularly president Andre Wateel, were out for their heads, but would never touch them if they were Para-Dice Riders. The response was immediate and positive. First came the beer and then came the patches. Not expecting visitors, the Para-Dice Riders didn't have enough patches to go around, but promised they'd have some more made. What the gracious hosts didn't know, and wouldn't find out until it was too late, was that it wasn't fear of Wateel that sent the Loners downtown. Instead, Stadnick had convinced them to infiltrate the Para-Dice Riders by dangling a Hells Angels prospective membership in the event they managed to take over.

Despite years of peaceful coexistence, there was very little affection between the Para-Dice Riders and Satan's Choice. The two big clubs, which had aligned mostly to present a united front to the Hells Angels, had grown suspicious of each other once large-scale patch-overs had begun. And when they met at a Victoria Day protest over police road-side stops, insults and threats started flying. Ironically, the presence of many uniformed and mounted Toronto police officers prevented any actual violence. Although no shots were fired and no punches were thrown, a different kind of war had begun in Ontario: a cold war in which the Para-Dice Riders and Satan's Choice scrambled for new members and new chapters in an effort to retain their chunk of the Ontario pie.

Farther down the road in Hamilton, Ion William Croitoru had no idea of what was going on, but soon became a major player. A hard-core Hamilton boy who carried 285 solid pounds on his 6-foot frame, Croitoru was famous in some quarters, but it hadn't made him particularly wealthy. When the World Wrestling Foundation hit its peak in the late 1980s, they needed guys for their stars to beat up on, and Croitoru fit the description. He was big, funny looking and ethnic (Romanian, but he generally ended up playing, in the long tradition of wrestling villains, a Turk). Even better, he had the ability to act like a fool in front of millions of people. While the likes of Hulk Hogan were throwing him around, Croitoru—who wrestled under the name Johnny K-9—enthralled audiences with his silent-picture actor–style theatrics.

But he didn't impress the people who ran the WWF. He got fewer and fewer assignments and got none after a 1991 conviction for assault and cocaine trafficking sent him to prison for six months. When he emerged, he signed up with Middle Tennessee Wrestling, a much smaller organization, and wrestled under the name Taras Bulba, after the greatest hero in Cossack history. Before long, he moved up to Jim Cornette's Smokey Mountain Wrestling, where he became a champion under the name Bruiser Bedlam. But it didn't matter how well he did in the minor leagues, when he walked around the streets of Hamilton, when people asked him for his autograph, when they bought him a beer at the Running Pump, he was Johnny K-9.

By the time Cornette's league ran out of money, Croitoru had assumed the Johnny K-9 personality outside the ring and even managed to get a bank account under that name. In the spring of 1996, he didn't have a job but continued to lift weights daily just in case a wrestling promoter called. Before long, he found some workout partners. One of them, a man police will identify only by the pseudonym Jimmy Rich, suggested that he, K-9 and another friend, Gary Noble, ride up to Toronto and visit the Satan's Choice clubhouse. The three weightlifters with shaved heads were welcomed warmly and given the opportunity to start a Satan's Choice prospective chapter in Hamilton after a short initiation in which they were obliged to act as bartenders and security guards at the Toronto clubhouse. After they had proven their worth, Noble purchased an old restaurant at 269 Lottridge Ave., just north of Barton Street, for $40,000, to serve as a clubhouse.

The Outlaws, weakened by a series of arrests as the result of an informant turned by Harris, did nothing to oppose the new chapter. And Stadnick, who'd stopped wooing Satan's Choice by that time and had switched his focus to the Para-Dice Riders, couldn't stop it either. Although Stadnick always tried to maintain a polite relationship with Outlaws boss Mario "the Wop" Parente, both of them realized they were each other's enemy and that Hamilton was, at least for the moment, Outlaws territory. Both Stadnick and Stockford were extra cautious when they were in their home town. Stockford told Kane once about hearing his doorbell ring one evening and looking out the window to see a guy on his porch with a pizza box. Since Stockford hadn't ordered any pizza, he didn't answer. Stadnick, of course, was a more valuable as well as a more visible target than Stockford, who Harris said almost never wore his colors in Ontario. The diminutive biker chief was walking down Main Street in Hamilton when a pickup truck stopped beside him. Before he could turn around to see who it was, there were a pair of large muscular arms around him. It wouldn't be easy to kidnap Walter Stadnick, though, and the intended victim managed to get out of his assailant's grasp and send him to the ground with a well-placed kick. Stadnick saw the metallic flash of a handgun as the passenger started getting out of the truck, and he started running, eventually getting to safety. He recognized both men as Outlaws.

Stadnick had other enemies as well. Steinert, who had repeatedly angered Stadnick with ambitions that often overlapped his own, started stomping on his turf. Under strict secrecy, Steinert began using Donald "Bam Bam" Magnussen, who had been Stadnick's bodyguard and good friend, to distribute cocaine in Thunder Bay, Ontario. Although there's no hard evidence that Stadnick or any of his allies knew what was going on, Steinert got into trouble at about the same time. Although he'd lived in Canada since he was eight, Steinert had never bothered to apply for Canadian citizenship. After repeated anonymous tips, the immigration department of Citizenship Canada started investigating Steinert and putting the wheels of deportation into motion.

Stadnick did receive some good news that summer. Near the end of June, the quiet town of Port Perry, Ontario, was overrun with hundreds of bikers and dozens of Ontario Provincial Police (OPP) officers. The event was one of the biggest in biker history: the retirement of Bernie "the Frog" Guindon, the leading voice for Satan's Choice since becoming president in 1965. Although bikers came from all over Canada, no Hells Angels or Para-Dice Riders were invited. That fact made police speculate that tensions were heating up and that a war was imminent. Stadnick, instead, saw opportunity. He was well aware that Guindon had built and then re-built the Satan's Choice empire in Ontario. Despite numerous arrests and the loss of most of their chapters, including Hamilton, to the

Outlaws while Guindon was in prison, Satan's Choice had rebounded to become the No. 2 gang in Ontario, behind only their old brothers in the Outlaws. They had, according to police, an enviable cash flow from drug sales, prostitution, strippers and other businesses and no lack of manpower ready to move product or bust heads. No doubt Stadnick was intrigued by the prospect of patching over such an established and successful network and he had tried to achieve it through negotiating with Guindon over the years. But with Guindon now out of the way, Stadnick began to make plans for an eventual takeover.

So did Ontario's police forces. With a mandate to bring down one biker gang every year until they were all gone, Guindon's retirement brought their focus to Satan's Choice (although at least one biker claimed that Guindon had been tipped off by an OPP officer that the raid was coming down and he'd be wise to leave the club immediately). On the morning of December 19, 1996, local police forces and the OPP, armed with warrants, raided every Satan's Choice clubhouse and visited the homes of every member, prospect and known associate. Before Christmas, 109 of the 125 active Satan's Choice members were under arrest. K-9, Noble, Rich and the two prospects they had gathered were all arrested in Hamilton.

What happened to them was typical of what most arrested bikers experienced. When bigger charges failed to stick due to lack of credible evidence or were plea-bargained out of significance, the Crown started nailing the bikers with proceeds of crime charges and confiscating their property. K-9, who claimed to have earned an average of $4,751 per year over the last eight years, had 48 items taken. At auction, his lot, including $7,802 in cash, two Harleys, a huge custom-built pink leather sofa and a six-foot-high laminated poster of James Dean, found a quick and anonymous taker. Like most other members of Satan's Choice, K-9 was a lot poorer for the experience, but soon back on the streets.

* * *

The Hells Angels had their own problems. After being warned about his weight by his doctor and losing more than 70 pounds, on February

23, 1996, Robert "Ti-Maigre" Richard suffered a massive coronary and died. Just as important, however, was the fact that Carcajou had conducted a series of raids on Hells Angels' interests in Quebec City. Starting with club associate Clément Allard, who was caught with $20 million in fake $20 bills on March 14, Carcajou raids led to 35 arrests and the confiscation of enough guns and drugs to put a serious dent in the gang's bottom line.

A few days after Richard's funeral, his former protégé, Steinert, exerted himself in a surprisingly public way—by getting himself a piece of Quebec history, Château Lavigueur. On the night of April 14, 1986, 18-year-old Yves Lavigueur answered the door of his run-down home in Lachine to meet a poorly dressed man who was yelling something at him in English. He slammed the door in the stranger's face and forgot about the incident until the next day when the same man showed up again with a friend. Lavigueur was about to call the police when the stranger's friend spoke to him in French, saying "Mr. Murphy has some important news for you." Lavigueur let them inside and they sat on the family couch with Yves' father, Jean-Guy.

Through his interpreter, William Murphy reminded Jean-Guy about how his lost wallet had been returned anonymously. Although he'd given back all of Lavigueur's cash and identification, Murphy had kept a 6/49 lottery ticket he'd found inside. It hit. The winnings were $7.8 million. After the celebrations were over, Jean-Guy decided to split the tax-free windfall evenly with four relatives and Murphy, each receiving $1.3 million. It was a story that delighted the entire province, but soon went bad and drew even more interest. The family moved into a palatial home in the luxurious part of Ile-Jésus, just north of Laval, which the media quickly named Château Lavigueur (the Lavigueur Mansion). As soon as they moved in, the hard-drinking, simple Lavigueurs started embarrassing themselves and the tabloids caught every bit of it. It played like a real-life version of *The Beverly Hillbillies* gone terribly wrong. When they finally ran out of money in 1995, the city put the house up for sale and the Lavigueurs retreated back to Lachine. So intense was the public interest that an admission fee of $25 to view the mansion was instituted to keep the curious out.

Two friends of the Death Riders who had been hurt in the Bar Le Harley explosion in September purchased the house. While they were working on renovations like bullet-proof windows and video cameras, a reporter asked Richard Turcot (the man whose name was on the deed) if he was an associate of the Hells Angels. He said "no" and refused to answer any more questions. When the fortification was complete, Steinert, whom the Hells Angels had sent north to control the Death Riders, moved into Château Lavigueur. The opulent setting did more than just serve as a palace for the man who considered himself king of Laval and as a place to conduct Death Riders business. When he found out that an old friend, Stéphane Chouinard, had come into some money and was interested in making some porn videos, Steinert offered him the use of Château Lavigueur—as long as the host could be one of the on-camera participants and get a cut of sales.

A lull in the violence in the summer of 1996 had Montrealers feeling pretty good about their city and about Carcajou. Some editorial writers were bleating that the war was over and some politicians were suggesting reducing Carcajou's budget or even disbanding it altogether now that its mission had been accomplished. That feeling of calm was shattered on the morning of August 22 when three bombs exploded in the suburbs. The next day, the RCMP, following a Kane tip, made a frightening discovery. When Gagné got out of prison in April, he sent a message to Boucher that he was looking for work. Two days later, Gagné's mother got him out of bed to tell him he had visitors. It was Boucher and his right-hand man Tousignant. They took him for a ride.

Just southwest of Maisonneuve–Hochelaga, in a neighborhood called Verdun, Boucher pointed out the Rock Machine's headquarters. Then he put his fist in front of Gagné's face. When he was sure Gagné was looking, he quickly extended his fingers, mimicking an explosion. No words, no sound effects. He asked Gagné if he understood. Gagné said he did. Boucher handed him $1,000 and Tousignant drove him home. After many frustrated attempts to get a clear shot at the clubhouse, Gagné finally got his hands on a stolen Hydro Quebec van, a vehicle so commonplace and anonymous it was almost below suspicion. He packed it with over 200 pounds of dynamite in five camping coolers, each with its own remote-controlled detonator. The day it was supposed to go off, the RCMP found it parked on one of the busiest streets of Verdun, not far from the Rock Machine clubhouse. Forensic tests indicated that the blast would have been powerful enough to have killed dozens in a shrapnel storm and even cause major structural damage to nearby buildings.

Although Kane's information had prevented another potential Desrosiers situation, he was also committing crimes with impunity and costing the RCMP a lot of money. Since he was the only source the police had inside the Hells Angels, they were obliged to believe what he said. Still, many cops speculated that he was behind or at least involved in a number of crimes, including the bomb that killed Desrosiers. But if he denied it, there was little they could do.

When Roland Lebrasseur's body was found on a deserted roadside in the South Shore community of Brossard, the police asked Kane what he knew about him. Kane told them that Lebrasseur had taken a job as a driver for Carroll's escort agency. When he met more Hells Angels, he boasted that he knew how to make bombs. Since they knew he was a Canadian Armed Forces veteran, they let him hang around. But he never made any bombs; he didn't actually know how. Instead, he started snorting tons of cocaine and racking up debts with the wrong people, particularly Carroll, who was chronically short of cash despite his high rank and numerous businesses. What Kane did not tell them was that, at a party in February, a drunk and stoned Lebrasseur had made a play for Patricia, Kane's new girlfriend. When she rebuffed him, he told her about Josée and Kane's three kids. Patricia not only told Kane it was over, she left the city. Kane also didn't tell police that before the sun rose on the morning of March 3, he drove Lebrasseur out to an unlit field far from any houses and told him to get out of the car, put three holes in his head and chest, then drove home.

Although the RCMP was paying him $4,000 every two weeks and he was still earning for the Hells Angels, Kane told them that he needed something more. Begging like a spoiled teenager, Kane told them that all the important Hells Angels ran businesses and that it would increase his credibility if he had one too. After some discussion, the RCMP gave him $30,325 to start *Rencontres Selectes*, a gay dating magazine where men placed racy ads looking for partners. The bulk of the profits would come from larger ads for strip joints, phone sex lines and escort services, many of which were owned or at least influenced by Kane's friends. After it succeeded, he told them, he could morph it into a gay club in Montreal and start making real money. A high-school dropout, Kane knew nothing about graphic design and even less about publishing, so his handlers at the RCMP came up with a business plan and even designed the first issue. He was playing them for fools. Kane did little meaningful work on the magazine and it folded after just three taxpayer-funded issues. He did, however, get what he'd wanted in the first place—access to gay men.

Aimé Simard was a sad and lonely young man from Quebec City who lived with his mother. Despite a habit of petty thefts and frauds, Simard studied police technology in college. After an instructor told him no police force would ever want an officer as short and fat as he was, Simard quit school and went back to his mother's house. When charges for passing rubber checks and using fake identification started piling up, he fled to Hamilton, where his father had relatives. But there was little work there for a college dropout who didn't speak English, so he returned once again to his mother's house. Before long he landed in prison and ran afoul of a tough cocaine dealer. After he was freed, he went to the Quebec City police and offered to inform on the dealer. The police, many of whom knew that Simard had always wanted to be a cop, were surprised he didn't ask for anything in return.

After word spread that Simard was an informant, he started carrying a handgun with him wherever he went. When his weight ballooned to 355 pounds, he convinced the provincial government to pay to have his stomach stapled. Determined to start life over again as a thinner man, Simard enrolled in nursing school. After a fellow student noticed and asked about the gun, Simard was arrested for possession of a restricted weapon and for pointing it at a classmate (a charge he denied). He received a sentence of 18 months. On a weekend pass he was issued just before a parole hearing, he decided to celebrate by going dancing. That night a passing cop happened to see him hiding his gun under the seat of his Jeep; Simard went back to prison to serve the rest of his term and a few months more. As soon as he got out, Simard moved back into his mother's house under her two conditions—that he get a job and go back to school. While working as a night clerk at the Château Mont-Ste-Anne and studying criminology in the day (still holding out hope of being a cop, despite his record), he placed an ad in *Recontres Selectes* under the bisexual category. After a few phone conversations, Kane told him he'd be stopping by Quebec City on the way to Halifax. During a date that included sex in his mother's bed, Simard recognized a tattoo on Kane's arm that identified him as a Hells Angel.

Kane went to Halifax under the orders of Carroll, who was appalled at the mess his old chapter had become since he'd left. Without their leader, the Hells Angels in Halifax weren't interested in anything but partying and had lost their grip on the prostitution and, particularly, drug markets. They had piled up massive debts with Carroll, and with other drug dealers who they had allowed to take over their territory. Kane was meeting up with Carroll's old friend Paul Wilson, a well-known owner of several Halifax bars, to deal with the chapter and recruit a small army of tougher young men to take back the city.

* * *

While Stadnick was moving his chess pieces around the board in hopes of an Ontario takeover, things started to unravel a bit in Winnipeg. Although Stadnick had done a remarkable job with the Redliners, his puppet gang there, all the really experienced bikers in Winnipeg ran with Los Brovos or the Spartans, and the best of them were Los Brovos. While the Redliners looked good as bodyguards and threw a decent party, it was with the members of Los Brovos that Stadnick did his real business. He trusted them to sell Hells Angels drugs in Winnipeg and, in the spring of 1996, told Ernie Dew, their president, to prepare to become a prospective Hells Angels chapter.

In an effort to extend more goodwill and to demonstrate the brotherhood between chapters, Mike McCrea, who was running the Halifax chapter while Carroll was in Montreal, invited David Boyko, a former president of Los Brovos and still one of the most popular members, out east for a party. At first, Boyko didn't want to go, but when

McCrea insisted, he agreed. He didn't have a good time for long. One of the other guests at the party was Magnussen, and they didn't get along. Drunk and stoned by the time Boyko arrived, Magnussen had gained his current boss's brashness and pride, but had none of Steinert's charm to temper it. Magnussen had lost a great deal of money in a bad drug deal in Winnipeg the previous year and blamed Los Brovos. He'd never liked Boyko and, since he was the first member of Los Brovos he'd seen in a long time, he took out his anger on him.

The big man they called "Bam Bam" approached Boyko with his fists clenched and demanded to know where his money was. Boyko tried to calm him down, saying he didn't know what he was talking about. Before he could finish, Magnussen took a swing. The fight didn't last long. A group of guests pulled them apart and threw Magnussen out. Later that weekend, Boyko's body was found on a gravel road in nearby Dartmouth.

The news devastated many in Los Brovos, where Boyko was extraordinarily well-liked (the primary reason Stadnick had urged McCrea to invite him to Halifax). His funeral was a hugely lavish affair with members of Los Brovos, the rival Spartans and clubs from all over the prairies (primarily the Grim Reapers of Alberta) in attendance. McCrea attended in hopes that it would help convince the bikers in Winnipeg that Boyko's death was an isolated incident, a bit of one-on-one violence that had nothing to do with the Hells Angels. It didn't work. Nobody at the funeral would acknowledge his presence and the members of Los Brovos turned their backs whenever he approached.

Although some Hells Angels in Montreal told him to give up on Winnipeg—some even believed he might be murdered for revenge—Stadnick wouldn't entertain the thought. He'd worked too hard on Winnipeg, particularly on Los Brovos, and he wasn't about to allow some idiot to waste it. Back in Winnipeg, the members of Los Brovos seethed in relative silence for a couple of months until the night of May 11, when a drug deal between a number of their associates and three members of the Redliners went bad. There was no negotiation. The three unlucky Redliners were beaten, kicked, burned, sliced and mutilated beyond recognition, with much of the torture occurring before their deaths. Perhaps the killers were symbolically taking out their frustration on Stadnick or the Hells Angels, because when he arrived in Winnipeg to help make peace, two members of Los Brovos met him at the airport. They weren't exactly friendly, but they didn't kill him either.

Chapter 9

With the implications of Richard "Crow" Émond's assassination still sinking in, the Rock Machine murdered a second full-patch Hells Angel on December 16, 1996. Quebec City member Bruno Van Lerberghe was eating a plate of fries and gravy in Bar Rest-O-Broue II in Vanier when a gunman shot him in the face and fled on foot. In addition to taking down a second full-patch, Van Lerberghe's murder also extended the shooting war to Quebec City, which had until then escaped much of the violence Montreal had suffered. Before New Year's, three more men would be shot in the area, all of them with connections to biker gangs.

Even the Nomads weren't safe. The day after Van Lerberghe's murder, the elite bikers effectively lost a member for the first time. When Richard "Rick" Vallée was on trial for conspiracy to murder Robert Luduc, a Joker he felt wasn't working hard enough, few expected a conviction. The only major witness to give evidence against him was Serge Quesnel, and discrediting his testimony had become routine in Quebec. When he was acquitted, the Jokers in the audience applauded. But Vallée had one more matter to take care of before he could leave. On another floor of the same courthouse, Vallée participated in a hearing with the U.S. Drug Enforcement Agency, which was seeking his extradition so he could stand trial for the murder of one of their informants.

Back in 1993, Lee Carter was a bartender at a bowling alley in Champlain, N.Y., just south of the Canadian border. After Vallée approached the clean-cut young man about ferrying "a package" (the DEA said it was cocaine) from New York City to Montreal, Carter went to police. Vallée was arrested, but before he could stand trial, Carter's Porsche exploded and he was killed—parts of his car landed on the roof of the bowling alley and his right leg was found under another car 30 feet away. It's a fact well known to Hells Angels that U.S. penalties are usually much harsher than Canadian ones and that prosecutors were often more effective in convincing juries of bikers' guilt. Although they didn't ask for the death penalty, which would have jeopardized the extradition order, the DEA had a strong case. Vallée knew he would likely go to an American prison for life. He was taken away in handcuffs to await another hearing. Before it came, Vallée was sent to a hospital for surgery on an abscess in his jaw. When a guard took him to the shower, he was confronted by a man who put a gun to his head. Vallée and his accomplice tied and gagged the guard and Vallée went home, packed his bags and flew to Costa Rica with a passport bearing the name Guy Turner.

Although civic governments had been begging for strong anti-gang laws, none had been passed. When a strip club manager in Lac-Saint-Charles happened upon a bomb at the bar's front door on New Year's Day, it was clear that the war had moved to the Quebec City area. When he heard that a real estate agent had shown a nearby mansion to some bikers, Richard Blondin took action. The mayor of Saint-Nicolas, the suburb where the Hells Angels had their clubhouse, he drafted a bill that would outlaw the fortification of buildings. Although it wouldn't apply to existing buildings, he hoped that it would prevent the Hells Angels from acquiring any more buildings for puppet clubs or having any other clubs move in.

Two weeks later, Quebec public security minister, Robert Perrault, who replaced Ménard after the Desrosiers incident, started a task force of SQ and local police to help identify bars and other establishments connected with the Hells Angels or Rock Machine.

By the end of January, the Groupe Régional d'Intervention sur le Crime Organisé (GRICO) had closed down two biker bars in Quebec

City. But no amount of lobbying by Perrault would get the federal government to pass the anti-gang law that police forces in Quebec wanted. Their plan was to make membership in what the government identified as a gang illegal and allow police to arrest a member of an organization like the Hells Angels and worry about specific charges later. That would be far different from the usually successful Racketeer-Influenced and Corrupt Organizations (RICO) law in the U.S., which had failed twice when used against the Hells Angels, and would almost certainly contravene the Canadian Charter of Rights and Freedoms. Instead, they got Bill C-95, which instituted minimum sentences for crimes committed "for the benefit of, at the direction of or in association with" a criminal organization and which also says: "Every one who . . . participates in or substantially contributes to the activities of a criminal organization knowing that any or all of the members of the organization engage in or have, within the preceding five years, engaged in the commission of a series of indictable offenses . . . of which the maximum punishment is imprisonment for five years or more . . . is guilty of an indictable offense and liable to imprisonment for a term not exceeding fourteen years."

In effect, if the federal government can prove that a person is part of a group in which the member knows its members have committed crimes in the last five years, he or she is liable to imprisonment. That passage struck a chord with the leadership of the Hells Angels. After a suggestion one police officer said came directly from Stadnick, eight members who had no convictions over the last five years split off and formed a new chapter with a name reminiscent of the old Sorel vs. Laval days: Hells Angels Montreal South.

But while police were getting more legal power, they were losing manpower. After Carol Daigle and Louis-Jacques Deschênes were arrested for plotting to kill Nomad Normand "Biff" Hamel, the Montreal police pulled out of Carcajou. "Those were the top guys in the Dark Circle. With them gone, they must have thought that was the end of the Alliance," said an SQ officer who was sure Montreal's pull-out doomed the task force. "It was like they declared the Hells Angels the winners and then went home."

But the bombs kept on coming. On March 11, 1997, a man crashed a Jeep Cherokee into the Quebec City Hells Angels clubhouse in Saint-Nicolas, jumped out and then triggered a remote-controlled bomb. The blast was huge, knocking off the front door of the heavily fortified building and shattering windows for blocks. When a newspaper ran a picture of a month-old baby in a crib full of broken glass, public outrage boiled over into action. On March 16, a group of over 600 Saint-Nicolas residents held a protest outside the Hells Angels clubhouse. While members inside videotaped the protest's ringleaders, angered citizens gave speeches, sang songs and chanted slogans about how much they wanted the bikers to leave. When Blondin, long a foe of the bikers, arrived to give a speech, the crowd fell silent. He threw away his notes, looked at the clubhouse and said: "allez" ("go away"). It worked. On March 24, the clubhouse went up for sale. The Hells Angels planned to move to a quieter neighborhood.

After four bombs went off in ten days in Montreal, it was obvious that the war was raging again. Unable to get any more help from Ottawa, municipalities took their own initiative. The city of Montreal closed the clubhouses of the Rockers and the Rock Machine over little-used safety regulations. Their huge metal doors and bullet-proof glass prevented escape or rescue in the event of a fire. Although both clubs quickly made the necessary renovations and moved back in, their buildings were far less secure. Chicoutimi, a city largely untouched by the biker war, responded to the founding of a local puppet club (Satan's Guard) by passing a law that would allow the seizure of loud motorcycles. The Satan's Guard moved to nearby Jonquière, taking Autoroute 70, just outside the Chicoutimi line, when they rode out of town.

* * *

Still enraged over the Boyko murder, Stadnick took action. Although Kane told the RCMP that Carroll had hired Tousignant to murder Magnussen, it's hard to believe Stadnick wasn't actually behind it. Not only had Magnussen compromised Stadnick's years of work in Winnipeg—potentially putting his very life in danger—he'd turned his back on his old friend and teamed up with Stadnick's biggest rival, Steinert. Magnussen's death would go a long way toward cooling tempers out west and would also weaken Steinert's position considerably.

When Tousignant did nothing for months, Stadnick, Stockford and Carroll met with Kane and offered him $10,000 for the job. Magnussen was a friend of his (which is probably why he was chosen), but Kane knew it was unwise for someone in his position to say no to a Nomad, let alone three of them, so he accepted.

Although Kane was a murderer, he didn't like the thought of killing his friend, no matter how much it would help his career; and he was frightened of what Steinert would do if he found out. So Kane went to the RCMP and told them about the plot. The police sent two of their most convincing men to Magnussen's house. On two occasions, the officers spoke to him about how much danger he was in (without mentioning names) and offered him police protection if he'd turn informant.

Magnussen refused, later saying he laughed at the cops and threw them out of the house (a claim the police denied). Kane had no choice. He was preparing himself to murder Magnussen when Boucher found out about the plot and called an emergency meeting of the Nomads. He pointed out to the three conspirators that it was unthinkable under club rules for a prospect to kill a full-patch member and that, if they wanted Magnussen dead, one of them would have to do it. He suggested that Stadnick, who had the most to gain by Magnussen's elimination, should be the one.

Before anyone could strike, Magnussen got himself into deeper trouble. Drunk and stoned, Magnussen got into a shouting match with a young man who'd made fun of him in a bar in downtown Montreal. Never much of a debater, the huge Magnussen resorted to his fists and boots, beating the young man nearly to death. It was another very bad decision. The victim turned out to be Leonardo Rizzuto, son of Montreal mafia boss Vito Rizzuto. The small-time drug dealer and enforcer from Thunder Bay had made yet another powerful enemy in Montreal.

Freed from the task of killing Magnussen, Kane accepted another contract from Carroll. Paul Wilson, Carroll's friend in Halifax, had called him to complain about a man who had been their common friend. Robert MacFarlane was one of the richest men in Halifax. He'd started one of the East Coast's first cellular phone companies and, some say, sold cocaine as his primary business. Despite a waterfront house, a yacht and a beautiful young wife, MacFarlane grew bored and started consuming massive amounts of drugs and alcohol. And, like so many men, he became violent when he was drunk. A large, strong man with a decided mean streak, MacFarlane threw his weight around in local bars—often getting into fights or stiffing on his bill—and nobody had the courage to stop him. He'd decided to terrorize Wilson's Reflections bar and had been arrested for threatening to set fire to the establishment and, later, for sexually assaulting a waitress. Wilson wanted him stopped and Carroll, who was anxious to reassert the club in Halifax, wanted him dead. MacFarlane was not just a jerk; he was also a fairly successful drug dealer, exactly the kind that had cowed the local bikers into submission.

For $25,000 Kane agreed to the job. He took along Simard, who had relocated to Montreal and become Kane's driver and secret lover. Fitting the profile of drug runners—Quebec plates on a nondescript car driven at exactly the speed limit by two men with goatees and leather jackets—they were stopped by RCMP officers on the Trans-Canada Highway just outside Fredericton, New Brunswick. When Kane objected to a search, the police had no cause to hold them and let them go. Kane later joked that he'd saved the officers' lives because Simard, who had a handgun tucked under his belt, had always longed to kill a cop.

Kane and Simard tailed MacFarlane for three days before they finally found him alone. When they saw his black Jeep Grand Cherokee speed by, they followed in their rented white Buick. MacFarlane led them down St. Margaret's Bay Road out of town and into the Lakeside Industrial Park on the shore of Ragged Lake. Kane and Simard drove past as they noticed another car pull in and park beside MacFarlane's Jeep. It was Claude Blanchard, an old friend of the intended victim's, who'd arrived to look at the car collection MacFarlane kept in a warehouse. When Blanchard and his dog, Jazz, got out of the car, MacFarlane was complaining about being followed by some cops in a white car. As if on cue, Kane and Simard pulled up.

MacFarlane told Blanchard to wait while he dealt with them, but he followed because Jazz had already run over to greet the visitors. After

MacFarlane asked them "what the fuck they wanted," Simard rolled down the driver's window, pointed a revolver at him and pulled the trigger. Click. Nothing. Jazz and Blanchard took off and MacFarlane tried to get back to his car, about 100 feet away. After three more pulls, the hammer found a cartridge and Simard shot MacFarlane in the chest. As MacFarlane dropped and staggered to get up, Simard got out of the car to get a better shot. Frustrated with the still jamming .38, he pulled a 9mm out of the waistband of the rain pants he had over his jeans. The gun caught on the snap and the pants were around Simard's ankles when he pumped another shot into MacFarlane, who went down again. After he struggled out of his pants, Simard walked over to where MacFarlane's body lay and put two more bullets into his neck. Kane got out of the car, walked over to MacFarlane's body and fired two shots. They were just for show. Forensic officers later found the bullets from Kane's gun deeply embedded in the mud beside MacFarlane's head.

Things began looking up for the rest of the Hells Angels in Quebec. While they were being transported to trial on April 4, Hells Angels Louis "Mèlou" Roy and Sylvain "Baptiste" Thiffault were surprised to see Rock Machine associate Robert Hardy shoved into the same armored truck. When the doors opened again at the courthouse, Hardy was carted away in an ambulance, fighting for his life. With only Quesnel's easily discredited testimony against them, both bikers were sure they would be acquitted; they were, in fact, released on bail. Shortly after they returned to Trois-Rivières, six members of area puppet gangs disappeared. Without any explanation to wives or girlfriends, the homes of each of the men were visited by other bikers who cleaned them out of anything that could be traced back to their clubs.

The Hells Angels' lucky streak continued in the spring when Carcajou, weakened but not out of the picture, came down hard on the Alliance. On May 20, they arrested Giovanni Cazzetta (who had rejoined the gang after his release from prison) and Richard Matticks, second in command of the East End Gang, on drug charges. Later that day, they caught Serge "Merlin" Cyr and charged him with attempted murder; his intended victim had been Boucher. The next day, 23 people were arrested on a variety of charges after a raid on 24 locations associated with the Rock Machine. Carcajou also confiscated $4 million in assets, including 350 sticks of dynamite that had been stolen from a construction site in Rimouski. Two days later, a pair of Rock Machine associates carrying handguns and cocaine were arrested just off the 401 in Tilbury, Ontario, less than 30 miles from the U.S. border.

The gang was struck by another set of arrests after Carcajou officers discovered how Rock Machine members and associates were supplying their dealers in Donnacona prison. A priest who ministered to the prisoners was caught by a member of the Rock Machine while having sex with an inmate. The biker threatened to tell the authorities unless the priest, who was never searched by the guards, agreed to act as a drug mule. Reluctantly, he agreed. When they were finally caught, the priest and his supplier, a former policeman whose stepson (another Rock Machine associate) was the inside contact for the scheme, went to different prisons.

Things were going so badly for the Rock Machine that Fred Faucher, who had been vaulted to third in command of the club after arrests and murders had thinned out the top ranks, secretly wrote a letter to the Bandidos in Sweden. The Bandidos were a Texas-based gang with a patch that featured a pudgy, stereotypical Mexican bandit in an oversized sombrero, armed with a pistol and what appears to be a pirate sword. They were rapidly growing in power and numbers throughout the world. The Bandidos in Sweden were fighting a war with the Hells Angels and managing to keep them at bay. Although the Scandinavian war didn't have nearly as much bloodshed as the one in Quebec, both sides frequently used automatic weapons and military-issue grenades and rocket launchers. Looking for friends, advice and weapons, Faucher asked the Swedish Bandidos if they would be interested in a merger.

* * *

Things were tough all over. After Operation Dismantle, Satan's Choice struggled to rebuild. Most of the members had gotten out of jail, but the club was in financial disarray after the cops took and then auctioned off most of their possessions. Hamilton was no different. Back in the role of president, Johnny K-9 leaned heavily on his members to make more money. Besides pushing them to sell more pot, cocaine, steroids and counterfeit cash, he also expected members to take more jobs as enforcers and debt collectors for the mafia.

When he announced that the club was demanding a bigger share of its members' profits, Jimmy Rich complained. On the morning of July 27, 1997, Rich answered a knock on the front door of his home. It was K-9. Without a word, he beat the living shit out of Rich. Two days later, K-9 visited Rich at Hamilton General Hospital. After admiring the job he'd done, K-9 produced the ownership for Rich's Harley (he'd grabbed it when he rummaged through Rich's house after the beating and before the ambulance arrived) and demanded Rich sign it over. Since K-9 had already beaten him severely in front of his house in broad daylight, Rich realized he'd have little problem killing him in a hospital room. He signed over the bike and, when he got out, went back to work for K-9, who rode his new bike every day.

* * *

At Kane's next meeting with the RCMP, they asked him if he knew Simard. Kane assured him he did and described him as "unpredictable" and violent. He also described him as about 150 pounds, although (stomach-stapling and all), Simard was actually closer to double that figure. The rest of the sketch was accurate, though; after the MacFarlane killing, Simard considered himself something of a badass. Just days after he returned to Quebec City, he murdered a man who mentioned a crime Simard had committed back in Montréal.

After a Jamaican holiday with Kane and his two sons, Simard returned to Montreal. He started hanging around with some of Kane's friends who called themselves the Commandos. They were a bunch of biker wannabes who did dirty work for the Rockers. When a job came up, Simard was told it was his turn. As chance would have it, a team made up of small-time street-level dealers who worked for the Rockers were slated to play a similar team of Rock Machine associates in an East Montreal ball hockey league. Convinced the visitors needed to realize they were on Rockers' turf, Commandos boss Pierre Provencher told Simard to take care of Jean-Marc Caissy, the team's best player and a rising star who many thought would eventually become a full-patch member of the Rock Machine.

To make sure Simard knew what he meant, Provencher told him to "make it ugly." Simard did his job. He hung around the parking lot until the game finished and walked up to a man who fit Caissy's description. After a jovial "hey, Caissy" determined his identity and got him to turn around, Simard shot Caissy in the face five times. After the murder, he headed to Pro-Gym, a Rockers and Hells Angels hangout, to lift weights and brag about the killing. Sloppily, he left the .357 Magnum in his locker. Further emboldened, Simard took another job the following night. A small-time dealer, like the ones Simard defended at the hockey arena, had stiffed a Rocker on a debt; he had been spotted at a video game arcade in the East End. Simard and seven other toughs affiliated with the Rockers waited for the boy to emerge. When he did, Simard smacked him on the back of his head with a baseball bat and kept swinging until his victim was twitching involuntarily on the sidewalk.

Although Simard was proving his worth as a weapon, he was angering many of his peers by constantly talking about his exploits, often in public places. In the middle of a war, with Carcajou agents and informants everywhere, that kind of thing was dangerous. The other Commandos steered clear of him. Kane, who was no longer interested in being his lover, decided it was time to turn him in. He told the RCMP it was Simard who had killed Caissy.

The official RCMP story was that a janitor at the Pro-Gym cut the lock off Simard's locker after the gym closed, discovered the gun and called the police. After matching the other items in the locker to video from the security camera in the gym's entrance, police matched Simard to the weapon. But many Hells Angels and Rockers left their stuff in their lockers overnight and the cleaning staff knew better than to disturb them. When the police tracked him down, Simard broke down almost immediately. In exchange for his confession to the Caissy murder and information on the Commandos and Rockers, he would receive a 20-year sentence with a chance of parole after serving 12, as well as

liposuction and financial help after he left prison. Immediately, he rat-
ted on fellow Commandos Provencher, Steven Falls, Patrick Ménard-
Pascone and Gregory "Picasso" Wooley. Part of Simard's deal was that
he also enumerate all of the crimes he'd ever committed that had not
been discovered. The police promised that they wouldn't prosecute him
for them; they just wanted to close the books on old unsolved cases.
Simard quickly agreed and rattled off the names of the people he'd shot
or beaten. One name surprised the police: Robert MacFarlane.

It was a busy time for Kane. He'd just bought a house near
Steinert's mansion and Gilles "Trooper" Matthieu had sponsored
him for prospective Nomads membership. On April 30, at what he
thought was a routine meeting with his Montreal RCMP contacts in
the Longueuil Ramada, Kane was arrested by Halifax RCMP for the
murder of Robert MacFarlane. After a two-hour flight to the RCMP's
Nova Scotia headquarters in Bible Hill, the interrogators started in
on him. No matter what the question was, Kane's answer was always
the same "I don't know fuck-all." The Halifax officers didn't give up as
easily as Simard. Although working with Carroll, Stockford, Stadnick
and Steinert had improved his English to the point where he understood every word the officers were saying, they brought in a French-
speaking interrogator. He was even less successful.

When they told him they had him trapped, that they had enough
evidence to put him away for a long, long time, Kane looked his interrogators up and down, and said: "Okay, take me to court." But the
Halifax RCMP wasn't entirely out of ammunition. After the video
cameras were turned off, two detectives looked him in the eye and told
him that they knew he was an informant for the RCMP in Montreal
and, if that information just happened to get out, Kane would be killed
the moment the bars closed behind him. He called their bluff. After
the spectacular and repeated failure of informants like Serge Quesnel,
Kane realized he didn't have too much to fear from Simard, whose
credibility was even easier to pick apart. Kane wasn't going to make a
deal with the Halifax RCMP; he wouldn't even accept their offer of
protective custody. He'd take his chances in jail—it was Simard's word
against his.

* * *

The recent spate of arrests had weakened the Alliance and convinced the Hells Angels they were on the ropes. With the war winding down, the Hells Angels became increasingly focused on their enemies in the authorities and within their own organization. An edict even came down from the Nomads that Hells Angels and their associates stop wearing their colors in public and reduce the size and number of parties. After the police found the bomb in the Hydro van on August 23, Boucher became convinced there was a snitch in the Hells Angels.

The cops knew exactly where the van was and what to look for; it didn't seem possible for them to know what was going on without a tip. Worse yet, an SQ officer flippantly let it slip that they had a mole in the Hells Angels' inner circle. Cops try to intimidate suspects with claims like that all the time, but this time Boucher thought there was more to it, especially after other officers got angry at the one who told him. Although he'd been loyal to him in prison, Stéphane "Godasse" Gagné was Boucher's prime suspect. It was his bomb the police mysteriously found and Boucher figured that Gagné could have chickened out of his first job, especially with the Desrosiers incident fresh in everyone's memory.

His fears were unfounded. Gagné was proving his worth with the Rockers. While serving under the watch of Boucher's right-hand man, Tousignant, and Paul "Fonfon" Fontaine, Gagné distinguished himself as a drug salesman and frequently lobbied to prove his worth to the club in other ways. Before they'd let him join a "football team" (what the Montreal Hells Angels called their killing squads), they told him he had to wait. But Gagné was too ambitious and impatient for that. Christian Bellemare was an old friend of his and had been selling his drugs since the days before Gagné got involved with the Hells Angels. Their long-standing friendship had allowed Bellemare a certain amount of leeway as far as debts were concerned, but when he'd run up a $12,000 tab at the same time Gagné needed to prove a point, he was in big trouble.

In the spring of 1997, Gagné and another would-be Rocker, Steve Boies, invited Bellemare up to a party in the Laurentians. After they got good and drunk at a chalet bar, Gagné suggested they go outside for a joint. When they were out of sight of the chalet windows, Gagné pulled out a gun. Realizing he was the intended victim, Bellemare took off and started climbing over one of the snowbanks that surrounded the parking lot. Just as he was getting over the top, Gagné shot him and Bellemare tumbled over backwards onto the pavement. They were surprised to see he wasn't dead, so Gagné grabbed the barely conscious man by the shirt, pointed the gun at his forehead and pulled the trigger. It jammed. Exasperated, he put his hands around Bellemare's throat and started squeezing. When Gagné was satisfied the man was dead, he left the body where it was, and he and Boies kicked enough snow over it so it wouldn't be discovered until they were back in Montreal. The plan probably would have worked if they had killed Bellemare, but they hadn't. Strangled merely into unconsciousness, the victim dug himself out of the snow and made it back into the bar where a waitress called 911. Although Gagné had not managed to kill anybody, he'd made his point. He was certainly willing to become a murderer.

Boucher was becoming obsessed with the idea that he had a rat in his midst. Since he couldn't find out who was telling the cops about what the Hells Angels were doing, his plan was to make the cops too scared to do anything about it. Under his new plan, the Hells Angels would murder police officers, prosecutors, judges and others who tried to put members behind bars, thereby inciting enough fear in the authorities to leave the Hells Angels alone and to ensure that, even if a biker was arrested, he'd never be convicted. Of course, the plan also had a personal side. Like many organized crime leaders, Boucher had very little love for authority figures and he wouldn't have minded seeing a few of them dead. So to kick off the operation, Boucher targeted the people he hated most, the ones he considered stupid and beneath his contempt, the ones who had treated him the worst over the years: prison guards. And, although Boucher didn't realize it, with Kane behind bars, there would be nobody to warn the RCMP.

True to the Nomads' philosophy, Boucher pushed the job down to his underlings, Tousignant and Fontaine. Although both men had a great desire to please their boss, neither wanted to take on such a hazardous job. According to Vincent, the man who claimed to be friends with both Boucher and Stadnick at the time, the belief among Montrealers at the time was that when a biker killed another biker, the police and prosecutors considered it a natural part of the business they were in. When a biker killed a civilian, it was sad but fairly routine. But if a biker were to kill an authority figure, he would be in real trouble. But Boucher wanted a prison guard dead, so it had to happen. This was the kind of job that normally would have fallen to Kane, but he was in jail awaiting trial on the MacFarlane murder, so Tousignant and Fontaine turned to another eager young thug, Stéphane "Godasse" Gagné.

They could hardly have picked a better candidate. Gagné was obsessed with becoming a Hells Angel, and he had a personal grudge against prison guards. Not only had they thrown him into the heart of Rock Machine territory in Bordeaux, but a group of seven guards had beaten him severely in Sorel. He jumped at the chance to take one down. As with many East Enders, when Gagné thought of jail or prison, he thought of the nearby facility in Rivière-des-Prairies, a sort of holding pen for maximum-security prisoners on their way to court. After he cased the prison several times under the cover of darkness, Gagné found a section of the chain-link fence he could crawl under. From there, he found a spot in the trees where he could watch the parking lot. After a few nights, he fixed on a target.

Of all the cars that arrived and left—mostly rusted old minivans or cheerless economy cars—one stood out. Five nights a week, a man in a suit, who left earlier than all the others at shift change, strode into a brilliantly white spotless Buick Park Avenue that was always parked in the closest spot to the door. Clearly, he was someone important. Not wanting to take any chances, Gagné followed him out of the parking lot one night. Gagné knew that unless he got his victim on the highway, he'd never be able to get away from the crime scene. He was disappointed when he tailed the man in the big white Buick. Instead of turning off on the Autoroute Métropolitaine into the suburbs, the Buick kept driving down Boulevard Henri-Bourassa into the city. Disappointed, Gagné was mentally running through his list of potential victims when he got an urgent page to report to Boucher's office.

When he arrived at Rue Bennett, Tousignant was waiting outside. He took Gagné to a bar and told him that Boucher was getting impatient for results and that they would be working together from now on. The plan was simple. Gagné and Tousignant would follow a prison guard onto the Autoroute Métropolitaine on a motorcycle, kill him just before the bridge to Laval, cross over, dump the bike in a mall parking lot and drive away in a stolen car. When it came time to do the job on June 26, Tousignant picked the most un-Harley bike he could find, a wildly low-slung silver Suzuki Katana racer. The two men sped to Rivière-des-Prairies and waited in the darkness until shift change. When the first guard left in an old Jeep Cherokee, they followed him until he passed the Autoroute turnoff. Tousignant then stopped the Suzuki, turned it around and twisted his right wrist until they were back at the prison.

Just as they arrived, they saw a short, heavyset guard get into a white Plymouth Voyageur and drive out of the parking lot. Tousignant followed. When the minivan turned onto the Autoroute Métropolitaine, the bikers knew they'd found their quarry. Diane Lavigne, the daughter of a veteran prison guard and one of the first women ever to serve as a guard in Quebec, was driving in the slow lane. She only took the Autoroute Métropolitaine about a mile before she turned off on the Chemin-des-40 Arpents to her house in St-Eustache. Tousignant brought the Suzuki even with the minivan. Gagné pulled out his revolver and fired into the open window three times. He hit her twice, the second one passed through her arm and her left lung before coming to a stop in her backbone. She was dead before the Voyageur came to a stop on the shoulder. Tousignant then sped into Laval, where they dumped the bike, burned their clothes and fled in a stolen Voyageur. Danielle Leclair was another Rivière-des-Prairies guard; she was driving on Autoroute Métropolitaine about a quarter mile behind Lavigne. She saw the Suzuki, even swerved to avoid it at one point, and heard some cracking noises. When she recognized Lavigne's minivan by the side of the road, she considered stopping, but didn't.

When news of the murder hit the media the next day, Gagné, Tousignant, Fontaine, Boucher and others celebrated. They were surprised to find out the victim was a woman and, after some ribbing, Boucher put his arm around Gagné and told him not to feel bad. He didn't. After receiving his Rockers prospective membership, Gagné

interpreted their gratitude as an indication that he was one more murder away from his full patch. But it would have to wait. About a week
later, a young drug dealer was driving around the East End in a stolen
car when he spotted Gagné wearing his Rockers patch (Fontaine and
Tousignant earned prospective Nomads memberships). Eager to make
his own Rock Machine prospective patch, the driver plowed his car
into Gagné's Harley and fled. Gagné suffered injuries bad enough to
keep him out of commission until late August. When he emerged, he
resumed his duties as a drug dealer and started planning for another
hit. Fontaine advised against hitting another prison guard. Without
any information from Kane, Lavigne's murder was being treated as an
isolated incident. Although the hit was professionally done, some ele-
ments—like the Japanese bike—put the police off the scent. Another,
similar killing might make it obvious who the real killers were. But
Fontaine was missing the point. Boucher's master plan was to de-
stabilize the Quebec government and make them fear the Hells Angels.
Following a model set down by the cocaine barons of Colombia,
Boucher wanted to terrorize the police and judiciary into submission.
Making it obvious was a key element to success. The next victim would
be another prison guard.

On September 3, Gagné and Fontaine were hiding in the trees
at Rivière-des-Prairies when they selected a victim. They followed
Richard Auclair and Gagné suggested they kill him at a stoplight just
before he turned onto the Autoroute. Fontaine, who had appeared nervous to his partner from the start, begged off, saying he didn't think
the escape route was safe. Gagné disagreed, but respected his decision.
On the ride home, Fontaine revealed that he was having a problem
with killing a guard. "Killing a Rock Machine—that doesn't bother
me; they're our enemies," he said, pointing out that he had no grudge
against the guards. "They mean nothing to me." He also wanted to
make sure that Gagné knew that if they were caught they were guaranteed 25-year sentences. Fontaine's arguments didn't have much effect on his partner, though. Gagné had already murdered one guard
and was desperate for his full patch.

They were back in the woods again on September 8. When
Boucher found out that it was Fontaine who had hesitated, he wanted

to know why. Fontaine said he didn't like the risk of taking motorcycles, so Boucher got him a little Mazda 323 hatchback and a Dodge Caravan minivan. Not only was Fontaine back on the job, but Boucher suggested he be the triggerman, although Gagné would carry a gun for backup.

That morning, 12 buses left from Rivière-des-Prairies to pick up prisoners and, when one turned toward where the getaway Caravan was parked, the bikers followed it in the Mazda. As government vehicles must, the bus stopped when it came to a railway crossing. Robert Corriveau, the relief driver, was in the front passenger seat when he saw a fat man dressed in black in front of the bus. He appeared to have a gun. Before he could say anything, Fontaine climbed onto the hood of the bus and emptied his .357 Magnum in the direction of Pierre Rondeau, the driver. Through a shower of tiny glass cubes, three bullets entered his body. One bounced around inside, shredding most of his internal organs. Stunned, Corriveau watched as Fontaine slid off the hood and ran away, but he didn't see Gagné until he heard the click. Gagné's 9 mm, aimed at Corriveau's head, had jammed. Corriveau hid under the dashboard. Gagné slid off the hood and calmly walked around to the right-hand side of the bus. Through the window in the door he could see Corriveau huddled in a ball and he shot every bullet he had before leaving. Somehow, every one of them missed Corriveau; but one hit Rondeau, whose heart was still faintly beating.

While Boucher was waging war on prison guards, the violence escalated again as the summer wound down. On the same night, two Hells Angels–associated bars were hit by Molotov cocktails and someone set fire to Sensations, Steinert's stripper/escort agency. Although many considered the fire just another salvo in what appeared to be an endless war, Steinert had enough enemies within his own club and in the mafia that it could have been almost anyone.

Further ambiguity arose on August 23. Louis "Mèlou" Roy was getting out of his black Mercedes in the parking lot of his father's motel when a masked man shot him four times and ran into a nearby getaway car. Police guarded Roy in the hospital and when he awoke a special team of investigators was sent in. Roy refused to answer any questions that the "pigs" asked and eventually threw them out of his room. They withdrew their protection and one was quoted (anonymously) by a newspaper speculating that it was the Hells Angels who had made the attempted hit in retaliation for Roy's bringing the bothersome Quesnel into the loop.

* * *

It was also the summer of Stadnick's masterful western surprise. Even from the beginning, he had left Boucher largely to his own devices in Quebec, stepping in only as he saw an opportunity for or a threat to his own interests. The result had been a slogging, blood-and-guts war in which bombings were commonplace, shootings were routine, innocent victims were part of doing business and the government of Quebec became the ultimate target. That wasn't Stadnick's way. He'd always rather buy a rival a beer than kick his head in. He knew that the way to succeed in the organized crime business is to seduce your rivals into working for you and give the police nothing to hang you with. That's how he conquered Alberta.

Like most places in Canada, the United States and Western Europe in the '60s and '70s, Alberta suffered through a period where disaffected young men jumped on motorcycles, wore leather jackets and went wild in the name of freedom. And like those other places, they saw the biggest and strongest groups of bikers swallow up or get rid of the smaller and weaker ones. At one point in the '70s, police say there were 35 distinct outlaw motorcycle gangs in the province. A half-dozen years later, there were four. The smallest of them, the Ghost Riders of Lethbridge, had survived mainly because of a strong working relationship with other Ghost Riders on the West Coast. But when Yves "Le Boss" Buteau extended prospective Hells Angels membership to the Satan's Angels in British Columbia, he did so under the condition that they get rid of all their competition in the area. In July 1978, the B.C. chapter of the Ghost Riders and Satan's Angels faced off and the Ghost Riders were routed. Without their Pacific Coast allies, the Lethbridge chapter knew they were an endangered species. When representatives of the Grim Reapers,

Alberta's biggest gang, showed up at their clubhouse with guns in November 1980, the Ghost Riders didn't fight. They just gave up their patches and retired.

The Hells Angels interfered in the Alberta gang wars again in 1980 when the Satan's Angels formed an alliance with the smallest surviving club, the Rebels. With the threat of the Satan's Angels (and, by extension, the Hells Angels) looming, the Grim Reapers called off plans to exterminate the Rebels and trained their sights on Calgary's King's Crew instead. In the spring and summer of 1983, Alberta endured a small-scale biker war. It started when the Grim Reapers showed up at the King's Crew clubhouse with guns and demanded the colors of everyone inside. Their burned, still-recognizable remains were sent to a Calgary paper to add public humiliation to the private one already suffered. The King's Crew vowed revenge and bombed an Edmonton Harley dealership which was associated with the Grim Reapers, but caused little damage. The Grim Reapers launched a crushing attack of bombings, shootings and abductions that caused the King's Crew to stop hostilities and go underground before Labor Day.

As tensions simmered between the Grim Reapers and the Rebels, the B.C. Hells Angels stepped in. They suggested that the Grim Reapers, based in Edmonton, and the Rebels, based in Calgary, divide the province. The Grim Reapers would take the north and the Rebels the south. Of course, the Hells Angels would supply drugs to both gangs. When a few members of the King's Crew regrouped and the Grim Reapers were poised to crush them again, the B.C. Hells Angels stepped in and guaranteed their survival. Before long, all three Alberta gangs were begging to become Hells Angels. Despite their involvement with all the gangs in Alberta, the B.C. Hells Angels—some say on orders from Stadnick—refused to grant any of them prospective membership.

When Stadnick himself started coming west, at first partying with all three clubs in Winnipeg, he started feeling the Alberta gangs out for their strength, their reach in their respective drug markets, and the quality of their leadership. In the summer of 1996, he decided that the Grim Reapers (who had since opened a chapter in Calgary, violating their agreement with the Rebels) were the best gang in

Alberta, and he offered them prospective membership. But there was a catch. Traditionally, members of prospect clubs wear half patches, but Stadnick convinced the Grim Reapers to wear their old colors while prospecting. The concept wasn't entirely unprecedented. The Aliens of New York City retained their patch while prospecting because they weren't sure they even wanted to be Hells Angels, and they were powerful enough to force the Hells Angels to bend the rules for them.

The Grim Reapers were no Aliens, but that's how Stadnick sold it to them—keep your own colors while prospecting—as though the Grim Reapers were trying the Hells Angels' colors out. But if the Grim Reapers were trying to play it cool, they failed. Not only did their 1996 Christmas card identify them as Hells Angels prospects, but so did the answering machine in their clubhouse. But it flew beneath the radar of local police and media. Although the frequent presence of luminaries such as Stadnick and de facto B.C. chief Rick Ciarniello, raised red flags, it raised the wrong ones. When a hundred rooms were reserved in a Red Deer hotel for a fictitious motorcycle racing company, reporters began frantically writing about how the Hells Angels were going to move a chapter to Alberta (like the Demon Keepers) or start a new one (like the Redliners), but they were caught off guard by what actually happened.

The people of Alberta, many of whom were there because they were fed up with the regulation and bureaucracy of the rest of Canada, welcomed the Hells Angels with open arms. Not only did published polls indicate that the overwhelming majority of Albertans believed the Hells Angels had a right to exist, they came out in droves to meet them. So did the police. At provincial boundary crossings, police set up roadblocks. They stopped everyone who looked like an outlaw biker and forced them to produce their license, registration and insurance papers. Familiar with the way police do things, the Hells Angels were ready and made it through without any major incidents. What they weren't ready for was what waited for them on the other side: cheers and applause.

Curious Albertans took pictures of the Hells Angels, often posing with their families and children, and asked them to sign autographs. Not since the days when the California hippies fatuously referred to them as "the people's police," had the Hells Angels been so warmly embraced. When the party finally ended on July 23, the

Grim Reapers' two chapters became the Hells Angels Edmonton and Calgary, the Rebels were granted prospect status in Red Deer and the King's Crew had their continued existence ensured as a puppet club for all of them.

The Albertans proved their worth almost immediately. A week after the party, longtime Grim Reaper and new Hells Angel Terry Malec applied for a Firearms Acquisition Certificate and was turned down. Since he already had two FACs for guns he'd used for years while hunting, he was surprised. When he found out why he'd been turned down, he was angry. Despite the fact that Malec had no criminal record, RCMP officer Joe Coulombe refused to approve his application because he was a Hells Angel. Predictably, both sides assembled their lawyers and had it out in court. The RCMP brought in a biker expert from Montreal who spoke of the horrors the war had brought to Quebec, but it was in vain. Judge Jeanne Burch ruled that Malec had the same right to a gun as any other Canadian without a record, no matter what jacket he wore. It was a huge judgment. The Alberta courts said, as the bikers had always maintained, that being a member of the Hells Angels does not make you a criminal.

But Stadnick didn't coast. Ever PR-savvy, he managed to make the most out of a horrifying turn of events in Winnipeg. In September, a pair of full-patch Spartans and two friends were arrested after they lured a teen-age girl into their clubhouse and violently raped her. It was a crime eerily similar to one that sent Spartans' chief Darwin Sylvester and a friend to prison on 1979, a crime many Winnipeggers remembered. Although Stadnick had already distanced himself from the Spartans and Redliners, he made sure everybody important knew that it was Los Brovos who were the Hells Angels' favorites in the area. He knew that if he could ensure that Los Brovos had a distinct identity in the public perception, they would look like "good" bikers in simple juxtaposition to the Spartans.

His plan came to fruition on October 18, when hundreds of Hells Angels and associates flooded into the city, ostensibly to celebrate Los Brovos' 30th anniversary. Large crowds turned out, although they weren't as blindly enthusiastic as the ones in Alberta a few months before. There were few skeptics, however, when the bikers arrived at

Los Brovos' east end clubhouse. Elmwood is the poorest section of Winnipeg and is home to many recent immigrants and First Nations families who had little reason to fear the bikers. When Los Brovos threw a massive street party, neighbors came out in droves. When reporters and photographers arrived, one smart biker got an idea. He got a visiting Joker to stand beside a hot dog cart and buy some neighborhood kids hot dogs, then instructed a cameraman from the *Winnipeg Free Press* to take a picture. It was pure theatrics, and it worked. The staged photo ran the next day with a caption that called it an example of "biker kindness."

But it wasn't just a social call. By the time the visitors left, Winnipeg had a prospective Hells Angels chapter. Later, chapter president Ernie Dew told reporters that, for him, the deciding factor was that Stadnick had already patched over the Grim Reapers, Los Brovos' old allies in the fight to keep the Hells Angels out of the prairies. Before he left, Stadnick sent over some of his toughest Quebec bikers to tell the Redliners they were disbanded. Not only had they not done enough to become Hells Angels, they weren't even fit to be a puppet club. Now that their purpose for existing was moot, they were in the way—except for one man. Bernie Dubois, the only Redliner who had proven himself a consistent money-maker for the club, was invited to join his old enemies in Los Brovos.

Stadnick gained more for the club and for himself than just new chapters. While the Hells Angels he'd left in Quebec had turned the corner in their war with the Rock Machine Alliance and moved onto bigger things, it had been costly and ugly. The media and public perceived Boucher as the architect of all the violence and had thoroughly demonized him. When he wasn't holed up in his Rue Bennett bunker listening to talk-radio callers demand his head, he was wearing body armor and surrounded by a brigade of bodyguards as police and would-be assassins stalked his every move. Stadnick, on the other hand, moved stealthily and comfortably throughout the country as the chapters in British Columbia dominated the drug and sex trades there with near-immunity to prosecution and the prairie bikers he'd personally brought into the fold rode through the streets to public acclaim and applause. Under what one source (a Rockers associate from

Montreal) claimed was Stadnick's urging, even Carroll had emerged from his drunken haze and restaked the Hells Angels' claim to Halifax and the East Coast. Stadnick's philosophy had played out almost precisely as planned. While ordering their underlings to do the dirty work, the Nomads had proven almost impervious to prosecution (the only exception, Vallée, was arrested for crimes committed before he was a Nomad), the Rock Machine were on the run and the Hells Angels had spread their influence throughout the country.

But it was also apparent that his quest was far from complete. Ontario still remained tantalizingly out of his grasp. Although he had managed to sneak his men into the Para-Dice Riders, they were still a minority voice—and hardly one known for its intelligence or stability—in the province's third-biggest club. He was a hunted man in his own hometown and, although he had managed to get a trickle of drugs into the area, his partners in Satan's Choice were making the real money. Still, it wasn't in Stadnick's nature to give up. He had a plan for Ontario, just as he had had for the rest of the country. There was just one annoying problem to deal with first. Steinert and Magnussen had to be stopped.

Chapter 10

His hand was shaking when he put down the phone. Although they had known each other for a while and had been married for a month, Scott Steinert's wife had never seen him scared before. He'd just gotten off the phone with his right-hand man, Donald Magnussen. She knew better than to ask what was wrong.

Although he enjoyed a rich sex life both on and off camera and owned five different escort agencies, Steinert had remained at least nominally with Louise, his girlfriend since high school. That changed in 1996, when he visited a restaurateur he had business dealings with, saw the man's daughter and immediately fell in love. Before long, he dumped Louise, moved Magnussen out of the mansion and into one of the three houses he'd had built on the grounds, and married the girl.

Many people who knew Steinert thought the marriage was an attempt to stave off immigration officials who were inching ever closer to his deportation as his appeals ran out. When his legal avenues dried up, Steinert approached some contacts in the nearby Kahnawake Mohawk territory about getting them to draw up some papers that stated he was a full-status member of the Mohawk Nation. First Nations status would allow him to live in Canada or the United States free of government interference. That plan fell through on September 23, 1997, when the Royal Canadian Mounted Police (RCMP) raided Kahnawake. Although the primary reason for the assault was to stem the flow of illegal weapons coming through the Mohawk territory, the widespread arrests effectively ended Steinert's attempt to claim First Nations status. Other sources claim the marriage was real and that Steinert was truly in love. "He even gave up the porno," pointed out one Death Riders associate.

And, on November 4, 1997, his wife saw the big man cry. The same thing happened at the little house outside where Magnussen hung up the phone, hugged his girlfriend and wept before saying goodbye. Earlier in the day, Steinert had received an important message that said he and Magnussen were to report to an urgent meeting with the Nomads that night. When he called Magnussen and they discussed it, they both realized it wouldn't be a party in their honor.

The consensus among forensic investigators is that the more grisly the mode of killing, the more hate the murderer has for the victim. If that's true, somebody really hated Steinert and Magnussen. It has never been positively determined who killed them, if they made it to the Nomads meeting or even if the meeting took place. What is clear is that on November 4, 1997, Steinert and Magnussen were beaten to death with hammers. Their horribly battered bodies were then wrapped in plastic, taken almost 200 miles downriver and dumped in the St. Lawrence at the historic village of Beauport.

While they were at the bottom of the river, two warrants were issued for Steinert's arrest. The police found evidence of drug dealing and immigration officials wanted to see him after he missed an extradition hearing. When he couldn't be found, the province seized Château Lavigueur and auctioned it off. While the paperwork was being straightened out, the former Steinert compound was put under 24-hour surveillance to foil any Hells Angels' attempts to burn it down.

* * *

Martin Clavel was a somewhat bumbling member of the Rock Machine who was arrested by the Sûreté du Québec (SQ) on August 27, 1997. The only thing special about his arrest was that he possessed something that had never been seen in Canada before: a "Support Your Local Bandidos" T-shirt. The press ran with it, widely reporting that the Bandidos were reinforcing the Rock Machine. But while the Hells Angels would never allow a non-member to wear their name or logo, the Bandidos will sell their gear to anyone. With that in mind, some voices claimed it was hype; but the Rock Machine, which was losing the war against the Hells Angels in Quebec, were looking for friends wherever they could find them.

Fred Faucher's letter to the Swedish Bandidos had paid dividends. The reply he received read, in part: "It is with great interest that we have read about the situation in Quebec. It's much the same conditions here in Scandinavia. We would like to hear more." Faucher and fellow Rock Machine members Paul "Sasquatch" Porter and Johnny Plescio were invited to the Bandidos Euro Run, where they met with, and were interviewed by, the international president from Texas and presidents from chapters in Sweden, France and Australia. Less than a month later, the Bandidos and Hells Angels signed a peace treaty on live national television in Denmark.

While many observers declared this pact ended hostilities between the Bandidos and Hells Angels worldwide, the opposite is actually true. The pact was a farce. Representatives of the Danish, Swedish and Norwegian governments had met with the leaders of both gangs and told them to sign the deal or their organizations would be outlawed. Realizing that none of those countries would hesitate to bring their militaries into the fight, the bikers signed. But it didn't make them friends and it didn't change things in Quebec. The Bandidos in Sweden—and more importantly, in Texas—were still very keen on the Rock Machine, and very much the enemies of the Hells Angels.

The potential for a merger took a step forward on September 11, 1997, when the Rock Machine's top two members—Claude "Ti-Loup" Vézina and Dany Légaré—went to prison on drug charges resulting from a raid in May. With them gone, Faucher—the man who had initiated the Rock Machine–Bandidos' alignment in the first place—became the highest-ranking member of the gang in Quebec City. His first executive decision was to repay his hosts in Europe with a party in Quebec. At the Loews Le Concorde hotel in Quebec City, Faucher threw a lavish party for the Bandidos, who attended from around the world. One notable Bandido who didn't make the party was Danish member Jan "Clark" Jensen, who had been deported from Canada two weeks earlier because of his lengthy criminal record. When a Quebec City uniformed officer recognized two Rock Machine associates on the sidewalk in front of the hotel, then noticed a mass of Harleys in the parking lot, he called for backup. When they arrived, they arrested six locals on outstanding warrants and deported Bandidos international vice-president George Wegers, the highest-ranking person at the party, back to the United States.

* * *

Prison guards and employees in Quebec were in a state of panic in the fall of 1997. Two of their peers had been professionally murdered and police had no real supects and no hard evidence. But the guards themselves were ready to make their own less formal investigation. Working day in and day out with many people who'd enjoy seeing them dead, the guards could make educated guesses as to which groups and individuals would be able to carry out such an elaborate plan. Many of them remembered the list of their names and home addresses found in a prisoner's cell in Archambault prison back in 1992. Even if the police didn't realize it, or didn't say it out loud, the prison guards knew who was killing them—the Hells Angels.

That fall, anxious guards noticed people taking pictures of their houses and cars. Some reported being followed as they drove to and from work and even on their jobs. Their panic turned to terror on October 14, when a prison guard's house was burglarized. While his most saleable items—TV, VCR, computer—were left untouched, the thieves did take something far more frightening—two complete guard uniforms, two extra shirts and a pair of handcuffs. Fed up with a lack of help from police, the prison guards took the investigation into their own hands. A combination of their own recollections and a brief, sometimes brutal, questioning of every man on his way into Bordeaux prison soon led them to the accurate conclusion that Stéphane "Godasse" Gagné had at least something to do with the murders. It made sense—

he was a vicious thug out to prove a point and he had experienced some really bad times with guards. Among the other names bandied about were André "Toots" Tousignant and Paul "Fonfon" Fontaine, who were also involved. As prisoners were released from Bordeaux and other institutions, they took what they'd learned from the guards' unsubtle investigation directly to the Hells Angels.

Serge "Pasha" Boutin was a successful drug dealer for the Pelletier brothers. He ran their operations in Montreal's gay village. When the war broke out, he sided with the Hells Angels and assumed the same role as a member of the Rockers. Just before Halloween, one of his street-level dealers—fresh out of Bordeaux—told him what the guards were saying. The next time he saw them, Boutin called Gagné and Fontaine into his office. He told them that the guards were spreading rumors that they were the killers. When neither said anything, Boutin waited until they left and called Boucher. Boucher then called Gagné and set up a meeting on the busy corner of Rue Ontario and Avenue de Lorimer. He told Gagné that the prison guards knew he was the murderer, and that they knew this because he was such a bastard to them behind bars. Gagné struggled to maintain his composure. He left the meeting wondering if he would be eliminated as a threat to Hells Angels' security.

A few days later, Mom Boucher arranged to meet Gagné on the sidewalk in front of his Rue Bennett headquarters. When he got there, Gagné started gushing about all the security precautions he had taken and that if the guards suspected him it was because he had fought with them in Sorel. Boucher calmed him down and told him it was time to hit another "screw." Gagné didn't understand; the police were everywhere and everybody knew the Hells Angels were behind the prison guard murders. Boucher laughed. "Not to worry, we'll do the police, we'll do judges and prosecutors too," he told Gagné. "But that's not for you, dear Godasse, you've already done your job." Then he gave Gagné a different assignment. He was to tail members of Montreal's Italian mafia in an inconspicuous gray Chrysler and videotape them using a camera concealed in a box of tissues. Nobody ever told him, but Gagné was sure Boucher was planning a war against the mafia.

Although the prison guards and public were outraged by what they perceived as a lack of action regarding the guard assassinations, the

Montreal police were quietly and effectively chipping away at the biker infrastructure. Under the codename Project HARM (Hells Angels, Rock Machine), police were buying drugs in bars undercover, then arresting the vendors and closing the establishments. It was running smoothly until the night of December 4, when four plainclothes cops were sent to bring down an escort agency in Rosemount that was known to have biker connections. When a frantic call for backup came in, the only available officer was André Bouchard, commander of the Montreal police. When he arrived he saw four cops, guns drawn, surrounded by 15 bikers and their women. The cops were screaming at the bikers, telling them to get on the floor. But the bikers were clearly unafraid of the officers and one even threatened them, saying, "You think you can shoot us all?"

Bouchard, a veteran of the days when officers beat up bikers on sight, made the difference. Arriving in his full dress uniform, complete with gold braid and gongs, he approached the biggest biker, sized him up, holstered his gun and then punched him in the jaw. The biker went down in a heap and the others got on the floor.

The police had stumbled upon treasure. In the back of the escort agency, they found a map of Montreal annotated with every Hells Angels–associated bar, complete with their contacts and whose responsibility it was to get them drugs. Armed with that information, Bouchard sent out every available officer that night. Before sunrise, the Montreal police arrested 28 Hells Angels associates, confiscated $2.5 million in drugs, 18 cars and 67 illegal weapons. But like a diamond amongst gold dust, they also found Steve Boies. There seemed to be little special about him, a regular street-level dealer, but when the police found almost four kilos of cocaine stashed in his house in Berthierville and a pager that linked him to a bombing attempt on a Rock Machine clubhouse, it was enough to put him away for a long, long time and he knew it. Boies then pulled out his get-out-of-jail-free card and started talking. He had some important friends and they had done some bad things.

Boucher, Gagné and Tousignant didn't know about the arrests. They were at Boucher's South Shore farmhouse going over the final details of an ambitious plan. The 20th anniversary of the Hells Angels in Canada was approaching and a celebration was scheduled for the following night. Boucher surmised that if the Rock Machine had any fight left in them, they'd almost certainly have to strike then. As part of a comprehensive overall security plan, he had rented two helicopters with the plan of putting Tousignant in one and Gagné in the other. They would circle the Sorel clubhouse and shoot any invaders from above. After much of the meeting was over, Gagné received a call on his cell phone and excused himself. Taking Tousignant's car, he sped down Route 132 until he came across a phone booth (Hells Angels never discuss anything of importance over cell phones) in Verchères. He called Benoît Cliche, his lawyer, back. It was bad news. Boies had been caught and had turned informant. Gagné sped home to St-Hubert, grabbed his wife, packed a few bags and got back on the road. He hadn't gotten very far on his way east when his wife convinced him to find a place to stay for the night. When he spotted a motel just outside St-Hyacinthe at 11 p.m., he stopped. As soon as he opened the door, he saw the lights and heard the sirens. The SQ had been tailing him since he'd left Montreal.

Back at the SQ offices in Montreal, Gagné sat in an interrogation room across the table from a faintly familiar face. His interrogator was Sgt. Robert Pigeon, the same officer who had made the arrest that sent him to Bordeaux in 1994. Pigeon told Gagné he knew about the attempted murder of Christian Bellemare. Gagné told him he wasn't going to talk and asked to call his lawyer. According to Gagné's later testimony, he tried three times between 3:00 and 3:30 a.m., but Cliche did not answer. Gagné returned to his seat and declared again that he had nothing to say. Pigeon knew Gagné and was pretty sure he lacked the intellect or ambition to mount two very intricate and successful attacks on the prison guards, especially when he recalled how poorly he'd pulled off the attempt on Bellemare's life. His theory was that if Gagné was actually just the triggerman (as Boies had assumed), he was the SQ's only chance at catching the architect of the assassinations. That man, Pigeon correctly surmised, was Boucher. Gagné called his lawyer again at 6:24 a.m.; there was still no answer. When he returned, he looked at his questioner and asked, "If I talk, how many years will I get?"

It says a lot about either Pigeon's persuasiveness or Gagné's character that he folded. In truth, Boies had told the police little of value. The only mention of Gagné that wasn't pure speculation was a reference to his asking Boies to clean his garage and get rid of some clothes. But Gagné didn't know that. After consulting with his wife, he made the deal. Another fact Gagné did not know until Pigeon told him was that he was liable for the murder of Pierre Rondeau, the second prison guard. Although he had never actually intended to shoot Rondeau, one of the bullets he'd shot at Robert Corriveau had hit him. Forensic experts determined that the bullet entered Rondeau's body before he died, making Gagné at least partially responsible for his murder. In Canada, the murder of two officials guarantees a mandatory 25-year sentence with no hope of parole. If the charge implicating him in Rondeau's murder was dropped, Gagné would face a 25-year sentence with a chance at parole after 15 years for the murder of Diane Lavigne. The police also offered $400 a month in cash and to drop any charges against his wife. Before talking to his lawyer, Gagné spilled his guts.

* * *

That night, December 4, the Hells Angels threw their anniversary party. It wasn't what they had envisioned. When Gagné didn't show—everyone knew he was to get his full patch that night—and the police laid off, it was obvious what had happened. Serge "Pasha" Boutin had been arrested that day and, as soon as he got out on bail, he told Boucher that Boies was definitely talking and that Gagné looked like he was about to break. Boucher assumed as much. He sent Tousignant out to get information. Although he couldn't confirm that Gagné was talking, he did tell his boss that he'd tried repeatedly to contact Hells Angels lawyers and none had responded. Boucher told Tousignant, who was one of two people (the other was Fontaine) who could link him to the murders, to stay in town.

A few hours later, Tousignant called again, complaining that he wasn't getting anywhere with the lawyers. Boucher told him not to worry and to meet him at his house as soon as he could. The moment he hung up the phone, Boucher called Sorel and asked them to send over some tough guys. The police never saw Tousignant alive again.

At Gagné's initial hearing on December 8, Cliche approached his former client, but the biker wouldn't speak to him. During the proceedings, Cliche asked the judge if he could confer with Gagné, but he was rebuffed again. Finally, the police informed Cliche that Gagné no longer desired his services. Fearing the worst, Boucher shut down the Nomads' Rue Bennett headquarters.

On the morning of December 18, moments after Gagné signed his confession, an arrest warrant was issued for Boucher. They knew where to find him. He had been receiving treatment for a tumor in his throat every Thursday and when he was finished, the police arrested him at the front doors of Notre-Dame hospital. He was scheduled for arraignment the next afternoon, but at 9 a.m., a Pontiac Trans-Am crashed through the doors of the courthouse. Although many assumed it was a bomb or an attempt to free Boucher, it was actually just a courthouse janitor who had a grudge against his employers.

* * *

Donny Peterson is quite a guy. A former president of the Para-Dice Riders who used to go by the nickname "Sleaze," Peterson is a definitive example of the way many bikers have tried to clean up their images. He has a successful business, Heavy-Duty Cycles in the east end of Toronto, claims not to smoke or drink, doesn't have a criminal record and even says he used to work as a social worker, although he doesn't say which organization he worked for, and none has claimed him. He gained some notoriety as a columnist writing about motorcycle repair and the Canadian Embassy in Cuba even flew him to Havana to help with a fledgling Harley riders' group there.

But many police officers have different memories of Peterson. "He used to be one of the most badass bikers in Ontario," said an Ontario Provincial Police (OPP) officer who didn't want to be identified. "He just remade himself and revised his personal history." Before long, the cleaned-up version of Peterson became a desired guest in Toronto social circles, and he met prominent investor and philanthropist Gareth Seltzer. Like lots of rich guys, Seltzer had bought a Harley.

Although he loved his bike, he didn't like the fact that police stopped him whenever they saw him and made him produce his license, registration and insurance before letting him proceed. Peterson commiserated and the two agreed that the cops were being unfair to bikers. But Seltzer wasn't just any rich guy; he was also chairman of the Empire Club of Canada. When Peterson filed suit against the OPP, Seltzer invited him to speak before the Empire Club, an honor he shared with such luminaries as Ronald Reagan, the Dalai Lama and many Canadian prime ministers. He was welcomed warmly. After a speech in which he joked about being labeled a "bad guy" and finished with "it can be very strange where you end up in life," Peterson spoke with individual heavyweights like constitutional law expert Peter Hogg and devised a strategy. He eventually lost his case, but gained even more respect in legitimate circles and later served on a provincial government committee that helped develop standards for training mechanics.

While Peterson and the Para-Dice Riders were flying high, things weren't going so well for their rivals in Satan's Choice. With information gleaned from Operation Dismantle, the police raided clubhouses again. One of the bikers they arrested was Jimmy Rich. He wasn't a nice guy—having already amassed a long record of drug possession, trafficking in drugs and stolen goods and even sexual assault—but the police knew he was not a decision maker. Even so, they were surprised at how quickly he gave up his brothers. Using information from Rich, the Hamilton police arrested Johnny K-9, his right-hand man Gary Noble, and four others in connection with a bomb that, exploded at a Sudbury police station on December 15, 1996. At the time, police were mystified by the attack and could determine no motive. Rich told them that it was part of the Hamilton chapter's initiation into Satan's Choice.

According to police, K-9 and Jure "Joey" Juretta traveled north on orders from the Toronto chapter and presented the Sudbury chapter with a gift-wrapped package. Inside the box was a bomb. Sudbury president Michael Dubé had a score to settle. He and Brian Davis, another member from Sudbury, were hosting the prospective Hamilton members at Solid Gold, a local strip joint, when the manager asked them to take off their colors. They refused and were given the boot when police arrived. Dubé swore revenge. A little more than a week later, K-9 and Juretta showed up with the bomb. Davis had just placed it in the trunk of his car and was about to drive it to Solid Gold when Dubé came running out of the clubhouse. He told him about a change in plans. Another member's girlfriend was dancing at Solid Gold and they couldn't risk harming her. He told him to take the bomb to the police station instead. Davis laughed. The cops were the real problem anyway. Although nobody was hurt, the blast blew a big hole in a wall of the station and made it clear someone was out to get the cops in Sudbury.

On the cold, rainy morning of April 16, 1998, the Hamilton police showed up at the Satan's Choice Lottridge Street clubhouse with warrants, a construction crew and the bomb disposal unit. Under proceeds of crime legislation, the government took ownership and the police were anxious to see what was inside. The first thing that went was the grinning devil's head Satan's Choice logo on the front door. To at least one officer's disappointment, a detailed search revealed no bombs, weapons or explosives. Instead, they took possession of the club's pool table, TV, stereo, surveillance equipment and office furniture. "We said we'd monitor them closely, and we have," said Bruce Elwood, head of the Hamilton–Wentworth police's investigative services. "We'd really like to put them out of business."

The next day, K-9 walked into the Hamilton Police headquarters on King William Street downtown. Ever the showman, he took a few minutes to joke around with a few cops he knew and to sign a couple of autographs. After a 30-minute meeting with the cops, in which he learned that Rich had switched sides, his mood changed. Storming out of the station, he told a reporter, "I got no fucking comment! No comment! Fuck you!" Surprised, the reporter took a moment to withdraw. Noble stepped between the two men and told the reporter to "beat it." He did.

K-9 knew he was in trouble. In addition to nailing Satan's Choice for selling pot, hash, cocaine, steroids and counterfeit money, the police also told him they knew about the protection fees and kickbacks he was charging local "adult entertainment" establishments. Not only did they arrest them, they did something far worse—they made the chapter homeless. Records show that ownership of the clubhouse at 269 Lottridge was transferred from Gary Adrian Noble to "Her Majesty the Queen in Right of Canada."

With biker crimes frequently making the front page and the failure of their neighbors in Quebec to convict Boucher, the Ontario RCMP,

OPP and local police forces from Hamilton, Toronto, Ottawa, Durham, York, Peel, Halton and Thunder Bay formed the Provincial Special Squad, a task force dedicated to sharing resources and information in the fight against biker gangs. A week later, 17 more Satan's Choice—this time from Toronto—were arrested on a variety of charges.

Juretta and Davis were convicted of conspiracy on November 9, 1999. K-9 was found guilty of trafficking marijuana and steroids. Dubé hanged himself in his cell while awaiting trial.

* * *

Denis Belleau, one of the founding members of the Rock Machine and a former friend of Boucher's from the SS, died after taking four shots to his head after leaving a Quebec City restaurant on February 20, 1998. Clearly, putting Mom Boucher behind bars didn't end the war. About a week later, the charred remains of a human were found hidden in a field in suburban Bromont, Quebec. The corpse was so badly burned that only its size identified it as male at first. Almost three weeks passed before its identity could be determined; it was Tousignant, who had been killed with a bullet to the back of his head and another to his chest before his body was set aflame.

Catching Boucher was one thing; what to do with him was another. Unwilling to allow him to mix with any prison population, the authorities housed him in the brand-new maximum security wing of Montreal's Maison Tanguay prison for women. "We didn't want 200 guys applauding when he showed up, like he's some kind of hero," said Réjean Leguard, head of Quebec's prison guards' union. There weren't any guys—or women—either. Alone in the wing, Boucher saw no other inmates. He did see ten officers dedicated entirely to watching him. For Boucher's safety, guards were only allowed in his cell in pairs and all guard-Boucher interaction was videotaped.

Those precautions were taken because the guards were, understandably, loath to come in contact with the man who was dedicated to seeing all of them dead or at least too terrorized to do their jobs. And they had little faith in the courts to convict him or to give him an appropriate penalty if convicted. Since beginning his career as a biker,

Boucher had been convicted 43 times, usually on weapons charges, and had spent a total of about two years in prison, most of that coming from the aggravated sexual assault conviction he sustained just before he joined the Hells Angels. Réne Domingue, a prosecutor who had been foiled many times in his attempts to put bikers behind bars, summed up their frustrated opinion of the justice system when he said: "Considering the success rates of cases solved against the Hells Angels, I'd say they kill with impunity."

The guards' anger prevented Boucher from getting to court for his March 19 preliminary hearing. No guards would drive him there. "It's like you're a father and someone has raped your daughter and then you're being asked to drive him to court," Leguard said. "We have a problem with anyone who participates in the murder of a peace officer." As if pushing them further, Boucher asked for a transfer to Rivière-des-Prairies, the facility the murdered guards had worked in. Despite his own private exercise equipment, TV, VCR, sound system and video game, Boucher complained that keeping him alone in Tanguay was inhumane. His request was denied.

The guards would get much angrier. Although Gagné was a willing, even enthusiastic witness, there was little he could say about Boucher. He'd received his orders from Tousignant and Fontaine and had committed the murders with them. He could certainly indict them, but while the police were rushing to incriminate and arrest Boucher, they'd gotten away. By the time the trial started, Tousignant was dead and Fontaine, though many believed he'd been executed too, was actually hidden in the Trois-Rivières clubhouse. What little discussion Gagné had had with Boucher on the subject had been oblique and his testimony against him was largely speculative. On November 27, the courthouse was crowded with bikers. During the trial, the courtroom had been full of them. According to the RCMP, bikers paid people $200 for their seats in court.

Although they never wore their colors in court, it was obvious to other spectators—and the jury—who they were. The courthouse was also full of cops: besides the usual complement, 15 more were hidden in the courtroom next to Boucher's and Commander Bouchard of the Montreal police brought 20 of his own men. After a closing speech by Judge Jean-Guy Boilard that Crown prosecutor Jacques Dagenais said totally refuted Gagné's credibility, the jurors returned a not-guilty verdict. Boucher asked if he was free to go. He was. As soon as the shackles snapped off his ankles, he was lifted onto the shoulders of cheering bikers and led from the courthouse. After a terse "no comment" to reporters, he was taken into a waiting van. With hundreds of police watching, Boucher's driver ran a red light. Nobody stopped them; there was no point. Stadnick's Nomads philosophy had worked to perfection. Nomad Boucher ordered Hells Angels Tousignant and Fontaine to kill prison guards. They, in turn, hired Rocker Gagné. And when he got caught and squealed, Boucher was insulated. It seemed the Nomads would be impossible to stop.

Less than a month later, on December 18, Judge Felix Cacchione sat in a Halifax courtroom and berated two RCMP officers. After saying that there was "a deliberate attempt by certain officers to influence the Court" and that "the officers displayed a propensity to change their evidence as the need arose," he set Dany Kane free. Although he informed on almost everyone he'd ever met, Simard's testimony didn't lead to a single conviction other than his own. Back in Montreal, Kane received news that he would become a full-patch Rocker, something he had wanted for years. Patricia, the girlfriend who left him after the Lebrasseur incident, was back with him and they were expecting a child, his fourth, and they bought a large house in suburban St-Luc. With expenses mounting, he went back to work, first collecting debts, then selling steroids and small amounts of cocaine. Seeking even more cash, he also went back to work for the police.

* * *

While Boucher and Kane were still behind bars, the fight against the Rock Machine not only continued, but escalated. On July 28, Rock Machine leader Richard "Bam-Bam" Lagacé left the Ben Weider Health Club near his home in Saint-Lin-des-Laurentides as he had almost every day of his adult life. Before he got to the sidewalk, two masked men shot him five times. The assassins, however, had no getaway plan, so they forced their way into a woman's home, where one held his gun to her head until she gave them her car keys. They dumped her red Nissan Sentra and the weapons in a cemetery about 16 miles down Boulevard Ste-Sophie. Lagacé's replacement was Johnny Plescio, one of the representatives the Rock Machine had sent to Europe to meet with the Bandidos. His reign didn't last long. On September 8, Plescio answered the door at his Laval home and was shot 11 times.

Later that month, lawns all over Montreal were deluged with leaves and many residents of the West End neighborhoods of Dorval and Pointe Claire called Bo-Pelouse, a landscaping company that also specializes in leaf and snow removal. The following morning, every house that had a Bo-Pelouse sign on its lawn also had a threatening letter stuffed in its mailbox. Written in "joual," colloquial Quebecois French, and peppered with curses, the letter threatened customers against using the services of Bo-Pelouse. It was signed by the Ontario Hells Angels. Since there weren't any official Hells Angels in Ontario (Stadnick and Stockford were from the province and lived there but, as Nomads, were part of the Quebec Hells Angels), the police knew it was a scam right away. A rival lawn-care company was simply trying to take advantage of the violence.

* * *

While Boucher escaped conviction for the murders of the prison guards, he did spend ten months in Tanguay and was widely regarded as public enemy No. 1 in Montreal. Stadnick, on the other hand, had an almost spotless record. In 1971, he was caught with a small amount of hash; on November 5, 1987, he blew over the blood alcohol limit at a traffic stop outside Hamilton and was fined $750. Just over seven years later he was apprehended for driving 108 km/h (67 miles per hour) in a 100 km/h (62 miles per hour) zone on the 401 just east of Napanee and received a $47.50 ticket. He paid it promptly.

After his success in Alberta and Winnipeg, things were looking up for Stadnick and the Hells Angels in Ontario. With K-9 and Juretta among their many members in prison, Satan's Choice posed little threat. Through his connections with the Loners, Stadnick had made serious inroads with the Para-Dice Riders and partied with them often.

According to police, they also served as excellent salesmen for drugs couriered in from Montreal. Even the Outlaws, who had once made him a hunted man in his own hometown, didn't scare him any more.

Although they had come around to the idea of setting up a puppet gang—the Black Pistons had three chapters in Ontario and did some of the Outlaws' dirty work—it was too late. Informants recruited years earlier by Sergeant John Harris of the Hamilton Police were paying huge dividends, as the Outlaws were being arrested on a regular basis. And Ontario courts proved tougher than their Quebec counterparts. Those Outlaws who did not receive prison sentences had probation terms that severely limited their ability to commit crimes or even meet with their associates. Richard Williams, president of the Sault Ste. Marie chapter, was arrested for allegedly uttering a death threat in front of a cop. Later that year, Thomas Culliton of the St. Catharines chapter went down for attempted murder after he stabbed his girlfriend in their Fonthill home.

Even Mario "the Wop" Parente, national and Hamilton chapter president, was put away. He was found guilty of killing local tough guy Jimmy Lewis with a double-barreled shotgun blast to the gut. While awaiting trial in Hamilton jail, Parente was attacked by a fellow prisoner with a knife. Although the other man managed to get Parente on the floor, prison guards broke up the fight before much damage could be done. "He tried to poke his eyes out, but the injuries were minor," said Hamilton–Wentworth police inspector Dave Bowen. Parente refused medical attention and declined to testify against his assailant.

At his trial, Parente's lawyer pointed out that Lewis's brother was at the scene of the killing and was armed with a handgun. He said that Parente only intended to fight with Lewis, but when he saw the other men and the gun, he knew he had to fire to save his life. Neither Parente nor his lawyer indicated why Parente shot Lewis instead of the armed man, but the excuse managed to get him a surprisingly light sentence—three and a half years. "With Parente out of the picture, the Outlaws were pretty much done in Hamilton," said Harris. "They didn't have much reason to keep going."

Realistically, there was no effective biker threat in Hamilton any more. But the bikers, powerful as they were, had never run Hamilton anyway. Instead they had acted as runners, dealers and enforcers in what the RCMP called "the most mafia-controlled city in Canada." The Italian stranglehold on Hamilton eased slightly in May 1997 when godfather John "Johnny Pops" Papalia and his No. 2, Carmen Barillaro, were murdered. "I was one of the first officers in Papalia's place after he was killed," said Sgt. Steve Pacey. "All he had was a big-screen TV, a VCR and stacks and stacks of gangster movies; it was so sad—like he never enjoyed the fruits of his labor." As soon as Papalia was buried, a young mafioso named Pasquale "Pat" Musitano assumed control of the city. Although widely regarded as brutally efficient, Musitano lacked Papalia's professionalism and humility, and the younger Don's hubris soon brought him down. Ken Murdock, the man Musitano had paid to murder Papalia and Barillaro, was arrested on extortion charges in the fall of 1998. When the police played a tape of Musitano and his brother, Angelo, mocking the hit man and joking about having him murdered, Murdock gave them up. When the Musitanos were arrested on October 23, it marked the first time in more than 75 years that the city didn't have a prominent godfather.

Stadnick swooped in. Police and newspapers reported him riding through Hamilton in full colors, partying with Satan's Choice in Toronto and meeting with Para-Dice Riders in Niagara Falls. With its proximity to the U.S. border, its huge casino and its image as an anything-goes tourist town, Niagara Falls became a much sought-after prize for bikers no longer afraid of mafia repercussions. When Stadnick showed his face in the area on April 13, 1999, newspapers from Fort Erie to Toronto ran front-page stories about how the Hells Angels were scouting clubs for an eventual takeover.

While others quibbled that Stadnick's presence in Southern Ontario was nothing new (Niagara Falls and Toronto are both less than an hour's drive from Hamilton), they failed to take into account the context—the local biker gangs were in no shape to prevent a Hells Angels invasion— or the nuance—Stadnick had never felt confident enough to ride around Ontario in full colors before the events of 1999. Stadnick was indeed in Southern Ontario scouting bikers and locations suitable for the Hells Angels and there was little to stop him. And nobody was more excited than the bikers, who wanted a chance at the brass ring. "There was a lot of excitement about the Hells Angels—it was like these small-time players got a chance at the big ticket," said Cal Broeker, an undercover RCMP agent who managed to ride with the Para-Dice Riders at the time. "To them, it was the opportunity of a lifetime."

And for Stadnick, it appeared to be his first chance at fulfilling a lifelong goal. On a flight from Montreal to Winnipeg, he told Stéphane Sirois, a veteran Rocker and a good friend, about his ultimate goal. "*The Hells Angels only, throughout Canada, with no other biker clubs*," Stadnick said. And then he put his dreams into focus. He wanted the Hells Angels to be so powerful and united in Canada that chapters would be unnecessary—a Hells Angel would be a Hells Angel. Instead of indicating which chapter the member belonged to, the bottom rockers on their jackets would simply read "Canada."

But the vacuum of organized crime power in Ontario did not go unnoticed by others. Before the Hells Angels could move, the Rock Machine made a shocking announcement. With the help of the Bandidos, the Rock Machine had finally become what the Hells Angels had mocked them for not being—a motorcycle gang. Starting with nine Toronto Outlaws who were tired of watching their own club fall apart under police pressure, the Rock Machine announced the formation of chapters in Toronto, Kingston and Sarnia, at the narrows of the St. Clair River across from Port Huron, Michigan.

The irony did not elude Stadnick, but it didn't please him, either. After a bloody five-year war in Quebec that left more than 160 dead and the Hells Angels soundly despised, the Rock Machine had appeared to be on their knees. Then, with a flourish, they did what Stadnick and the Hells Angels had always wanted to do but never managed: they opened chapters in Ontario, in Toronto yet. Before long, the busy Ontario highways—the 401, the QEW—were the home range of a new set of bikers. Like almost all motorcycle clubs, they wore jackets based on those worn by the Hells Angels. But theirs said "Rock Machine" on the top rocker and the winged skull was replaced by an eagle's head. And, no matter which chapter its owner belonged to, the bottom rocker simply read "Canada."

The surprising turn of events didn't discourage Stadnick. Quite the opposite. The sudden success of his old rivals on his home turf pushed him back to the old drawing board. A desire to get even, to reverse the fortunes of both clubs, led him to a plan more ambitious than any in biker history.

He almost didn't get a chance. While Stadnick was far from the household name that Boucher had become, his successes around the country had led police to believe that he was the real power and intelligence behind the Hells Angels in Canada. It was an astute conclusion. Boucher, for all his bravado and tactical ability, was little more than a soldier (though a flamboyant one) whose task was to subdue Quebec to make it safe for Nomads operations. While he was risking his life and freedom on the frontlines in Montreal, Stadnick was flying first-class around the country spending thousands on parties so the club could make millions in drug sales. After much conversation, biker cops around the country came to a unanimous decision—getting Stadnick would cripple, if not stop, the Hells Angels.

The operation was in its infancy when the Hells Angels held their 22nd anniversary party in Sherbrooke on December 4, 1999. Although officers were under express orders not to stay in the same hotels as bikers, Guy Ouellette, the SQ's biker expert and media mouthpiece, and his good friend Rick Perrault checked into the Hôtel Delta right in front of at least two dozen bikers. If it was a power move, it failed. Every biker in Quebec knew who Ouellette was. His face showed up on every TV report about bikers and his name was in every newspaper article.

As he and Perrault ate breakfast in the hotel restaurant, two members of the local Hells Angels puppet gang, the Scorpions, broke into their room and made off with a laptop. Thinking it was Ouellette's, they were pleased, but when they found out what they really had, they were ecstatic. Perrault was not only the OPP's top biker intelligence officer at their Kingston base, but he also served as translator between Ontario and Quebec police forces. "Pretty well everything they told us and we told them went through Perrault," said Sgt. Pacey. With the information from Perrault's computer, the Scorpions delivered almost everything every cop in Canada knew about every biker in the country. For years, the contents of Perrault's Dell would come back to haunt the police. In raid after raid, pictures of, and vital information relating to, members and associates of the Rock Machine, Outlaws and other rival groups that had come from Perrault's computer turned up.

The single most important folder on Perrault's desktop was simply called "Operation." Inside were detailed plans for a joint RCMP-OPP-SQ operation to bring down Stadnick. Not only did the files contain everything the police knew about Stadnick from observation and informants, but it detailed police tactics and strategy. With all of their cards showing, the police got out of the game—at least temporarily. The operation to arrest Stadnick was called off. "We didn't have a lot of choice," said Pacey. When the information reached him, Stadnick knew where all the bugs were, whose phone was tapped and, sometimes, who the rats were.

None of the informants were identified by name in the files. But the Nomads worked long and hard to figure out who they were by putting together dates and places. One meeting in particular struck a note in the memory of Normand Robitaille. From the information in one informant's file, he triangulated the date, the place and the discussion and came up with a name—Claude De Serres. A small-time dealer who worked for Serge "Pasha" Boutin in the gay village, De Serres had decided to go straight and serve as an informer for the SQ.

On February 21, 2000, Robitaille called Boutin, who was vacationing in the Dominican Republic, and told him what he thought. Boutin understood. He cut his trip short, returned to snowy Montreal and called De Serres. The two were old friends and De Serres was a top producer, so he readily accepted when Boutin invited him up to his chalet in the Laurentians for a weekend of skiing and partying. Both men had ulterior motives. Sure that Boutin would say something incriminating, De Serres arrived at the chalet with a recording device taped to his back. Police followed him up into the mountains but lost him in a snowstorm. When they finally arrived, they found his body by the side of a gravel road, partially obscured by a snow bank. It still had the recorder attached. When the police played the tape, they heard a man (not Boutin) ask De Serres, "Why do you work for the police?" De Serres didn't get a chance to tell them why. The last sounds the police heard on the tape were the four shots that ended his life.

After De Serres's death, Carcajou officers met with Kane and told him to quit the Rockers and get out of town. Information from Perrault's laptop could easily pinpoint him as an informant and the De Serres incident showed exactly how the Hells Angels handled rats. Kane scoffed. Not only was he hanging around with his biker friends but he was actually recorded joking with some Nomads that De Serres was "one informant who wouldn't be able to testify." When he showed up on March 10, some officers reported they were sure Kane was ready to give up. Quite the opposite—he was there to deal. Up to this point, Kane had been an informant. He gave information that the police could use to uncover Hells Angels activities, but not use in court. Now he was willing to take the next step. He offered to testify against his brothers if his conditions were met.

When the negotiations were finished, Kane had hammered out quite a deal. Police offered to defend him under a system similar to the FBI's Witness Protection Program, give him $1.75 million in three installments, another $63,000 up front as a signing bonus, $2,000 a week for living expenses, $3,000 in legal fees, $1,500 for a handgun he said he needed to serve as a bodyguard, $1,500 to take care of his suspended driver's license, $1,000 for a wedding present for a Nomad and $600 for two new suits. In exchange, he wrote a confession detailing all of his crimes and promised to testify. It took ten pages for Kane to recount everything he'd done and when he was finished, he asked the police for more money.

He may have switched sides officially, but he didn't stop working for the Hells Angels. Three weeks after he signed his confession, Kane, who was still trying to prove himself by acting as a gofer for the Nomads, was driving "Wolf" Carroll to a license bureau in Montreal. Carroll was, as usual, complaining about how things were going for him in Halifax. In particular, he was talking about Kirk Mersereau. Kirk was the brother of Randy Mersereau, a former Hells Angel who had left the club to strike out on his own. Not only had Randy weakened and insulted the Hells Angels by leaving and becoming one of their competitors on the streets of Halifax, but rumor had it that he had been talking with the Bandidos about starting a local chapter. There was no way the Hells Angels, in particular the Nomads, could allow him to survive if they were to achieve their national agenda.

208 | Chapter 10

And Carroll admitted there was a great deal of pressure "from above" to solidify the Hells Angels' standing on the East Coast. When they learned that Randy was attempting to contract out the murders of Carroll, Boucher and Mike McCrea, president of the Halifax Chapter while Carroll was in Montreal, he became their top priority. Kane told his RCMP handlers that Carroll called him with a plan to kill or intimidate their allies into submission, and then send the Jokers and Scorpions into Halifax to reclaim the city for the Hells Angels.

On the next day, September 23, 1999, a bomb blasted through Mersereau's car dealership in Truro, Nova Scotia. Windows were shattered and seven employees were injured. Randy Mersereau stumbled out into the street with blood on his head and torn clothes, but he was not seriously hurt. Kane told the police that McCrea was behind the bombing, but no arrests were made. He also told them that Randy Mersereau didn't have long to live. About a month later, Kane and Carroll got into Kane's car and got on the road to Halifax. As Kane turned off Route 132 to Route 185 in Rivière-du-Loup, he saw police lights in his rearview mirror. Officially, the SQ officer stopped him for speeding, but he was actually a tipped-off Carcajou officer attempting to prevent a murder in Halifax. Carroll was surprised when Kane allowed the cop to search the car. When he found Kane's .38 and Carroll's Mac-10, the bikers were put under arrest, cuffed and put in jail until members of the Trois-Rivières chapter could post bail.

It didn't matter. As soon as he got back to Montreal, Carroll got on the phone. Someone—maybe Carroll, maybe someone on his behalf—put together a local team in Halifax to take Randy Mersereau out. Although his body was never found, nobody ever saw Randy Mersereau again after October 31, 1999. His car was found, with the keys still inside, on the shoulder of Highway 102, just outside Truro. The police had no leads and the crime was never solved, although Kane later reported that Randy Mersereau had been killed by Hells Angels associates and had been buried in a forest near the highway. Kane didn't give very many details, but he did point out that there were many people other than Carroll who wanted to see the Mersereaus dead.

Boucher didn't care about the Mersereaus or the state of the club outside the Montreal urban community. With the Rock Machine subdued and the police and courts proven impotent against him, Boucher wanted to enjoy his spoils and rub it in their faces. In April 2000, Boucher and nine of his most intimidating Hells Angels and Rockers drove up to Anjou in the East End to have coffee. They took some seats at the Au Bon Pain in the Place Versailles shopping center. In full colors, Boucher and his men enjoyed their coffee and pastries in seats normally reserved for the homicide and anti-gang officers of the Montreal police, who had an office on the fourth floor of the mall.

At first, officers joked that having him downstairs just made it easier to watch him, but when he kept doing it every morning for a week, it became apparent to the police that Boucher was making a public show of his power. Commander Bouchard, the top officer at the station and the toughest cop in Montreal, was almost certainly the primary target of Boucher's psychological assault. Bouchard had an idea: he'd bug the tables at Au Bon Pain. But Boucher had anticipated that move and frequently brought his lawyer along. It's against the law in Canada to record lawyer–client conversations. Advised of this by his lawyers, Bouchard instead sent 20 cops to watch the bikers. His plan was to irritate them enough to utter a threat and then arrest them all. The charges wouldn't stick, but it would piss Boucher off. Nothing happened. The next day, he sent down 30 cops. That was enough. Boucher and his men left, but they'd come back from time to time.

A week later, on April 17, Nomad Normand "Biff" Hamel drove his wife and son to their pediatrician's office in Montreal. Formerly Boucher's right-hand man, Hamel had been sent to Laval to act as godfather of the Death Riders puppet gang after Scott Steinert was killed. He wasn't any luckier. As he got out of his Mercedes in the doctor's parking lot, he saw two masked men approaching. That was all the warning he needed. He ran as fast as he could, while his wife and son retreated back into the car. He didn't make it out of the lot; he was killed by two gunshot wounds to the head. The first Nomad and the third full-patch Hells Angel to be killed in the war, Hamel became front-page news throughout Montreal. Many commentators assumed that the Rock Machine had assassinated him and that the war was back on. But if they had taken the time to drive past any of the clubhouses in the area, they would have noticed that no flags were at half-staff.

The Hells Angels were not grieving. With Hamel out of the way, the Death Riders were quickly reorganized as the Hells Angels Montreal North, under the supervision of full-patch Sorel members Stéphane "Fesses" Plouffe and Benoît Frenette.

Boucher had other tasks on his agenda besides irritating cops and restaffing Laval. A friend of his got into debt with the wrong guy. André "Dédé" Desjardins was a former construction union chief from the Olympic era who had a reputation as a man who would use any resources at his disposal to get his way. "He was a tough guy. But at the same time you have to remember labor relations back then were tough as well," said Henri Masse, president of the Quebec Federation of Labour. "During strikes, employers would use thugs and dogs and other means."

After leaving union politics, police say Desjardins turned very successfully to loan sharking. After quickly amassing a fortune reported to be more than $25 million, he moved to the Dominican Republic and was so entrenched there that police said that no construction happened in the country without Desjardins getting a cut. But he still did plenty of business in Montreal and when Boucher asked for a breakfast meeting, they agreed on Shawn's in the East End on April 25. Boucher asked Desjardins to forgive his friend's debt. Desjardins said "no way." With interest, the friend was now in for $400,000 and that was just too much for him to get away with. Boucher didn't offer money; he didn't offer any reasons for Desjardins to relent other than the fact that Boucher and his men were running the show in Montreal now.

It didn't impress Desjardins, who had been around a lot longer than Boucher and had some powerful friends of his own. Unable to reach any sort of agreement, Desjardins asked if they could continue their discussion later. Boucher suggested the same place, same time on the following day. On the morning of April 26, Desjardins and a burly friend were sitting at the best table in Shawn's as waitresses in bikinis poured coffee. Just after 9:15 a.m., Desjardins' cell phone rang. Rather than speak inside the restaurant, Desjardins walked out to the parking lot. As he opened the door to his Cadillac SUV, he was shot 11 times by a masked assailant, who left a silencer-equipped handgun at the scene and fled into a waiting van. Police consulted traffic cameras in the area, but found no leads.

Twenty minutes after the murder, the police recorded a call from a tapped Montreal phone to the Dominican. The only words spoken (in French) were "Okay, go ahead." At 10:30 a.m., someone broke into Desjardins' condo in Puerto Plata and stole the contents of his safe. With Desjardins out of the picture, *Journal de Montreal* reporter Michel Auger wrote that criminals would have to go to the Hells Angels for their loan-sharking and money-laundering needs.

The next day, Boucher had his morning coffee at Au Bon Pain. He was met there by Commander Bouchard, who asked him what he knew about Desjardins' murder. Boucher told him to talk to his lawyer. He did. That afternoon, the Montreal police had a brief, polite meeting with Boucher and his lawyer, Gilbert Frigon. Boucher said that he'd met with Desjardins at Shawn's to discuss the weather in the Dominican and that he knew nothing about the murder. "Sad thing," he said. He also promised to call them back "if he heard anything."

Chapter 11

Desjardins' murder wasn't about a debt. The friend wasn't even a Hells Angel. He was an associate of Montreal's Rizzuto crime family. Although Stéphane Gagné had told police that Boucher's ultimate goal was to drive the mafia out of Montreal, Boucher knew it would be unwise to launch another war against a bigger, more entrenched enemy, so he chose to work with them instead. Their common interest was cocaine.

The Nomads had an enviable business model. Five of them—Boucher, Robitaille, Denis Houle, André Chouinard and Michel Rose—administered what the club called The Table. They imported cocaine and distributed it to every Hells Angels chapter (except Sherbrooke, which had cut an earlier deal), puppet club and associated dealer in Quebec. Members of The Table received $5,000 a week, plus 10 percent of the profits on sales of their drugs. The cocaine came to The Table primarily from the Mejia Twins cartel in Colombia, although a much smaller amount came from contacts in Bolivia, Amsterdam and New York. The Table's man in Colombia was Guy Lepage.

A hulking ex-cop who'd been kicked off the Montreal force for corruption, Guy Lepage arrived at the Mejias's distribution center in Barranquilla in the summer of 1997 and stayed at the palatial estate of José Miguel Carvajal—a senior executive in the cartel. After brief negotiations, Carvajal and Lepage worked out an ingenious and effective plan. The Colombians would get cocaine to a Hells Angels operative in Miami, who would then get mules to drive it up to Montreal for distribution.

The only problem with the system was that it couldn't handle large volumes. Cocaine shipments through Lepage averaged less than 500 kilos a month, far less than the Hells Angels needed to corner the Montreal market, let alone all of Canada. With cost seemingly no object, Lepage (on orders from The Table) convinced the Colombians to ship 2,400 kilos of cocaine directly to Quebec. In October 1998, under cover of darkness, a medium-sized pleasure craft with Miami registry docked off the coast of Gaspé, Quebec. Seven SUVs were waiting on shore. When they loaded, the cars took off at regular intervals towards Montreal. They all took slightly different routes to confuse police. As the last SUV drove through the Gaspé Peninsula, a Sûreté du Québec officer in the tiny village of Ste-Anne-des-Monts thought there was something strange about a scruffy-looking young man of about 20 driving a brand-new Chevrolet Trailblazer at exactly the speed limit just after sunrise, so he pulled him over. A quick search revealed 480 kilos of cocaine and a pager with the telephone numbers of Lepage and fellow suspected cocaine importers Raymond and Sandra Craig. But the rest of the shipment got through. With some minor alterations in delivery methods, the Gaspé landing spot became the Hells Angels' primary cocaine source.

No matter how effectively The Table could get cocaine into Quebec, there was no way they could get enough to run the mafia out of business. With years of experience and thousands of contacts and associates in every major city between Barranquilla and Montreal, the mafia could import drugs nearly at will. Rather than a war, the Nomads wanted an alliance.

On June 21, 2000, Robitaille, Chouinard and Rose went to a fancy Italian restaurant in Laval to meet with Vito Rizzuto, his right-hand man Tony Mucci and two other tough-looking Italians. Mom Boucher had promised he'd attend, but didn't show up. That was fine with Rizzuto, who scrupulously avoided meeting with any well-known underworld figures, and none was better known than

Boucher. After it was agreed that the Italians and the bikers would work together, dividing the bounty of the Montreal drug market between them and defending it against outside influences, they moved on to lesser items. First, they set the minimum price for a kilo of cocaine on the streets of Quebec at $50,000. Anyone selling for less faced the death penalty. Second, they decided to split the proceeds of a telemarketing scam, aimed at Americans to make detection and prosecution more difficult, equally between the bikers, the mafia and the independent operators. Although the total take from the scam was about $1 million per week, it was by far the least important item on the agenda.

The partnership hinged on the agreement that the Hells Angels were required to eliminate any competitors, even if they fell within their own ranks. Considering the rampant slaughter of his former SS friends in the Rock Machine, Boucher showed no reluctance to murder even his closest associates if it meant the bottom line would improve.

Then, Louis "Mèlou" Roy, president of the Trois-Rivières Hells Angels, arrived in Montreal on June 21, with bad news for Boucher. A police raid on the Blatnois, a puppet gang based in nearby Grand-Mère, had been devastating and all of its important members plus several close associates were in jail. Robitaille told Roy not to worry, as that sort of thing happened from time to time and if he had been protecting himself properly, he had nothing to worry about from police.

He did, however, have a problem with the Nomads. Roy had been at the top of the underworld in Trois-Rivières for so long that he had built up an enviable fiefdom. He bought his cocaine from his own suppliers and set his price according to supply and demand. It was virtually always less, often quite a bit less, than $50,000 a kilo. Robitaille warned him that he should buy his cocaine from The Table. Roy refused. Robitaille told him that even if he didn't deal with The Table, his friendship with Boucher and other Nomads could keep him alive if he got in line with their retail price demand. Again Roy refused. He attended the Nomads' fifth anniversary party the following night and was never seen alive again.

Next on the Nomads' list were Raymond and Sandra Craig, the largest remaining independent drug dealers in Montreal. The Craigs could operate without interference from the mafia, Hells Angels and even the Colombian cartels because Sandra was the daughter of a powerful Bolivian drug lord. Before the deal with the Italians, the Craigs had been consistent and reliable cocaine suppliers for the Nomads. Now they were competitors. On August 29, the Craigs were driving home after a quiet night of dinner and drinks at one of the chalets in Ste-Adèle. They were stopped at a red light when Sandra heard a crash. Four bullets came through the back window, three of them penetrating Raymond's skull and killing him. The assassins, on a Suzuki Sidekick, assumed both people in the car were dead and sped away. It was the second attempt on Sandra's life in two months and she was scared. She went home and shut down her business.

* * *

Kirk Mersereau hadn't been very careful since his brother's death. He'd sworn revenge many times in Halifax and word eventually leaked to Paul Wilson and then to Carroll. Carroll flew to Nova Scotia and met with Mersereau. At first he tried to turn his enemy, indicating how rich he could become if he became a Hells Angel. Mersereau wouldn't budge. There was no way he'd do business with the people who'd killed his brother. Since he'd made it personal, Carroll finished the meeting by asking Mersereau if he'd put out a contract on his life. Mersereau didn't say that he had, but he didn't deny it, either. With no more to talk about, Carroll left. Three days later, on September 10, a neighbor drove up to Mersereau's isolated farmhouse because she hadn't heard from him in a while. She was about to knock on the front door when she noticed it was open. Inside, she heard what she thought was a baby softly crying. When she came in, she saw Mersereau's 18-month-old daughter exhaustedly trying to cry. She picked her up and carried her into the bedroom, where she found the bloodied bodies of Mersereau and his wife.

* * *

With his enemies either dead or made into friends, Boucher was not just a gangster—he was a celebrity. When Nomads prospect René

"Balloune" Charlebois was married on August 5, Boucher held the reception at his Contrecoeur farm, invited the tabloid press and hired Quebecoise pop star Ginette Reno to perform. When photos of Reno hugging and kissing Boucher appeared in *Allô Police*, she was soundly criticized in the mainstream media. Her response was a bizarrely pompous demi-apology in which she compared herself to Christ. "Jesus hung out with bad people," she told the *Journal de Montréal*, inferring that she was aware that the Hells Angels weren't solid citizens. "Are they killers and criminals 24 hours a day?" She couldn't use ignorance as an excuse. She'd also sung and partied at Paul "Fonfon" Fontaine's wedding the previous summer.

And she wasn't the only big-time celebrity who'd been linked with Boucher and the Hells Angels. José Théodore, star goaltender for the Montreal Canadiens, showed up in police photos drinking beer with some bikers in the Sorel clubhouse. When the SQ took the photos to the NHL head office in New York, their security department told Théodore to avoid the bikers, at least in public. He ignored them. When he and his father, Ted, were stopped on a golf course after playing 18 holes with some Hells Angels, he used a similar defense to Reno's—they might be bad guys, but hanging out with them doesn't make me bad. "My father taught me respect and good manners; he also showed me that honesty to one's self pays off," Théodore said. "If you are honest in your work, you're not afraid of looking at yourself in a mirror." Later that year, Théodore's father and half-brother were arrested for running a loan-sharking business out of the Montreal Casino.

While Boucher's star was rising, Kane's was sinking into self-doubt, blunted ambition, resentment and despair. He'd allowed the police to put video cameras, transmitting and recording devices in his home, his car and on his person. The police could tell he was beginning to feel exposed and vulnerable. His biker career was depressing him, too. While he had spent ten years of his life with the Hells Angels, killed for them, started clubs for them and gone to prison for them, he was still nothing more than a gofer. While he was still chauffering Robitaille around and waiting patiently while the Nomad did his business, Kane could see newer members of the gang surpassing him. Michel Rose had not only become a Nomad, but was riding around in his many luxury cars or custom Harleys or piloting one of his three racing boats. Even Gregory "Picasso" Wooley, who'd done way less than Kane had, had become Rockers president—and he was black, normally a hindrance to promotion in biker gangs.

Meanwhile, Kane was having big-time money problems. He'd foolishly guaranteed a loan that Denis Houle, one of the wealthiest Nomads and a member of The Table, had taken from the Sherbrooke chapter. When Houle didn't repay it, Robitaille pressed Kane to come up with the $80,000. Even more galling was the fact that The Table had just forgiven a $400,000 loan that the always unreliable Carroll had forgotten to repay.

By August, those close to Kane began to notice that he was emotional and depressed even by his own standards. On the morning of August 7, his common-law wife Patricia was extremely worried. So were the police. Benoît Roberge, the Montreal police officer attached to Carcajou who became Kane's contact after his falling out with the RCMP, had a 7 a.m. meeting with the informant and, when he didn't show up after 15 minutes, the cop paged him. But it was too late. At 8:30 a Rockers-supplied driver took Patricia and her son Steve home to Kane's house. She'd been at her mother's house the night before and had warned Kane not to deadbolt the front door. He had a habit of sleeping late and heavily the mornings after he'd been partying and, considering the mood he'd been in, she wouldn't put it past him to be snoring away inside.

She tried the front door. It was locked. Pissed off, she tried the garage door opener. The stiff metal door budged, but didn't open. She tried again with the same result. With the help of the driver, she tried to pry the door open enough for Steve to crawl in. As they heaved, Patricia could smell exhaust fumes and was startled when their cat, clearly upset, came running through the gap. When they managed to create a space big enough for Steve, he scooted under. As soon as he stood up, they heard him scream. "Dany!" Desperately, they kept pulling and the gap was eventually big enough for Patricia to get through. She rushed to the car. Kane was inside. He was sitting in the front seat of their Mercedes with the windows open and the engine running. He didn't appear to be breathing and she couldn't locate his pulse, but the color in his face and the warmness of his skin made her sure he was still alive. She ran into the house and dialed 911. It was 9:22 a.m. She told the driver to take Steve to her mother's house. Police arrived five minutes later with an ambulance not far behind. As Patricia watched in horror, they made no effort to revive Kane; rather, they routinely declared him dead at the scene. And once the suburban cops typed his name in the computer and saw his record and who his friends were, they sealed the house and took Patricia in for questioning. When he finally found out, Roberge was stunned. "It was a huge, huge shock," he said. "That guy was a little like a partner."

* * *

Life went on for the Hells Angels. Michel Auger, the *Journal de Montréal* reporter who most doggedly pursued the bikers and was often ahead of the police in his investigations, began to become more than a mild irritant. After a late-night meeting with the anti-gang squad at Place Versailles,

Auger drove his Subaru back to the newspaper's parking lot in the East End. As he was opening his trunk to retrieve his laptop, Auger felt a sudden pain in his shoulder. Then he heard the shots. When he turned around, he saw a masked man with an umbrella shooting at him. Auger went down and the assailant left him for dead. With what he thought was his last bit of strength, Auger called 911. Although he eventually recovered and is still investigating and typing away in an effort to expose criminals, he was sure he was going to die. Newspaper reports said he was shot six times, but Auger disagreed, saying: "I still don't know how many bullets hit me."

Montreal exploded with a righteous anger that hadn't been seen since a Hells Angels bomb killed 11-year-old Daniel Desrosiers in 1995. Boucher wasn't impressed. He'd seen it before and he knew it would pass. His new partners didn't share his stoicism. Rizzuto sent Boucher a message that he'd better do something quick to calm the situation immediately. According to police, Rizzuto was afraid that public outrage could force the feds into passing an organized crime bill similar to the Racketeer-Influenced and Corrupt Organizations (RICO) law in the United States. While RICO had failed twice against the Hells Angels, it had repeatedly weakened the mafia.

Boucher relented. He sent emissaries to Fred Faucher in Quebec City. Now the highest-ranking surviving member of the Rock Machine, Faucher was stunned by the invitation to meet with Boucher in Montreal to discuss a truce and perhaps a large-scale patch-over. Faucher called Salvatore Cazzetta in his U.S. prison cell and excitedly told him the news. Cazzetta was horrified. He told Faucher that his old SS partner couldn't be trusted; it was a trap that would almost certainly end in the Rock Machine's extermination. Faucher ignored him. On September 27, the bikers held a summit at a downtown Montreal hotel. When they emerged an hour later, Boucher and Faucher announced that the two sides had agreed to a truce. According to Patrick Héniault, a member of the Palmers (a Rock Machine-associated puppet gang similar to the Rockers), members from both sides ate dinner together that night at a fancy Rue Crescent restaurant and a few even went drinking together at area nightclubs. "It was the beginning of a new time," he said. "Everybody was happy that we're going to stop shooting at each other." The war was over.

* * *

No matter how often he came around, Ontario police never got used to Walter Stadnick. They followed his every move, snapped hundreds of photos and shot miles of videotape. Every time he arrived—usually in the company of nine or more members from the Sherbrooke chapter, where he was revered—the police sent a release to major media centers predicting a gang war. Stockford, who was harder to spot with his ordinary appearance and reluctance to wear his colors, passed with less fanfare, but he was watched almost as diligently. Ouellette and the other usual quote machines were dragged out to give their often contradictory opinions but the theme was always the same: the Hells Angels were coming and they were bringing violence with them.

They'd seen it before, and not just in Quebec. When the best members of Los Brovos earned Hells Angels prospect status in October

1997, they changed the complexion of Winnipeg. The prospective Winnipeg chapter learned that the Hells Angels' way does not allow for competition. With the Redliners out of the picture, the Winnipeg chapter set its sights on their old rivals, the Spartans. On the warm, moonlit night of May 29, 1998, Darwin Sylvester walked out of the Spartans' clubhouse on Chalmers Avenue. He'd had a few drinks, but he wasn't drunk. It didn't matter anyway, he never made it home. His body was never found.

Without the charismatic leadership of Sylvester, the Spartans didn't stand a chance. For good measure, Sylvester's good friend Bob Rosmus was, like many Hells Angels victims in Quebec, shot in the head. Without any serious competition, the former Los Brovos prospered and their promotion to full-patch Hells Angels appeared imminent.

A Winnipeg police officer who doesn't want to be identified was woken up from a deep sleep on the morning of July 21, 2000. The Hells Angels were coming and he was called into work. By the time he got dressed and drove into work, the biker procession had just passed to the north of Kenora, Ontario, about 125 miles from Winnipeg. When the convoy hit the Ontario–Manitoba line, the police were ready. It was a typical roadblock in which the cops checked the bikers' licenses, registration and insurance papers and ran them through their computers, hoping to find any ticketable offenses or outstanding warrants. There were no cheering crowds looking for autographs this time. Aware of the increased violence and drug sales their own Hells Angels had brought, the people of Winnipeg weren't about to welcome any more. But they couldn't stop them. Although he had not been national president, or even a chapter president, for some time, no biker dared ride in front of Stadnick. It was his project, his day and, according to insiders, his gang.

The ride ended at the newly fortified clubhouse, a former Filipino evangelical church, in Elmwood. Legions of cops, reporters and spectators surrounding the place had no idea what was going on inside until they heard a roar of approval. Within minutes, 12 former Los Brovos came out of the clubhouse, lined up and turned their backs to the audience. They'd earned their bottom rockers; they had become a Hells Angels chapter. Instead of Winnipeg, the rocker read "Manitoba."

Even the police couldn't help but get caught up in the festive atmosphere. Some of them applauded, not all of them sarcastically.

Stadnick worked with incredible alacrity in the prairies. With Hells Angels on both sides, Saskatchewan's two biggest biker gangs, the Rebels (not affiliated with the Calgary or Toronto gangs of the same name) of Saskatoon and the Apollos of Regina, applied for Hells Angels membership. After evaluating their men and operations, the Hells Angels granted prospect status to the Rebels on September 18, 1998. The Apollos were designated as a puppet club, subordinate to their former archrivals 160 miles north. One year later, there was a huge party in Saskatoon. Hells Angels and prospects from British Columbia, Alberta, Manitoba and Quebec showed up. According to one source, Stadnick rode in on a borrowed Harley. By the time the party was over the next morning, Saskatoon had a full-patch Hells Angels chapter. According to an RCMP report published six months later, "the Saskatoon Hells Angels' main source of income is from the sale of illicit drugs, particularly cocaine and marijuana."

With the Spartans more or less neutralized, the former Los Brovos were awarded the title Hells Angels Manitoba on December 22, 2000, just five months after they became prospects. One RCMP officer pointed out that the Manitoba designation was intended to intimidate the few remaining Spartans who were operating in nearby Brandon and some smaller rural communities. Immediately after their elevation to a full-patch chapter, the Hells Angels Manitoba started expanding their market by persuading independent dealers to deal only with them. When some balked, a message needed to be sent. Bradley Russell Anderson was one of Stadnick's original hand-picked Redliners. When the boss folded the company, Anderson went back on the streets to sell drugs. Although he bought the bulk of his drugs from Hells Angels, he could often find lower prices from other sources. Police sources said the Hells Angels told him he had to stop, and he promised he would. He didn't keep his promise, but the Hells Angels kept theirs. Anderson's bullet-riddled body was found north of the city two weeks after he received the ultimatum.

At about the same time that the Rock Machine was recruiting disgruntled Outlaws and setting up shop in Ontario, undercover

RCMP agent Cal Broeker was riding with the Para-Dice Riders. He wasn't a cop and he wasn't an informant. Broeker had been a successful businessman in upstate New York when an investigation linked him to organized crime groups—including bikers—in Montreal. Although he'd never done anything wrong and was acquitted, Broeker became fascinated with the men who had sullied his name and decided he wanted to do everything he could to uncover their crimes. He volunteered his services to the RCMP and they were more than happy to accept. In 1999, posing as a crooked accountant, he insinuated himself into the Para-Dice Riders. He wasn't a member or a prospect, but he was close enough to have a pretty good idea of what was going on. Stadnick's increased presence led him, and many others within Para-Dice Riders, to believe they were going to become a Hells Angels puppet club. And they were excited. "They were like small bit players who got the big ticket," said Broeker. "To them, it was the opportunity of a lifetime."

The police had the same idea. "When I talk to police in this province, their major concern with organized crime is really the bikers." said Ontario Solicitor-General David Tsubouchi on December 28, 1999. "It's pretty evident right now that the bikers are a priority with us." Realizing the biggest bikers were coming, Tsubouchi answered police requests for funding and manpower by increasing the Provincial Special Squad to 44 members and reorganized it as the Biker Enforcement Unit (BEU). "There will be no easy ride," he told newspapers.

The cops themselves didn't sound as sure. "I don't think we can stop it," said George Rooke, operations coordinator of the BEU. "But we are prepared for it." In case there were any people in Ontario who were still under the sway of the Hells Angels' old romantic image, he told *The Toronto Star*. "This isn't a bunch of guys riding bikes; this is big business. It's organized crime, and when you are dealing with organized crime you are dealing with individuals who have avenues and people entrenched in illegal activities in the province of Ontario— money laundering, drug trade, prostitution, stolen property, motor vehicle theft and extortion." The Hells Angels were coming, and everyone watching was sure they'd start small by patching over a few veteran bikers as they had in Alberta and Manitoba.

They were all wrong. The day after the saber-rattling comments by Tsubouchi and Rooke appeared in newspapers nationwide, a procession of bikers filed into the Sorel clubhouse. As soon as the first bikers started filing in, a herd of Quebec and Ontario cops gathered outside. What they saw was chilling. Besides the usual Quebec Hells and puppet gang crests, they saw bottom rockers from British Columbia, Alberta, Manitoba and Nova Scotia. "The only thing missing is Ontario," joked one OPP officer. He wasn't laughing for very long. When all the anticipated guests had arrived, parked their bikes and walked into the building, the air was once again filled with the rumble of Harley V-Twin engines through customized pipes. Around the corner came Ontario. More than 125 bikers—wearing the logos of the Para-Dice Riders, Satan's Choice, Last Chance and the Lobos—arrived en masse.

A few of the bikers acknowledged some of the cops they knew from their home towns; some mugged for newspaper and police surveillance cameras. The shock of their numbers shut the police and media up. Again, the calm was short-lived. There was a third rumble, far quieter than the others, but perhaps even more profound. The third and smallest group was made up of unlikely guests. Even the most cynical cops were shocked to see these patches arrive—about a dozen bikers, some sporting "Charlie," the Outlaws' trademark skull, and others with the Rock Machine's screaming eagle's head. The third group of bikers passed the crowd with little show of emotion as they filed past the stunned cops and reporters. The arrival of a beat-up old Chevy van made everything very clear to the spectators. Two big hang-arounds unloaded a heavy crate, which was clearly marked as containing an industrial-sized sewing machine.

As bikers filed out with their freshly attached winged skulls, the scale of the patch-over became evident. More than 150 Ontario bikers had become Hells Angels that day, without having to prospect or serve as puppet clubs first. "When Walter was hanging around with them, it became clear that he was after the Para-Dice Riders; and with Guindon retired, getting Satan's Choice made sense too," said John Harris. "But some of those other guys—they were useless, drug-addled wastes—it seems like he was getting desperate, letting anyone on a Harley wear the patch."

The cops did their best to regain some composure. A few of them started chanting "I'll live and die a Para-Dice Rider," the club's motto. It did nothing to dampen the bikers' enthusiasm. Freshly minted Hells Angels began to trot out of the Sorel headquarters. Some of the veterans ran over to cops and reporters they knew and showed off their patches like students displaying their diplomas to their families at graduation.

And nobody was happier than Walter Stadnick. Although it had taken years and there were a few close calls, Stadnick had managed to expand the Hells Angels across the country from their power base in Quebec. British Columbia? Hells Angels dominated. East Coast? With the rapid deployment of puppet gangs from Quebec and a few well-placed assassinations, Hells Angels once again dominated. The Prairies? Hells Angels dominated by chapters and puppet clubs throughout Alberta, Saskatchewan and Manitoba. And Ontario? Although a few pockets of resistance remained—mostly the four small Rock Machine chapters and the dozen or so Para-Dice Riders who refused to patch over—even Canada's richest province was now Hells Angels territory.

And while the successful prosecution of the war against the Rock Machine and the genuine fear he had sown in Quebec's government and population had made Maurice "Mom" Boucher a headline regular and a household word, it had also made him a target. He'd been in and out of prison so many times that he had an entire maximum security wing reserved only for him. And police and prosecutors were working 24/7 on a way to get him back in there. The only thing that kept him free was a strict adherence to the rules of insulation he'd learned from Stadnick when they set up the Nomads.

But through stealth, intelligence, charm and luck, Stadnick had managed to build the empire of his dreams. From sea to sea, he had a legion of bikers wearing his colors, selling his drugs and making him millions. He had hundreds of men at his disposal. Men who would work for him, go to prison for him and even kill for him. And all the police could do was follow him around and give him meaningless traffic tickets.

The little guy from Hamilton who didn't speak a word of French had not only taken over the Hells Angels, but, from an underworld standpoint, he ran the country. The wily Wild One had outlasted the Outlaws, the Rock Machine and his old bosses in the mafia. He'd subdued the Grim Reapers, the Rebels, the King's Crew, Los Brovos, the Spartans, Satan's Choice, the Para-Dice Riders, the Apollos, the Loners and dozens of others into becoming his men. He'd outwitted and outmaneuvered the police in such a way that he'd made them someone else's problem. Walter Stadnick, the horribly scarred little biker who preferred Armani to leather, had won.

Chapter 12

The other waitresses thought Hélène Brunet was nuts. She hated bikers and refused to serve them whenever they ate at Eggstra, the Montreal-Nord strip-mall café where she worked. The rest of the staff loved it when the bikers came in. Not only did they leave better tips than the few coins most of the deadbeats in the area gave them—so much so that they began to use a code name for bikers: "five bucks"—but they were exciting. It wasn't just Rockers or Death Riders from across the river in Laval, but real Hells Angels. Even Maurice "Mom" Boucher, the "baddest" and most famous of them all, would stop by every week or so for a plate of sausage and eggs. The other waitresses would often compete to serve the bikers, especially the ones they recognized from the newspaper.

But Brunet was adamant. She wanted no part of the bikers. She wasn't afraid of them, she maintained, just disgusted with their attitude. But on July 7, 2000, she didn't have a choice. Two guys she thought were bikers sat in the smoking area, and she was the only waitress on duty that morning who could work in that section. It didn't matter; anyway, there was a long-haired guy with a moustache in the non-smoking area too. If he wasn't a biker, he was a wannabe and they could be worse. Just as Brunet approached the bad guys' table to take their order, she heard a commotion and turned around. What she saw at first confused her.

A masked man had come into the restaurant and joined the long-haired man and both of them were carrying handguns. "I thought it was a joke," said Brunet. "You see that on TV—I didn't even think it was a real gun." They both were.

Before anyone could react, the masked man shot Bob Savard three times in the head. His face was in his eggs before Brunet realized what was going on. The other biker leapt to his feet and grabbed Brunet by her collar and the waistband of her pants. He held her in front of him and used her as a human shield. The long-haired man emptied his clip. Three bullets hit Brunet in the right leg and another one penetrated her right arm. The man who hid behind her, Normand Descôteaux, fled unharmed.

Savard and Descôteaux weren't bikers. But the assassins were. The hit that involved the unfortunate Brunet was a bit of Hells Angels strategy. Savard and Descôteaux were independent loan-sharks, eager to take over the business left over when André "Dédé" Desjardins was killed. It was just a little housecleaning for the Hells Angels. There was no room in Montreal for anyone who didn't play ball with the new lords of the underworld.

After recovering in hospital, Brunet became an anti-biker advocate and even sued Descôteaux and Boucher for the shooting. She has frequently been seen since with Josée-Anne Desrosiers, mother of the slain Daniel, at rallies, functions and media events. The Montreal tabloids have since named them the "Elles Angels."

Traditionally, women don't mean much to the Hells Angels. According to the club's original rules, a woman ranks far below a member's Harley and on a rung somewhat below his dog. That's why it's ironic (or perhaps fitting) that so many Hells Angels were brought down by two angry women.

France Charbonneau, a lawyer based in Montreal, had been working night and day since Boucher's acquittal for the prison guard murders. She pored over the court transcripts and compared them to precedent. Like many in the Québec legal community, she was horrified by the speech Judge Jean-Guy Boilard made just before sending the jury to deliberation, in which he described star witness Stéphane Gagné as "not credible" and pointed out that lying in court would probably save his life. On October 10, 2000, Charbonneau's dedication paid off. A three-judge panel for the Québec Court of Appeal unanimously agreed that there should be a new trial for the case against Boucher for the murder of the prison guards.

It was no problem for the police to find him, as they had him under constant surveillance. The hard part was deciding who would arrest and then hold him. Both the Sûreté du Québec (SQ) and the Montreal police claimed jurisdiction. Both wanted to be seen as the force that caught the mighty Boucher and neither side would back down. Finally, they worked out a deal in which two Montreal officers and two SQ men would apprehend him. The city cops would search and frisk him, but he would be held at the local SQ headquarters at Parthenais.

The following morning, Boucher got a call from his lawyer, Benoît Cliche. After telling him about the court decision, he set up a lunch meeting at a South Shore restaurant. Boucher was surprised. He did not expect to lose the appeal. But now he was going back to jail.

He had just worked out a plan with Cliche and Gilbert Frigon over lunch in which he would quietly surrender himself at a West End police station, when they spotted the cops outside. At 1 p.m., Boucher left the restaurant, was arrested, searched and cuffed before being stuffed into an SQ car and taken to Parthenais. According to police officers, he was so upset about the public arrest that he didn't stop swearing until after he was put in his cell.

* * *

The other woman would show up somewhat later. Before Dany Kane died, he managed to give the SQ an immense gift. Normand Robitaille, the Nomad he served as a de facto valet, had some business in Québec City, so he gave Kane his briefcase to protect. "It is extremely important this does not leave your sight," his boss had told him. "The contents are very important." As soon as Robitaille's car was out of sight, Kane got on the phone and set up a meeting with the SQ. He handed over the briefcase, the police photocopied every document inside, put them back in exactly the order they had found them in, and returned it to Kane.

Robitaille was none the wiser, but the cops found out more about the inner workings of the Nomads than they could have imagined. The papers inside the briefcase were accounting records for The Table and, although they were not entirely incriminating on their own, they indicated an immense amount of both drugs and money passing through the organization. They also contained the name of Jean-Richard "Race" Larivière, whom Kane had mentioned as a major drug distributor for The Table.

Carcajou immediately started tailing Larivière. When he stopped at 7415 Rue Beaubien Est, the cops were pretty sure it was a social call because Larivière came from Anjou. But then the police noticed that the front door of the high-rise was almost spinning with traffic. When they looked closer, they noticed that the overwhelming majority of people passing through the lobby were young and almost every one of them was carrying a bag of some sort clutched closely to their bodies. When the first set of officers were replaced by a more experienced group, reports began to be called in about the presence of well-known drug dealers and Hells Angels associates from Laval, Québec City, Trois-Rivières, the Eastern Townships and other parts of Québec.

Finding the apartment in the 75-unit high-rise wasn't difficult. An officer stationed in the lobby noticed that almost all elevator rides—and all that contained known or suspected drug dealers—stopped at the fifth floor. Armed with that information, the police checked utility records. They were suspiciously low for unit 504; clearly nobody lived there. Further, more specific surveillance showed the police that the Hells Angels had installed no extra security for the apartment that many would later refer to as "the Nomads National Bank." After acquiring the proper warrants, they copied the superintendent's key to the front door. Inside, they saw a setup more closely resembling an office than a home. As quickly as possible, they set up bugs, phone taps and video cameras.

The following day, they saw the inner workings of the Nomads' banking and drug distribution system. Time after time on grainy black and white video, the police saw dealers or their runners drop off bags of money and receive bags of drugs in return. Once the customer was gone, a Nomads associate named Robert Gauthier would take the money to another apartment in the same building for safekeeping. Another check of utility bills indicated they were using unit 403. Police broke in that night and found more office-style furniture, two PCs and a large safe—they quickly installed more video cameras and bugs.

A few days later, SQ Sergeant Pierre Boucher, commanding officer for what was now being called Project Ocean, had an idea. When the bank was closed, he got a Royal Canadian Mounted Police (RCMP) agent to sneak into 403 and copy the contents of both PCs. He was disappointed at the results. Although both computers had identical accounting software, neither had any data. But further examination of the videos showed that Nomads associate Stéphane Chagnon carefully inserted what looked like a disk or CD into one PC when he arrived in the morning and ejected it and then hid it every night. Boucher went into 403 that evening and recovered a 100 Mb Zip disk from under a rug, copied it and then returned it to the hiding spot. Jackpot. The disk contained spreadsheets revealing a massive amount of trade in what the police assumed was cocaine and hashish. Although code names were used for every transaction, it was clear what was going on. And a quick look into their records showed that both Gauthier and Chagnon were related to Nomad Michel Rose by marriage. Project Ocean officers broke into the 403 every night to copy the updated disk and to photograph the contents of the vault.

Although evidence was piling up, there was little the police could do unless they could tie the money to drugs and find out who the people hiding behind the codenames were. They got both when the second angry woman walked into the RCMP Montreal headquarters on January 24, 2001. Sandra Craig had survived two attempts on her life when the Hells Angels were removing their competition from the streets of Montreal. She'd lost her husband and her livelihood as a drug trafficker because the Nomads were making sure every dealer in the city bought from The Table. Now it was her turn to ruin their lives. After asking for and getting assurances from Sergeant Tom O'Neill that nothing she said would be used against her, she presented him with copies of some spreadsheets similar to what the police had found in apartment 403. He asked her to explain what they meant. She told him that they were records of cocaine and hashish sales between the Craigs and the bikers. He asked who her customers were. "André Chouinard and Michel Rose," she answered. O'Neill asked her to repeat what she had just said. "André Chouinard and Michel Rose," she said calmly. Police knew these names of the members of The Table.

Less than a week later, they struck. At night, police raided the Rue Beaubien apartments and two others that were used for nothing other than to count and store huge sums of cash. Altogether, they confiscated more than $5.6 million of the Nomads' money. When they arrested Chagnon as he showed up for work the following morning, they took his two cell phones, three pagers and his little black book of phone numbers. Inside, they got what they were looking for—a directory of who held each coded account. One of them, amusingly named Gertrude, belonged to Walter Stadnick and Donald Stockford.

* * *

Jean-Guy Bourgoin and Stéphane Sirois were two old friends going in different directions. Both were founding members of the Rockers, but Sirois had left the club in 1997. Police learned from informants that he left because his wife was afraid he'd get hurt. None of the other Rockers held it against him. "It's always that way," one of them told him. No hard feelings. Bourgoin, on the other hand, stayed in and went hardcore. According to police, he controlled the drug trade in Plateau Mont-Royal. In February 1995, he and Normand Robitaille were arrested for extortion. They demanded $450,000 from a local businessman with a severe cocaine habit and drove him to his bank to clean out his savings account. As they waited in the car, the intended victim told the bank manager what was going on. The police grabbed Bourgoin and Robitaille and charged them with forcible confinement, unauthorized possession of a firearm and concealing evidence. They were sentenced to 26 months in prison. In September 1998, Bourgoin was in trouble again. He was charged with assault after he attacked Montreal Alouettes linebacker Stephen Reid with a metal pipe in a bar fight, and spent 20 days in jail.

About the same time Bourgoin came out of prison, Sirois returned to the Rockers. His two-year tenure out of biker life had been moderately successful, but the news of massive payouts to informants at the height of the war caused him to rethink his career. Sirois—again, some say, at his wife's urging—called the RCMP about becoming an undercover agent-source. The cops jumped at the chance. Sirois was articulate, fearless and well-respected by the other bikers. The police knew he could not only infiltrate the bikers at the highest level, but he could also be a sympathetic character on the witness stand.

The Rockers welcomed him warmly and it didn't take long for Sirois to be reacquainted and trusted by heavyweights like Bourgoin. The RCMP put a recording device on his chest and asked him to talk to Bourgoin about three topics: money-laundering, drug sales and murder. He delivered on all three.

After a few beers at an East End strip club, Sirois told Bourgoin he had a little problem. Getting back into business had made him a lot of cash very quickly, and he needed a way to keep it from drawing too much attention. Bourgoin laughed and gave his old friend a playful punch on the arm. He told him he'd set him up with an accountant. "He's a hell of a guy, worked 25 years for the government and he was Rizzuto's accountant. He's always worked for those Italian guys," Bourgoin said. "You give him the cash, say 'here wash this for me'—and he will play with your money." While he said it, he made a washing motion with his hands.

A few weeks later, Sirois met with Bourgoin again, this time at the clubhouse. He didn't have to ask him for anything. Trusting his old friend, Bourgoin offered to cut him in on the action of a popular new product—bootleg Viagra. "I have it in industrial quantities," he said. Feigning skepticism, Sirois asked if it worked. Bourgoin laughed and told him that he should try it himself, saying: "You'll be as big as a horse." Using RCMP money, Sirois bought some. He never said if he tried it.

The RCMP learned a lot about the makeup of the Rockers through the Sirois tapes and his verbal reports. He told them about two associates who claimed to be full-patch Rockers to impress some girls. As soon as Bougoin found out, four real Rockers dragged the boasters into the clubhouse and beat them so severely that "they were on the floor, in convulsions." Sirois couldn't help looking shocked and disgusted.

Bourgoin tried to calm him down and explain the situation by pointing out that some of the Rockers would do anything to get ahead and they knew that the straightest road to the top of the Hells Angels' enforcer unit was through displays of savagery. "These guys all want to get promoted." Bourgoin told his old friend. "They're all mental cases, psychopaths." Even more revealing was the conversation Sirois had with Rocker Sébastien Beauchamp, who told him what bikers thought of ordinary citizens. "I look at people who get up at seven, get stuck in traffic just to work for ten bucks an hour, then come back at night," he said. "They're the fools; we're the ones who are sensible."

Still considering him a trusted confidant, Bourgoin invited Sirois out for a fancy sushi dinner in the West End. In fact, Bourgoin was considering recommending him for a promotion. Rather than the "baseball team" (the squad of Rockers who intimidated debtors and enemies with fists and bats), Bourgoin wanted Sirois to join the "football team" (the Rockers who eliminated enemies with guns and bombs). The work was less physically taxing, the pay was much higher and the chances for advancement were much greater. Sirois said he was interested, but that he needed more details, especially when it came to the cash. Bourgoin laughed and laid out the compensation package like any other prospective employer. The Hells Angels, Bourgoin said, would pay $100,000 for every full-patch Rock Machine member murdered, $50,000 for every prospect and $25,000 for every hangaround or known associate.

* * *

Ginette Martineau and Raymond Turgeon were exactly the kind of people Beauchamp was making fun of when he was talking to Sirois. She was 49, he was 52 and they lived together in a nondescript apartment in the suburbs. They worked together at Acces-Sport, a privately owned licensing office that handled automotive issues for the insurance bureau of Québec. Money was always tight and thrills were few and far between. So when a charming young man offered to pay Martineau for some information about some license plate numbers, she was eager to deal.

On January 17, 2000 Martineau handed her new friend a photocopy of the license and insurance information for a man named Marius

Poulin. It included his home address and phone number. She got $200 in return. Ten days later, Poulin was found dead in the stairwell of his apartment building.

Before she was caught, Martineau gave her friend another important file in exchange for $200. It was for Michel Auger, who had never visited their Rue Ontario store. "For some reason, he gave the newspaper building as his home address," said Randall Richmond, the prosecutor who tried Martineau. "And that's where they got him." It became increasingly clear that Martineau was passing information to the Hells Angels' executioners. "A man's life went for $200, that's what it amounted to," said Richmond, referring to Poulin. "It's pretty horrifying." Though they couldn't pin conspiracy on Martineau or Turgeon, they did manage to convict them on 25 breach-of-trust charges and the 25 charges of fraudulent use of insurance-board files. They both received sentences of five years. And, although they could never find the triggerman for the Auger shooting, Richmond did put the man who supplied the weapon, a Hells Angel's associate named Michel Vezina, behind bars. Vezina was sentenced to 59 months for trafficking the .22-caliber Ruger that Auger was shot with and a far more lethal Luigi Franchi submachine gun. It was his second conviction for trading illegal weapons in three years.

Significantly, an unnamed party requested four publication bans for the Martineau–Turgeon trial. Judge Maurice Galarneau granted them all. Under his orders, the media were not allowed to report what happened to the other people whose information was accessed; they could not report any speculation by lawyers or witnesses as to whom the information would have helped; they could not name the party who asked for the bans and, perhaps ridiculously, they could not reveal the subject Auger normally wrote about.

One person Auger wrote about frequently was Peter "Buddy" Paradis, one of the most powerful members of the Rock Machine. He didn't start out big. In 1981, at the less-than-legal age of 16, he started working as a stripper in Montreal's gay clubs. After two years on the stages and tables, Paradis learned a more lucrative trade—dealing drugs, mainly cocaine. He made a pretty good living as an independent until the war broke out and he was forced to pick sides. In June of 1994, he was one of many small-time dealers approached by Rock Machine founding member Renaud Jomphe to join their side. It was hard to say no.

Jomphe—known by some as the "King of Verdun"—was a well-known dealer long before the Rock Machine was an entity. Paradis agreed and his fortunes immediately improved. Jomphe sincerely liked Paradis, taught him the intricacies of the industry and gave him contacts that increased his reach. At the height of the war, on October 18, 1996, Jomphe went out for dinner at the Kim Hoa restaurant in Verdun with two of his henchmen, Christian Deschesnes and Raymond Laureau. It was his last supper. They were already drunk when a masked man approached their table and raked them with submachine-gun fire. Jomphe and Deschesnes died immediately and Laureau was injured severely enough to end his gangster career.

By that time, Paradis had shown he was smart, courageous and ready for the big time. They gave him Jomphe's old fiefdom. Not only did his income almost quadruple, but he also became a Rock Machine prospect. With added rewards came added responsibilities. On April 11, 1997, Paradis was driving through the East End with two of his dealers, Mario "Marteau" Filion and Simon "Chiki" Lambert, when Lambert spotted one of the enemy. Hells Angels-associated dealer Raymond Vincent was standing on a street corner as they passed by. Filion, who was driving, turned the corner and went around the block. Lambert put on a ski mask, pulled out a gun and rolled down his window. As they passed by again, Lambert shot Vincent three times. He later died in an area hospital.

Life as the boss wasn't always easy. When one of Paradis's dealers, Yan Bastieri, complained that Hells Angels associate Eric Perfechino was muscling in on his business, Paradis gave him a gun and told him to "do what you know you have to do." Perfechino was murdered a week later.

As the war intensified, Paradis never went anywhere without his bodyguard Daniel "Poutine" Leclerc. On the surprisingly cool summer night of August 10, 1998, Leclerc drove Paradis to his home in Lasalle. Neither driver nor passenger noticed the two men parked in the black Ford Taurus in front of the house. As Leclerc drove off, two masked men emerged from the Taurus and shot Paradis four times before escaping. After eight days in a downtown hospital and still weak, Paradis returned home.

As soon as he was healthy enough, Paradis went back to work. His contacts in the Rock Machine told him that the gang's brass was pleased with his efforts, but would not be reluctant to give his position to someone they considered more courageous if his recovery lingered on much longer. Things weren't going well for the Rock Machine and they needed money fast. The Hells Angels were winning the war and more and more street-level dealers were defecting from the faltering Alliance. But the "Hells" (as the Rock Machine called them) weren't the only enemy.

On March 9, 1999, Paradis and eight of his dealers were arrested by Carcajou. He made bail and, desperate for cash, quickly started trying to collect on his debts. In January 2000, Paradis sent his younger brother Robert (who'd been both shot and arrested in the previous year) and tough guy Jimmy Larivée to collect from a particularly annoying customer. Gilles Nolet supported his rather large cocaine habit by stealing jewelry, and he was always hanging around Paradis, hoping the coke would come out and they'd party. On one night out before Paradis was shot, Nolet told him that a Colombian had sold him a kilo of excellent coke and that he could have it for just $15,000. Paradis bought it and Nolet faded away. When the coke turned out to be so impure as to be practically worthless, Paradis put out word that he was coming for his money. The shooting and the arrest deferred the debt, but when Paradis was finally able to do something about it, he did. But before his little brother and Larivée could get to Nolet, he was murdered in a bar in Côte-Saint-Paul.

Things just weren't working out for Paradis in Montreal. His funds were drying up and his sources of income were being murdered, the Hells Angels had taken over his territory and his dealers, and the police had an excellent case against him. He was one of the first four people to be charged under C-95, Canada's new anti-gangster law. Facing a bleak future outside of prison and thinking about his wife and son, Paradis told his lawyer to cut him a deal. In exchange for a lighter sentence (12 years with a chance at early parole), Paradis promised to tell everything he knew about the Rock Machine, the Hells Angels and the criminal underworld in Montreal.

* * *

Paradis wasn't the only prominent member of the Rock Machine who lost faith in their ability to compete with the Hells Angels, at least in Montreal. At about the same time Paradis and his men were arrested, founding Rock Machine member and former SS man Paul "Sasquatch" Porter packed up his operation (including a few trustworthy dealers) and moved to Ottawa. With Hells Angels turning dealers all the time, the 6-foot 6-inch, 420-pound Porter found it increasingly difficult to hold onto his territory at the foot of the notorious Boulevard St-Laurent. But maintaining a staff wasn't the only problem Porter had in Montreal; he was also a conspicuous target. While driving his Chevy Dually pickup down Route 341 near the North Shore village of L'Épiphanie on May 31, 1997, Porter was passed by a Mustang. As the other car came even with his driver's side window, Porter reflexively turned his head. He saw a young man lower his window, draw a gun and unload a magazine of automatic fire. When Porter collected himself on the side of the road, he was surprised that all he had suffered was a scratch on his arm; the door of his pickup was full of holes and his bullet-proof vest would need replacing. Less than a year later, it happened again. Porter was driving in the East End when seven men opened fire on his truck. He put it in reverse and escaped without a scratch.

A few weeks later, he decided to move to Ontario. He and his old friend André "Curly" Sauvageau (another former SS man) were just beginning to make inroads into Ottawa's modest drug market and serve as godfathers for the Rock Machine's fledgling Kingston chapter when fellow Rock Machine member Joe Halak invited them to his Canadian Thunder motorcycle show in Georgetown, a quiet little town just west of Toronto. Although the Hells Angels didn't show up in person, they did send a gift. That morning, July 21, 2000, the *Toronto Sun* sent a technician to 341 Guelph St. in Georgetown to fix a newspaper box that had been malfunctioning for weeks; it had been giving away free newspapers. When the unsuspecting repairman arrived, he was surprised to find a box of 4,000 nails surrounding 2.2 kilos of C4 plastic explosive. Although police surmised that Porter was the intended target, there was little doubt that dozens of innocent motorcycle enthusiasts would have been killed or maimed if the bomb had exploded at the show.

On the outside, Porter was unaffected by the attempts on his life. When Boucher and Fred Faucher signed the truce that officially ended hostilities between the two gangs, Porter was front and center with his oversized leather jacket and its massive Rock Machine patch. Two months later, he crossed the lines. On December 27, 2000, just two days before Stadnick welcomed 150 new Ontario bikers to the Hells Angels, Porter switched sides, bringing Sauvageau and his dealer network with him. It was a tremendous loss for the Rock Machine and a huge victory for the Hells Angels. "It's not like going from the Conservatives to the Liberals; it's like going from the Hatfields to the McCoys," one Ontario Provincial Police (OPP) officer said. "He could never get away with something like that in the United States or in Europe, but Canada's a different place."

Many in the media have speculated that Porter's defection was due to his old friendship with Boucher from the SS days, but the reverse is probably true. Porter walked the Rock Machine walk during the war and was one of their most stalwart, if not overly aggressive, members. It was only once Boucher was back in Maison Tanguay for the prison guard murders that Porter would negotiate with the Hells Angels. "I think he blamed Boucher for the war," said one Hull-based dealer who claims to know Porter and Sauvageau well. "But he had no problem with Wally." And it must have been clear to him that with the rapid expansion of the Hells Angels nationwide, his chances for survival as one of the most prominent of their enemies were dwindling.

Stadnick was gracious in victory. Porter was not only accepted into the club, but he and his partners in Ottawa were reinforced with a few Québec Hells Angels and granted the title of Nomads Ottawa. It was not only an acknowledgment of Porter's worth to the Hells Angels, but also an indication of how serious were Stadnick's plan for Ontario. It was the third Nomads chapter in Canada, after one was set up in the

Vancouver suburb of Burnaby in September 1998 to control the rapidly expanding chapters on the West Coast. Just as the Hells Angels' name, logo and concept had proven desirable enough to franchise a generation earlier, Stadnick's Nomads idea had proven prosperous enough, and immune enough from prosecution, for it to be copied in other places with enough business to support an elite biker management team.

* * *

While the Hells Angels may have looked invincible from the inside, the police were gearing up for their own war with the gang. The RCMP, SQ, OPP and local police forces in Montreal, Québec City, Vancouver, Toronto and Hamilton came together for a project as large, far-reaching and unprecedented as Stadnick's massive patch-over had been. Armed with over 264,000 wiretaps, miles of videotape, hundreds of photographs and documents and the testimony of Stéphane Gagné, Stéphane Sirois, Peter Paradis, Sandra Craig and others, the allied police forces launched Operation Printemps.

As soon as all the documentary evidence was scanned and loaded onto CDs by the RCMP, a network of ERMs (Esquoades Regional Mixte or Regional Integrated Squads) involving 23 different police forces were set up in areas where Hells Angels and puppet club activity was particularly heavy—Montreal, Québec City, Trois-Rivières, Sherbrooke, Hull and Jonquière. "It was the first time that a long-term joint force operation had been put in place in Québec," said RCMP Sergeant Tom O'Neill, head of the Montreal ERM. "We had several JFOs in the past, but they generally had short-term mandates with one file, or they involved one group or one event. If we needed resources that were not available at one police force, we would go to another police force."

On the afternoon of March 26, 2001, two days before the huge operation was to launch, O'Neill hosted a meeting with hundreds of officers from various police forces. The crowded auditorium sat spellbound as O'Neill went through a long PowerPoint presentation detailing the evidence, the suspects and the strategies involved. Although most of the cops had an inkling that they were being gathered to arrest some Hells Angels, almost all of them were shocked at the size of the operation. "We were stunned," said one SQ officer. "It was like we were taking down the whole gang." The cops in attendance were so impressed with their mission that few said anything before O'Neill opened the floor to questions. Even then, the officers needed to take a moment to compose themselves. The scale of the operation was simply overwhelming. There were warrants for a total of 142 bikers (although four were assumed dead), including the entire Nomads, Rockers and Evil Ones clubs. Charges would include conspiracy, drug trafficking, money laundering, gangsterism and, of course, murder. When O'Neill finally finished, he was given a standing ovation. O'Neill later joked that he should have charged admission and sold popcorn.

As successful as the meeting was, O'Neill and the other managers of Operation Printemps couldn't help but worry. With as big an operation as they were planning it was critical that word not leak out. They weren't so much worried that one of the 2,000 officers might tell a wife or girlfriend what was going on, but they couldn't stop thinking about how Gagné and other informants had told them about how Boucher, Scott Steinert and others had bragged about contacts within the police. If even just one biker found out about the operation and spread word, it could be disastrous. Years of work and millions of tax dollars would be lost and hundreds of officers would be put into grave danger.

It started at 4:30 a.m. Paul, who manages a sporting goods shop, was walking his dog before heading downtown to open the store when he saw a convoy of police vehicles come speeding out of the Complex Sportif Claude Robillard. "I lost count after I saw 30 go by," he said. "They were in a big hurry and they had all their stuff." By midnight, police in Québec had conducted raids in more than 200 locations in 77 different municipalities, and 118 bikers and their associates were behind bars. Police also seized huge amounts of cash and biker property (including all three of Mom Boucher's South Shore homes) under proceeds of crimes legislation. Cooperating police forces in Ontario, Manitoba and British Columbia arrested ten more bikers, including Stockford. "We're talking about the most important operation of this kind that we've ever had," said Montreal police Commander André Durocher.

"It's unprecedented." Most of the big names in the Hells Angels— Normand Robitaille, Michel Rose and even Boucher's son Francis— were paraded past TV cameras on their way to jail. One news report showed a 77-year-old accountant, who had been laundering money for Hells Angels, uncovered by Project Ocean, pathetically asking the police not to put him in Bordeaux prison because he'd just had prostate surgery. Only one Nomad was not arrested: David "Wolf" Carroll, who had been named in many of Kane's reports. When his name was conspicuously absent from the list of those arrested, some in the media wondered in print if it was because he was an RCMP informant.

Operation Printemps was wildly successful, but it failed on one important count. The only Nomad the police failed to put behind bars that day was Stadnick. Some sources claim he was tipped off and making a run for it, while others counter that the giant take-down coincidentally fell on his anniversary with Kathi Anderson. Either way, Stadnick was in Jamaica when the arrests happened in Canada. When confronted, the Hamilton police claimed they knew he was gone, but they busted into his house anyway, just to be sure. "We knew where he was," Hamilton–Wentworth Chief Ken Robertson said the day after the raids. "And we know where he is. And it's only a matter of time before he faces the music like the rest of them."

But they were taking no chances. With the likelihood of Stadnick willingly returning to Hamilton to face charges slim, Steve Pacey, the Hamilton biker specialist, called O'Neill and told him where Stadnick was. While the RCMP and the Jamaican Defense Force SWAT team were arresting Stadnick in Jamaica, it was Pacey's responsibility to search Stadnick's house. Much of what he found, he expected. There were closets full of fancy clothes—"he had racks and racks of Armani suits and Kathi had expensive shoes out the wazoo," he said—and office equipment. He was struck by the cleanliness of the house and a decor far subtler that Stadnick's often flamboyant appearance would suggest. But what really surprised him were the pictures. "The inside of the house was full of photographs," he said. "Much of the wall space was devoted to framed pictures and there were piles and piles of photo albums everywhere."

These weren't mere holiday snaps; they chronicled Stadnick's entire career. "There were albums devoted to his recovery from the accident. You could see his progression; he might have wanted them for a lawsuit," said Pacey. "And there were all kinds of pictures of him with other bikers and even some celebrities." Pacey put the photos of Stadnick with the other Hells Angels and Nomads in chronological order and noticed that he edged ever closer to the front-row center position normally reserved for the president. In the office, he found a gallery of pictures he was sure gave Stadnick a huge amount of pride. In the photos, he was seen in friendly poses with a number of celebrities, including NHL players, NHL coach Pat Burns (a former cop), and a well-known African-American movie star. At this point, Pacey had to admit he was a bit impressed, but what he found in the night table drawer chilled him. There were a number of photos of rival bikers from the Rock Machine and other gangs. There was a picture of a man playing softball with the words "Tommy—RCMP informant" written on it. And, finally, there was a picture of Pacey himself. "You like to think you're pretty sharp and you know they're following you, but I still have no idea when and where they took that picture," he said. "I used to like to tell people I found it on her side of the bed; I'll bet Walter really appreciated that."

Chapter 13

They all underestimated France Charbonneau. They shouldn't have. The lawyer who reopened the prison guard murder case against Maurice "Mom" Boucher and would prosecute him was smart, creative and fearless. She brought a 79-1 record in murder cases into the courtroom and had no intention of letting Boucher get away again. She spent months of late nights and weekends studying the first trial trying to figure out what went wrong. She distilled it into three things—bikers in the courtroom intimidated the jury, Boucher's defense lawyer used his ample charisma and professionalism to seduce the jury, and the judge did everything he could to discredit the testimony of informant Stéphane Gagné.

When the second trial came around, it was far different from the first. Of course, there was a different judge. And as per Charbonneau's instructions, nobody was allowed into the spectators' area with any hint of insignia—no colors, no belt buckles, no labels, no nothing. You couldn't even have a polo player on your shirt. Charbonneau also decreed that Boucher and the jury be out of sight of all spectators except media: there would be no contact between Mom and his gang or any intimidation of the jury this time.

But there was little she could do about Jacques Larochelle, Boucher's slick high-priced lawyer, until he made what

Charbonneau believed was a huge mistake. When Larochelle found a slight discrepancy between Gagné's testimony in the interrogation room and what he said in court, he turned on the witness. Larochelle accused Gagné of lying and asked him to explain. "I had been awake for 25 hours when I said that," Gagné said, referring to his admission to Sergeant Robert Pigeon in the interrogation room years earlier. "I didn't know what I was saying." Larochelle sneered, "You didn't look tired to me." Charbonneau was stunned. Seizing the moment, she interrupted and shouted, "Let's see the videotape!"

The tape was played in court in glorious black and white. Gagné was babbling. His head was reeling and falling into his hands. Even through the grainy overexposed video, it was clear his eyes were unfocused and his skin was waxy. Gagné was exhausted to the point of collapse. And Larochelle's credibility was shot. When the jury came back, the foreman announced that all but one of them had reached a decision and she wasn't entirely sure what "reasonable doubt" meant. Once instructed by Judge Pierre Béliveau on the finer points of the law, they came back with a decision. On May 5, 2002, Maurice "Mom" Boucher was found guilty of two counts of murder for Diane Lavigne and Pierre Rondeau and one count of attempted murder for the shooting of Robert Corriveau. He betrayed almost no emotion as the bailiffs took him away.

One down, 128 to go. Actually, the defendants were broken down into groups representing their level of involvement. The first 98—Hells Angels, members of puppet gangs and other associates—were to be tried individually for crimes they had committed or for evidence found at the site of their arrest. The next 17—all Rockers—were to be tried en masse for gangsterism, drug trafficking and conspiracy to commit murder. And the final 13—all of the Nomads and a few prominent Rockers—were charged with gangsterism, drug trafficking, conspiracy to commit murder and 13 charges of first-degree murder. From the testimony of Rocker Stéphane Gagné and former Rocker turned RCMP agent Stéphane Sirois, the prosecution had managed to trace a handful of the 160 or so murders from the war back to the Nomads and Rockers.

The first of what the media would label mega-trials was an utter fiasco. For some reason, Jean-Guy Boilard, the man whose handling of the first Boucher case resulted in the need for another one, was selected to preside. In its opening argument, the prosecution entered 177 CDs as evidence. The defense immediately objected. Although the evidence on the disks amounted to no fewer than 693,000 pages of documents to go along with the 274,000 wiretapped conversations, 256,000 police logs and 211 videos, the defense wanted hard copies of everything on the CDs, claiming that documents on disk are much easier to forge or alter than those on paper. To support their claim, they brought in an expert witness from Vancouver. By happenstance, one of the prosecution team recognized him from another trial. The defense's "computer expert" was actually a guy who owned a paving company on the West Coast and had served as an expert witness on the subject of asphalt about a year earlier. Boilard refused the request to print.

The following day the entire seven-person defense team walked out of the courtroom, vowing not to return until their $500-a-day stipend from legal aid was doubled. Before an entire day was lost, Boilard raised their pay to an unprecedented $1,500 per day, on the condition they did no other work. Outraged, Quebec's attorney general Paul Bégin protested, pointing out that the trial was likely to cost over $2.5 million in lawyers' fees alone. Boilard held a press conference in which he threatened to suspend the trial if Bégin questioned his judgment again. Bégin backed down. The defense, looking at the biggest pay checks of their lives, started taking their time with their presentations and what had promised to be a long case started to appear endless.

Boilard's decision also affected the other mega-trial, where defense lawyers got a raise from $500 to $1,100 a day and worked just as slowly. With seven weeks of paid summer holidays, the trial dragged on. Justice Réjean Paul had a reputation as a tough, no-nonsense judge, but this case proved too much for him. The defense lawyers the bikers had collected were mostly boorish and unruly and did everything they could to delay and frustrate the proceedings. None was worse than Réal Charbonneau, who was representing a minor Rocker named Paul "Smurf" Brisebois. While Brisebois winked at his girlfriend in the audience, Charbonneau put on a show of rare insolence. He frequently ignored Paul's commands and spoke right over him, often using a distasteful mockery of low Quebecois slang.

According to one eyewitness, the defense lawyer even made what he believed was an obscene gesture toward the judge when he wasn't looking. Five months after the trial began, just a little more than 10 percent of the witnesses had been heard from. Paul had had enough. He cited Charbonneau with contempt and removed him from the case. He had no choice but to offer Brisebois the choice of getting a new lawyer, defending himself or being removed from the mega-trial and tried alone. Brisebois wasn't stupid; he took the third option and the trial became a bit less mega.

Boilard ran into more trouble almost as soon as he got back in the courtroom. Gilles Doré, a lawyer he had publicly scolded in court in another case, sent him a letter complaining about his actions, which he called "abusive." Boilard replied with an angrily worded letter of his own—a very bad idea. Doré leaked the response to the local media and they ran with it. A week after he wrote the letter, on July 22, 2002, Boilard stood up, told everyone gathered in the courtroom that because of a "reprimand," he believed that he no longer had "the moral authority, or even the necessary capacity," to preside over the bikers' trial. Despite the fact that 123 witnesses had testified, 1,114 exhibits had been shown and millions of taxpayers' dollars had been spent, Boilard took off his robe, muttered something about "retirement" and went home. Pierre Béliveau, the judge who presided over Boucher's conviction, was named to replace him but, as capable as he was, there was nothing he could do with the mess Boilard had left but declare a mistrial.

It took seven months for the courts to get the pieces back together for a new trial. During that period, seven bikers had plea bargained to lesser crimes, some receiving sentences as short as three years. Another, Normand "Pluche" Bélanger (Sirois maintained he handled the gang's ecstasy trade, mostly to high schoolers) called in sick. His doctor testified that Bélanger suffered from a veritable buffet of diseases, including diabetes, hypertension, cirrhosis of the liver and one other condition the judge wouldn't allow to be published. When asked how long Bélanger had to live, the doctor said "no more than ten months." Beliveau granted Bélanger a conditional release, so he could spend his final days with his eight-year-old daughter, on September 10. Fourteen months later, *The Montreal Mirror* reported that Bélanger was seen as he rented videos and took friends to "a downtown spaghetti restaurant" looking "chipper" and "youthful." Two weeks after Bélanger's release, fellow defendant René "Balloune" Charlebois asked to be excused for a toothache. He got one day off.

* * *

Of course, things were different for Walter Stadnick and Donald Stockford. Neither they nor their high-priced Toronto lawyers spoke much French. Alan D. Gold, former president of the Canadian Criminal Lawyers Association and Edward Greenspan, who had defended such luminaries as former Nova Scotia premier Gerald Regan, theatre magnate Garth Drabinsky and millionaire wife-killer Helmuth Buxbaum, represented an enviable dream team. Neither came for free. They asked Judge Jerry Zigman for an English-language trial (the prosecution wanted them to undergo a bilingual trial with Boucher, André Chouinard and Brisebois) and, on September 18, 2003, it was granted. They were flexing their muscles early.

But they didn't frighten Randall Richmond, Quebec's deputy chief prosecutor for organized crime, although he did later admit that he had studied and been influenced by Greenspan when he was in law school. Not only was Richmond fluent in English (like the defendants, he originally came from Hamilton), but he was the Crown's most informed and effective prosecutor. But so impressive were the imported lawyers that Michel Rose, a francophone, decided to be tried in English. "I cross-examined him in English and he passed," said Richmond. "The law says that you can be tried in either official language; it doesn't have to be your first language or even your best language. You simply have to have an acceptable grasp of it." Richmond described Rose's English as "good enough" and said: "It was clear he chose an English trial because he wanted Greenspan to represent him."

Despite having lived for almost two decades in Quebec, neither Stadnick nor Stockford appeared to have learned much French. "The only times I ever heard their voices was on wiretapped phone conversations, and they always spoke in English," said Richmond. "In fact, when other people, francophones, spoke with them, they always used English as well."

As with the previous trial, the defense team claimed ignorance of how to use the CD-mounted evidence and demanded that it all be printed and translated at government expense. The Crown agreed to translate and print all evidence it planned to bring into the trial. Unable to work out a deal, Gold and Greenspan then took the translation issue to the Supreme Court of Canada, which decided that the Crown need only translate and print what was necessary for its case. Although nothing was gained by either side, the translation issue delayed the case many weeks. "We consented to translating thousands of pages of evidence—we accepted it as part of doing a trial," said Richmond. "We actually translated much, much more than we planned to use."

With the preliminary issues finally out of the way, the trial began in earnest on March 1, 2004. On the very first day, Greenspan surprised everyone in the courtroom by entering a guilty plea on Rose's behalf. Eight other francophone bikers also pled guilty that day, including Nomad André Chouinard. Although they avoided a first-degree murder charge (which carries a mandatory 25-year sentence with no chance at parole), Rose and Chouinard did admit to the attempted murder of Sandra Craig and to importing more than four tons of Colombian cocaine into Quebec.

With Rose gone, Stadnick and Stockford were led into the bullet-proof Plexiglas cage that served as a defendants' box, their leg shackles rattling as they walked. Moments earlier, guards reported Stadnick sardonically chuckling with them and boasting that it wouldn't be long before he was free again. Once in court, however, both looked impassive and serious. Neither made any gesture or revealed any emotion as Richmond read the 23 charges, including 13 of first-degree murder, against them. When the long list of crimes he was alleged to have committed was finally finished, Stadnick leaned into his microphone and in a low, quiet and steady voice said, "not guilty."

Gold and the defense team led in a number of witnesses and supporting evidence that portrayed both defendants as well liked and respected family men. He pointed out that Stockford had no criminal record and that Stadnick's was slight, especially when compared to the other bikers on trial. The court heard about Stockford's legitimate career as a movie stuntman and about how he'd landed a small role in the big-budget Jennifer Lopez film *Angel Eyes*. No mention was made of West End Talent, the stripper agency Stockford and his wife, Christine, ran back in Hamilton, or the fact that Stadnick had never held a legitimate job.

The gangsterism and drug-trafficking cases against the bikers were very straightforward. The earlier trials had established the Nomads as fulfilling the requirements as a criminal organization as described by Bill C-95. Dozens of photographs and other documentary evidence were displayed before the court, establishing both Stadnick and Stockford as members of the Hells Angels and later, the Nomads. Although he did show that Stadnick was a particularly influential man within both groups, Richmond was never able to prove he was president, although the evidence supported it. In all of the posed group photos after the date in which Stadnick was alleged to have become president, he is sitting front-row center. And, after the same date, according to the testimony of police officers, Stadnick always rode on the front left of every biker procession they'd seen him in. Richmond brought in Guy Ouellette, the Sûreté du Québec's (SQ) oft-quoted biker expert, to testify that, in his opinion, those bits of respect from the other bikers indicated that Stadnick was indeed president.

Similarly, evidence and testimony that had already been introduced in the other mega-trials carried credibility against Stadnick and Stockford. The documents that Sandra Craig had provided were easily cross-referenced with those seized from the "Nomads National Bank" and from later arrests. Accounting records from March 30, 1999, to December 15, 2000, showed that $111,503,361 made its way through the Nomads with $10,158,110 coming from the Gertrude account for the purchase of 267 kilos of cocaine and 173 kg of hashish. Other documents revealed that the contact numbers for the Gertrude accounts led to phones and pagers used frequently and exclusively by Stadnick and Stockford.

It would, of course, be harder to prove them murderers. There was not a shred of admissible evidence that either Stadnick or Stockford had ever killed anyone. But Richmond had established that they were both very influential men and that other bikers, particularly Rockers, were bound to carry out their commands. "In the cases where we had physical evidence of the murders—DNA, fingerprints—the murderers had already pled guilty," said Richmond. "But just as a general is liable for any war crimes men under his command commit, we were convinced that Stadnick knew about the murders and did nothing to stop them." The defendants were accused, therefore, of being responsible for the murders of Pierre Beauchamps, Marc Belhumeur, Yvon Roy, Johnny Plescio, Jean Rosa, Pierre Bastien, Stéphane Morgan, Daniel Boulet, Richard Parent, Serge Hervieux, Tony Plescio, Patrick Turcotte, François Gagnon and Alain Brunette, as well as three counts of attempted murder in the cases of bombs that didn't achieve their intended purpose. "We had no surprise evidence against them," Richmond said afterward. "It was risky, a long-shot; I could have dropped the murder charges, but I felt that it was a theory that should be tested."

Because the defendants elected against a trial by jury, it was up to Justice Zigman alone to determine whether the state saw Stadnick and Stockford as gangsters, drug traffickers, murderers or all of the above. It didn't take him long. On September 13, 2004, Zigman declared the two men in the defendants' box guilty of gangsterism, drug trafficking and conspiracy to murder. There was not, he said, enough evidence to find them guilty of murder. Neither Stadnick nor Stockford showed any emotion as Zigman read his verdict or when he described them as "hardened criminals who show little or no hope of being able to straighten out their lives and cease participating in criminal activities. They are violent people who are a danger to society. They have expressed no remorse for their acts."

Both men received 20-year sentences, minus time served.

Chapter 14

"It was so cool; I can't hardly describe it," said Manny, an 18-year-old who happened to be waiting for a Fennell Bus on his way to his job at Mountain Plaza. "All these cops—with shields and guns and armor—were telling everyone to get off the block." Manny did what they said, but he waited with a bunch of other curious people just around the corner, all looking to see why the cops were so excited. Selling baseball caps for a bit more than minimum wage could wait. This was important.

Although it was just June 8, it was already getting hot. Hamilton, even the mountain, is known around the area for its oppressive heat and mugginess, and the summer of 2005 was already starting to get bad. Manny could see the cops sweating and suffering under their armor. "There's snipers on the roof of the bingo hall," said a girl about Manny's age. "They went up with these really big guns—I thought they were army guys at first—it was cool." And, when Manny squinted, he could see the barrels of the rifles over the roof of the Princess Bingo Centre. The girl then pointed to more snipers on top of the high-rise across the street.

Now Manny was really interested. At first he thought it was a bank robbery, but the banks were closer to Upper Wellington and from what he could see, the snipers were pointing their guns the other way, up toward East 14th. There was nothing worth robbing up that way.

Without being asked, an older bald guy told everybody what he thought. "It's for Chrétien," he said. "He's in town for Mac grad." Indeed the former prime minister was in Hamilton that day for Convocation at McMaster University, but Mac was down the mountain. There were no snipers on top of its libraries or classrooms, just an ordinary security detail with handguns and walkie-talkies. And Jean Chrétien had no business at the Princess Bingo Centre or any of the buildings around it.

As the spectators were discussing the reasons behind the armed occupation, the roadblock opened up and a fleet of cars, led by a marked Hamilton cop car with lights flashing, went down the otherwise deserted street. The third vehicle in line was a big black Chevrolet Suburban with blacked-out windows and the word "Canada" on the driver's door. It parked on East 14th, just outside the parking lot of the Crestmount Funeral Home. When the doors of the Suburban finally opened, Manny could see two guys in dark suits get out. As soon as they were standing up, they opened umbrellas. Then a third, smaller, man got out and hid behind the black umbrellas. He was followed by another guy in a suit. The four of them walked into the building past a lineup of cops in full riot gear. They also went by the funeral home's sign, which announced services for "Andrew Stadnik."

Walter Stadnick's 92-year-old father had died at home, about four blocks north of Crestmount, three days earlier. There was a small, nondescript announcement in the paper that said the service was limited to family and a few close friends. A couple dozen heavily armed Hamilton cops would arrive as well. Andrew's oldest son Eric had died a few years earlier from a heart attack and Gordon, who always had a problem with drugs and everything, had just gotten out of jail after getting into yet another fight. The youngest, and some say Andrew's favorite, had made it to the service despite living a long way away and under unique circumstances. Transported from the Special Handling Unit of Ste-Anne-des-Plaines maximum-security prison 400 miles away, the man Andrew had named Wolodumyr Stadnik was allowed a half hour of private visitation with his father's body. According to an observer who attended the funeral and briefly glimpsed Walter, the former biker king was silent and slipped away without incident. He'd arrived shortly after noon and by 1:00 p.m., he was on the road back to prison.

It would probably be his last time out of prison for a long time. Although his lawyer, Alan D. Gold, is mounting a long-promised appeal, few seem optimistic it will succeed. Randall Richmond, the Hamilton-born prosecutor who sent Stadnick away, doesn't seem very impressed. "Yeah, yeah, the appeal," he said. "I've been waiting for the defense to file their appeal, but it's been a long time. Walter Stadnick and Donald Stockford are in jail and I've got lots of other work to do."

Kathi Anderson, Stadnick's common-law wife of many years, still adamantly maintains that he is nothing more than a member of a motorcycle enthusiasts' club and that he was convicted on nothing more than conjecture and circumstantial evidence. If what they were saying was true, she points out, why hadn't she seen any of the millions that was supposed to have passed through her husband's hands? She's got a point. Although Anderson and Stadnick did live well in a nice house with Harleys, luxury cars and expensive wardrobes, theirs was a lifestyle more befitting a successful banker or real estate agent than an organized crime kingpin. His opponents say that the money was beside the point for Stadnick. Although he was willing to buy nice things for himself and Anderson, his real goal was to be in charge of the organization. The money was just a bonus.

Ten days after Stadnick and Stockford were convicted, Justice Jerry Zigman presided over their proceeds of crime trial. Noting that the pair had cleared over $2 million in profits from selling drugs from March 1999 to December 2000, he decided that each of the defendants would pay a $100,000 fine and forfeit their homes (or at least the equity they had in them) and all of their vehicles. Stockford also lost $34,000 in cash the police found in his home. Prosecutor Brigitte Bishop declared it a major victory, although she had asked Zigman to fine each man $10 million. Stadnick gave up three vehicles, including his Harley. Anderson and Stockford's wife, Christine, managed to reach a deal with the government in which they could keep their houses by paying the equity ($90,000 for Anderson and $50,000 for Stockford) through second mortgages.

The idea of Stadnick reducing his tenure in prison by turning informant stretches credulity far beyond the breaking point. Stadnick built the Canadian Hells Angels into his own empire, and he'd never do anything to harm it for a few measly years off his sentence. What would he do with them anyway? Get police protection and live a normal life with a job like some nobody? Although he'd astutely and efficiently run what amounted to one of the most profitable and powerful corporations in the country, he'd have nothing more than a high school education (specializing in auto shop) and a long prison term to put on his résumé. No, it makes far more sense to stick out his sentence and behave as the model prisoner in hopes of early parole. Depending on the opinion of the parole board, Stadnick should exit prison somewhere between the ages of 61 and 64. He could enjoy his retirement with the help of his friends or even rejoin the biker world, this time being even more careful than before.

Besides, things haven't worked out so well for the informers. Dany Kane is dead, probably by his own hand. Aimé Simard was stabbed more than 100 times in his cell in Prince Albert, Saskatchewan, about a week after he requested a transfer because he feared for his life. Stéphane Gagné and Serge Quesnel are still in jail. Yves "Apache" Trudeau spent seven years in protective custody and then was freed under a witness-protection program. After losing three government-supplied jobs, the mass murderer went on welfare. It worked out pretty well until he was discovered by police sodomizing an underage boy. In court, Trudeau pointed out that prison can be a very dangerous place for informants and pedophiles (not to mention mass murderers). The judge was not impressed; he was given four years and was stripped of his federal protection.

Most of the other bikers who played a big part in the great Hells Angels–Rock Machine war are now either dead or imprisoned. A census of Quebec prisons would reveal a veritable *Who's Who* of Nomads, Hells Angels, Rockers and other bikers. Most of them, like Stadnick, won't be out for a while. And some are with him in the SHU, the only supermax prison in Canada and the only one in which guards carry loaded weapons on routine patrols. At least one prisoner who was recently released from the SHU has told me that the old bikers, in particular the still-swaggering Boucher, are doing well and looking forward to their releases. He doesn't think that Boucher or any of the others wield any significant power outside the prisons but would likely be welcomed back into the clubs with positions of honor.

Stadnick, he said, mainly keeps to himself and a few close friends and generally falls under most people's radar. But it hasn't been all easy behind bars for the top bikers. Boucher has survived at least one murder attempt, perhaps more. On August 15, 2002, a 36-year-old inmate from Saskatchewan managed to get close enough to Boucher in the prisoners' dining hall to stab him once in the right underarm with a makeshift knife. Before he could strike again, a group of inmates who were surrounding Boucher wrestled the knife from him and attacked his assailant before guards stepped in. "The four guys with Mom grabbed the native guy, drove him into a shower stall, beat the living crap out of him and stabbed him 21 times," said a source who witnessed the incident.

Although Boucher was essentially unharmed (he required no medical attention), while his assailant eventually died from his wounds, it was a stark reminder that the Hells Angels are not the only gang, or even the most powerful gang, behind bars. The would-be assassin was a member of the Indian Posse, a gang made up of Native Canadians. Most inmates say they have far more members and power than the bikers in Canada's prisons.

With so many Hells Angels behind bars, especially the important ones, it's tempting to think of them as a weakened and declining empire. According to police forces all over the country, the opposite is true. While they may be the No. 2 gang in prisons, they are still solidly in front on the streets of Canadian cities and towns. With 34 chapters in Canada, the Hells Angels are still on top of the organized crime heap. Although police intelligence officers claim that their activity has been reduced in the Maritimes and Quebec, which is no surprise considering the massive number of arrests, those same officers admit that business is booming for the Hells Angels in Ontario and Western Canada. The Royal Canadian Mounted Police (RCMP) and Ontario Provincial Police (OPP) claim that the Toronto area has the greatest concentration of Hells Angels in the world. Things are even better for

them out West, where crystal meth use has reached epidemic propor-
tions. According to one Saskatchewan biker cop, "There's tons of crystal meth out there, and the Hells Angels are controlling it all."

A street-level dealer who recently moved from Toronto to
Edmonton told me, "These days, you can sell meth anywhere there's
white people . . . of course I get it from the bikers—that's what they're
famous for."

Perhaps more important is the fact that Stadnick's legacy lives
on. According to the Hells Angels head office, there are currently 22
Nomads chapters worldwide in places as disparate as Brazil, Finland
and Nevada. While the man himself is behind bars, he can feel secure
in the knowledge that his philosophical contribution has helped the
club immeasurably.

And, as the Hells Angels saved themselves by turning to selling illegal drugs in 1965, they have recently gone to legal means to
raise funds. Although the Hells Angels would never allow a non-
member to wear the winged skull logo or the name, the club has
opened a number of retail stores to sell what they call "support gear"—
licensed items with pro-biker designs and logos. With slogans like
"Support 81" (the 8 stands for H, the eighth letter of the alphabet and
1 for A) and ACAB (an acronym for All Cops Are Bastards), Hells
Angels–approved gear is selling like proverbial hotcakes. I visited one
of the two Toronto locations and almost bought a T-shirt. On a black
background, a muscular man with heavily tattooed arms on a Harley
is lovingly holding onto a smaller Harley with a toddler aboard.
The slogan reads "Big Red Machine/First Lesson." Other stores
have opened in places like Thunder Bay, Ontario; Moncton, New
Brunswick; and Charlottetown, Prince Edward Island. "Obviously
we want to make money off them," said Donny Peterson, the former
Para-Dice Rider who has become a de facto Hells Angels spokesman.
"And we do make good money off them." Another store is planned
for Halifax.

Of course, the authorities haven't stood still. Operations like
Project Dante in which the RCMP, OPP and Sûreté du Québec (SQ)
arrested 16 Hells Angels in the Kingston and Ottawa areas continue
and arrests pile up. Hit particularly hard have been the Bandidos, who

did eventually swallow up what remained of the Rock Machine, making the last remaining major Canadian motorcycle gang a subsidiary of an American super-club.

Advocates of tough anti-gang legislation cheered on June 30, 2005, when a Barrie, Ontario, judge ruled that the Hells Angels were indeed a "criminal organization." At the extortion trial of Woodbridge Hells Angels Steven "Tiger" Lindsay and Ray Bonner, Justice Michele Fuerst found them guilty not just of demanding $75,000 from a Barrie businessman, but also for having "presented themselves not as individuals, but as members of a group with a reputation for violence and intimidation." Since Lindsay and Bonner used nothing more than the man's fear of the Hells Angels to force him into payment, it was clear to Fuerst that the club was itself a weapon. Of course, Fuerst's ruling did not outlaw the Hells Angels, but it did open up members and associates to harsher penalties if they are convicted of any crime. As one Toronto-area biker said to me: "Great, now if I get into a bar fight, I can get 14 years tacked on to my sentence because of what some guys did in Quebec ten years ago."

But despite all the arrests and threats of harsh punishments, the bikers, especially the Hells Angels, continue to survive, even expand. "With Operation Springtime, we took out the brains of the organization," said one OPP officer. "But it didn't matter; they put together such a well-thought-out system that taking the managers out of the equation didn't affect it all that much." They can thank Walter Stadnick.

As has been the case for more than half a century, there are legions of young men who will work hard, humiliate themselves and give up everything they have just for a chance to wear the colors. I talked to an old friend of mine who counsels troubled youth in suburban Montreal. The boys he sees are from the very pool that biker gangs have always recruited from. Though some of them are smart, they are all doing poorly in school and most have had some trouble with the law. "If they have one common thread, it's the alienation," said the counselor. "That and a habit of wearing denim and leather." They're about the same age Daniel Desrosiers would be if he were still alive. Although none of them would admit that they want to join a motorcycle gang, every single one of them apes the biker look. They all know who "Mom" Boucher is and all of them know who the local puppet gang is.

I asked them about popular culture. Fewer than half knew who Jay-Z is and one declared that "nobody around here listens to rap." Instead, they maintain, all the kids are into Metallica, Slayer, Pantera and even Led Zeppelin, a band that broke up ten years before many of them were born. Theirs is an entirely different youth culture than the one they see on TV, one not significantly different from the one that informed Boucher, Stadnick and all the other big bikers.

* * *

One city where motorcycle gangs have never had a problem finding disaffected youth is Hamilton. A walk around downtown indicates that things aren't going very well for the city. Of all the storefronts on King Street, the main drag, the only ones that appear to be doing any business are the ones that deal in what at least some people would consider vice: tattoo shops, hemp shops, fast-food restaurants, pawn shops, bingo parlors and the like. At the corner of King and Hughson is a large building that used to be the S.S. Kresge department store. Poor cousin to the also-defunct Right House across the street, Kresge's was well known a generation ago for its bustling lunch counter and a pet shop that housed a parrot that could swear reasonably well in at least three languages. Now the curse words are written in black magic marker on the building's west wall where people wait for the Cannon and Barton buses. The store, later renamed Kmart, closed in 1994. Since 1998, the building has housed Delta Bingo, which had just lost its lease in the city's East End. There was some opposition to allowing a bingo parlor to move into one of downtown's most prominent buildings—one city councillor even called it a "symbol of poverty"—but it beat an empty building.

The back of Delta Bingo faces King William Street, the downtown's artsy district. There are bookstores and art galleries, nightclubs and restaurants and the city's massive police headquarters. One of the strip's most popular restaurants was La Costa, a family-style Mediterranean bistro with an adventurous menu and a respectable wine list. For 11 years, La Costa stood at the corner of King William and Hughson and won the "Best Italian Restaurant" title from the readers of *The Hamilton Spectator* eight times. But in a chain that spread from suburban Toronto to Calgary, the Hamilton location was the only La Costa that lost money. It even started with a bad omen: two days before it opened, a woman was stabbed to death on the sidewalk in front of the restaurant. "That poor woman. I couldn't believe what happened," said La Costa owner Chris Des Roches. "In the months that followed, it was a big struggle to get established; people wouldn't come downtown after that."

But as other stores closed and violent crime became more common downtown, fewer and fewer families came to Hamilton to eat out. Those that did often reported to Des Roches that they were harassed by aggressive panhandlers, had their cars broken into or were even mugged. A month after a random, almost fatal stabbing in the Jackson Square mall two blocks away, La Costa shut down its Hamilton franchise on July 5, 2004. "The downtown has deteriorated so much that people don't come downtown anymore; Gore Park is full of gangs," said Des Roches. "We really tried to keep it going; we did everything to keep customers happy. But when my customers tell us they are afraid to come down on Saturday night, you can't change that." The day the restaurant closed, there was a sign posted in the window that thanked loyal customers and explained that it was just too difficult to do business downtown. Within hours it was painted over.

About two miles to the northeast stood a narrow three-storey building with no windows and a giant metal door. The police had confiscated 269 Lottridge St. when they convicted Johnny K-9 and the Hamilton chapter of Satan's Choice with proceeds of crime offenses in 1998. They had been looking for a buyer for the lonely former variety store surrounded by factories almost ever since. In March 2002, they found someone. A man identified as John Q. Public bought the building for $40,000. He then leased it to an organization called The Foundation. Less than a year after Operation Printemps sent Stadnick and Stockford to jail, the Hells Angels returned to the city. The Foundation was one of six puppet clubs established in Southern Ontario that year. "Walter never wanted a Hells Angels' presence in town; he liked the idea of living away from the business," said Sergeant John Harris, a former biker cop who followed Stadnick's career. "But with him gone it didn't make much sense not to have one here; lots of the Toronto and Kitchener guys lived in or around Hamilton anyway."

Before long, the bikers refortified the building, installing a tall privacy fence with barbed wire, video surveillance equipment and concrete barriers in front of the wall that faces the street. Although the club featured some tough guys, they didn't impress a city that had seen Red Devils, Cossacks, Wild Ones, Outlaws and Satan's Choice, not to mention what was arguably Canada's biggest mafia concentration, the Barton–Sherman Gang, and plenty of skinhead, Asian and Jamaican gangs. "They weren't seen as a big deal," said Sergeant Steve Pacey, another Hamilton biker cop. "It wasn't like the Hells Angels. When Stadnick would walk into a bar in his colors, even as small as he was, he commanded a great deal of respect. The Foundation didn't have any of that; they were a joke."

They did have one moment in the sun, though. When heavy metal superstar Ozzy Osbourne played Hamilton's Copps Coliseum in 2002, The Foundation were invited as guests of the band and, after a rumor that a number of Outlaws would attend, they arrived in full colors. There weren't any incidents at the show, but their presence caused the city to consider banning gang colors at local events. "Yeah, who's gonna tell a biker to take his jacket off?" said one Copps ticket taker. According to police, some members of Ozzy's entourage went back to Lottridge Street for a party, but the man himself declined.

On March 9, 2005, less than six months after Stadnick and Stockford were convicted and sentenced, the Hells Angels moved into Hamilton. With a massive party that brought dozens of bikers to the Lottridge St. clubhouse, The Foundation finally got something that would give them respect on Hamilton's mean streets—Hells Angels colors. According to Pacey, it was the 16th chapter in Ontario. Naturally, the locals went crazy. Police chief Brian Mullan said that he was "extremely concerned . . . We'll do our utmost to ensure citizens of the city don't see more crime or violence." Newly elected Hamilton mayor Larry Di Ianni seemed caught unawares by the turn of events. "This is not the kind of club we want to see set up in our city," he said. "It took me by surprise. There has been motorcycle-gang activity in all the communities around here. I heard that consistently from the police. But to see an actual establishment of a clubhouse in our inner city is not an encouraging sign." SQ biker expert Guy Ouellette piped up that Stadnick would be delighted. I don't believe him.

* * *

I'm in the passenger seat of Harris's giant white police Suburban. I'm surrounded by computers, lights and shotguns. It's hot and the windows are open. Every time we stop, people talk to us. Harris leaves every person he talks to laughing. He's telling me stories about Stadnick, Stockford, Alvin Patterson and Mario Parente and a hundred other bikers. He laughs a lot. He swings the big truck around and checks in on a convenience store robbery. I grew up in Hamilton. We pass the hospital I was born in, my high school, a dozen friends' houses. We talk about crime, bikers, the mafia, cops, politicians, football. I tell Harris that I played football in high school. "I know," he says. That disturbs me a little. He tells me a story about a cop he convinced to move from Toronto to Hamilton. About how the next time he saw him, he asked him how it was going. "Well," the cop told him. "I've pulled my gun more times in six months in Hamilton than I did in ten years in Toronto." We drive up Lottridge Street to the Hells Angels' headquarters so I can take some pictures. Harris gets out of the truck and laughs.

"Who's in there?" I ask. "Would they know you?"

"Yeah, some of the older guys would," he replies. "They're mostly from the West Toronto chapter, guys who lived in Hamilton but didn't have a chapter until now—bunch of muscle-heads, you won't find a Walter Stadnick in there now." But they don't need another Stadnick. His work is done.

* * *

I have spoken with plenty of bikers in Quebec, Western Canada and the United States, but in Ontario, they mostly won't talk. So I recruited an old friend from high school named Brian, specifically because he used to sell drugs and claims to know some bikers. We meet in a seedy

Hamilton bar. There are four of them. Long hair, jeans, leather jackets. No colors. Plenty of tattoos, but nothing that identifies them as Hells Angels, prospects or even hangarounds. I pay for the jugs of beer.

We talk. As always, they start in with the bullshit about how biker gangs—they call them "clubs"—do plenty of good in the community (like toy drives and other charitable events) and that the mainstream media never report it. The fact is that they do report it, or at least they used to. Bikers do, in fact, participate in many charitable functions, especially around Christmas, and I have no doubt that many needy people genuinely benefit from their generosity. But the newspaper editors I know are reluctant to cover such events for fear of being labeled gullible pawns in what would appear to be an obvious, if not ham-handed, PR ploy.

Then, as I have heard many times before, the bikers rattle off a list of cops who have been accused or convicted of crimes, as though the news of a half-dozen crooked cops should make me consider hiring the Hells Angels to protect me from the OPP. Then they talk, as bikers always do, about the anti-gangster legislation—what they call the "guilt by association" law. Here, I admit, they have a point. But then I bring up the Hells Angels' paradox. There is nothing more valuable, more necessary to the Hells Angels than their image as outlaws, yet they cry foul whenever anyone accuses them of breaking the law. I couldn't prove it in a court of law, but the table agrees that a very big part of being a Hells Angel is not just having a disregard for the law, but a desire to break the law. They consider it wrong to label the Hells Angels a criminal organization, but they also acknowledge that it is one. They continue to drink the beer I pay for but tell me nothing that I haven't heard a million times before from cops and street-level dealers.

When I asked Harris and Pacey where I'd meet some real local Hells Angels, they listed pretty much the same bars. One strikes Brian's fancy and we drive four blocks north. It's hard not to recognize the neighborhood. The jail is across the street, Hamilton General is in sight, and the Hells Angels clubhouse is just a few blocks to the east. When I pull open the purple metal doors of Hamilton Strip, Brian jokes, "In nice cities, they call it a 'gentlemen's club' or 'adult entertainment,' but here in Hamilton, it's just 'the Strip.'"

The first thing I see is a red-and-white sign that says the wearing of gang colors is prohibited. Beside the sign is a gaudy red-and-white Molsons ad declaring, "I am Canadian." Once past the second set of doors, it is another world. Although it is a bright, sunny Saturday afternoon, at first glance it appears pitch black in there. There are hundreds of tiny multicolored bulbs, but they do little to illuminate what's going on. My eyes never really adjust. Brian, excited, gets us seats near the stage. The first thing I notice is the L-shaped bar with much of the area out of sight of the stage. More goes on here than just stripping, it would appear. On the stage, which still has the name "Hanrahan's" inlaid in it, although the bar hasn't been called that for years, is a black dancer who is pushing the line between voluptuous and fat. She's working hard to acknowledge, while at the same time avoid, a patron, also black, who is very drunk and determined to get to know her better. Behind her is a small motorcycle—what they call a pocket bike—styled to look like a Harley and painted red and white. The pixel board above her advertises "The Edge 102.1." Three snickering guys who look like they just walked off a golf course sit down in front of us and obscure our view of the stage.

Other patrons, particularly the big guys playing pool, and the staff are staring at me. I'm the only guy without a beer (I'm drinking a club soda) and I'm not paying attention to the show. I'm used to this, though. I'm a big white guy with a buzz cut, no tattoos and no piercings. Every time I walk into a bar, someone takes me for an undercover cop. Brian finishes his beer and heads off to the men's room. To get there he passes under two TVs playing rather dated-looking hardcore porn.

When he comes back to the table, he is almost running. He is 6-feet 3-inches and about 225 pounds. He has a weightlifter's body and is as tough as they come. I've seen him fight, I've seen him sell drugs and I've seen him run from cops, but I'd never seen him afraid. When he came back, he didn't sit down. He put his hands on the table and looked me square in the eyes. His face was white. "They know who you are," he told me. "And they want us to leave." His voice, for the first time I have ever heard, quavered. "I really think we should." Without looking to see if I was with him, he left. He never told me who "they" were, what they had said to him or why he was so scared—just that he didn't want to help me any more.

Index